GREEN BUSINESS

A Five-Part Model for Creating an Environmentally Responsible Company

Amy K. Townsend, Ph.D.

Schiffer Publishing Ltd®

4880 Lower Valley Road, Atglen, PA 19310 USA

Published by Schiffer Publishing Ltd.
4880 Lower Valley Road
Atglen, PA 19310
Phone: (610) 593-1777; Fax: (610) 593-2002
E-mail: Info@schifferbooks.com

For the largest selection of fine reference books on this and related subjects, please visit our web site at
www.schifferbooks.com
We are always looking for people to write books on new and related subjects. If you have an idea for a book
please contact us at the above address.

This book may be purchased from the publisher.
Include $3.95 for shipping.
Please try your bookstore first.
You may write for a free catalog.

In Europe, Schiffer books are distributed by
Bushwood Books
6 Marksbury Ave.
Kew Gardens
Surrey TW9 4JF England
Phone: 44 (0) 20 8392-8585; Fax: 44 (0) 20 8392-9876
E-mail: info@bushwoodbooks.co.uk
Free postage in the U.K., Europe; air mail at cost.

Library of Congress Cataloging-in-Publication Data

Townsend, A. K.
  Green business : a five part model for creating an environmentally responsible company / A.K. Townsend.
    p. cm.
  ISBN 0-7643-2503-5 (hardcover)
  1. Management—Environmental aspects. 2. Business enterprises—Environmental aspects. 3. Green products.
  I. Title.

HD30.255.T69 2006
658.4'083—dc22
                                                    2006019065

Covers and book designed by: Bruce Waters
Type set in Futura Bold/Huminest 521

ISBN: 0-7643-2503-5
Printed in China

Contents

Dedication

This book is dedicated to the late Julian Manduca, whose commitment to bettering Malta's environmental health inspired those who knew him.

Acknowledgments

I would like to extend my sincere thanks to all of those who have provided support – academic and otherwise – through the course of creating this book. My heartfelt gratitude goes out to the following individuals, who not only have helped me in this endeavor but also helped to enrich my life by sharing themselves along the way.

To my parents for your love and encouragement, which have served as a wellspring of support through the years.

To my friends for your patience with my long absences during which I spent far too much time at my computer and not enough time playing.

To my dissertation committee... Dr. Mitchell Thomashow, Dr. Alesia Maltz, and Dr. H. Leedom Lefferts, for your academic guidance, support, and sincere caring.

To my academic colleagues... Dr. Brad Daniel for your continuous encouragement, love, and patience when I'm in "work mode." Dr. Steve Chase for your expansive mind, laughter, and boundless enthusiasm. Lynn Levine for your forest expertise, coyote humor, and genuine warmth. Dr. Alison Ormsby for your brains, charisma, and "just do it" attitude. Diane Rusanowsky for your humble brilliance, unending endurance, and commitment to excellence. Rowland Russell for your metaphoric humor and great hospitality. Carl Salsedo for your high energy and gardening stories. Dr. Elin Torell for your kind heart, great laugh, and ability to cut to the core of complex issues. Dr. Lee Ann Woolery for your strength and your deeply brilliant artistry.

To my professional colleagues and individuals who have inspired me along the journey... David Eisenberg for your dedication to making the world better through your work with straw bale building, incorporating sustainability into the building codes, and seeking ways to support visionary work. Dr. Jon Miles for your commitment to bringing students to the world of renewables and for your work in Malta. Bill Reed for your deep commitment and tireless efforts to make regenerative design a reality. Joel Glanzberg, Ben Haggard, Pamela Mang, and Tim Murphy of Regenesis, all of who introduced me to a new approach to regenerative design.

And to the Creator, without whom none of this would have been possible.

I am deeply grateful to you all.

Preface

In 1992, I took a one-year position as Research Fellow at a large environmental organization in Washington, D.C. My time there was spent on two projects, one of which was a domestic policy for sustainable development. Little did I know of the impact that my yearlong position would have on the direction of much of my later work.

One might imagine that an environmental organization's internal behaviors and resource use would be informed by its environmental mission and concerns. Over the course of my fellowship, however, I grew to realize that although the organization's efforts were focused on protecting multiple species and habitats, its internal business activities were little different than those of any other company. In fact, they were far from being "green," or environmentally friendly.

Though *sustainable development*, which necessitates considering the future impacts of current activities, became a buzzword in the environmental community in the early 1990s, environmental organizations often behaved like other large businesses. With little to no knowledge or awareness of green building, landscaping, or office supply sources, few organizations knew how to ensure that their internal behaviors were consistent with their conservation-related missions, goals, and activities.

Recognizing the lack of and the need for information regarding greening a company, I began to search for everything from green office supplies and equipment to energy-efficient lighting and non-toxic paints and carpets. That was the beginning of my interest in greening the human-built environment, particularly the workplace – be it a corporate headquarters, hotel, manufacturing plant, home office, government facility, or non-profit organization's workplace.

In 1993, I created the Institute for Global Environmental Strategies (later Sustainable Development International Corporation) with a mission of providing how-to information that would help organizations of all kinds to become more ecologically sustainable. Over the next four years, I conducted research and wrote numerous articles and a book, *The Smart Office*, which was published in 1997. *The Smart Office* explained how companies could become more environmentally friendly by creating healthier, more resource-efficient workplaces that, ultimately, save money, increase employee productivity, and help the environment. (The content of that book can be found on the Internet at *www.smartoffice.com*.)

Following its release, I continued to conduct research into the general topic of sustainability and also consulted for a few governments and organizations that were interested in becoming greener. During that period, I saw a sharp growth in the demand for greener buildings and products, new Federal requirements for greener building and purchasing, and an increased awareness within organizations regarding the importance of greening. Yet, much remained to be done. Although a few books had been published on creating greener businesses, what and how they greened varied, and most did not offer an ecologically based approach for greening. Instead, companies and other organizations tended to focus primarily on reducing or eliminating waste through resource efficiency, thereby saving money and reducing some of their environmental burdens at the same time. To a lesser extent, they focused on replacing toxic products with safer ones.

As important as today's wide variety of greening approaches have been in reducing companies' environmental harm, few can result in businesses that are environmentally harmless. At least two key pieces are missing in the green business field: 1) a holistic, standardized model that breaks the company into manageable conceptual parts and ensures that the company is greened in its entirety and 2) a detailed process, based in the environmental and social sciences, for greening the company. This book was written to fill the gap of the former, providing a five-part model that companies can use in their greening efforts. It is my hope that this book moves the green business dialogue forward and that it provides another stone in the path toward understanding sustainability. The latter issue – the need for a greening process based in the environmental and social sciences – will be taken up in a future book following further development.

Introduction

This chapter explores the growing interest in green business, offering examples of companies and industries that are working to become more environmentally friendly.

Overview

Companies around the world are working hard to improve their environmental performances, or become greener. Just two decades ago, many businesses viewed the environment as a constraint because the growing number of environmental regulations and laws forced them to integrate environmental concerns into their everyday practices. Today, however, a growing number of companies view the environment as an opportunity and as a model that will help to facilitate the creation of new products, services, and markets. Both social and environmental sustainability are becoming integral parts of mainstream companies' strategic planning (Rowledge, Barton, and Brady 1999). This trend is likely to continue. In other words, greening is here to stay.

Although the business of greening is fairly new, most companies in the U.S. have accepted some degree of greening as a priority (DeSimone and Popoff 1997). Even mainstream, multinational corporations have begun to align themselves with green concepts and values. For example, the company BP (formerly British Petroleum) has adopted the slogan "Beyond Petroleum" and touts its investments in renewable energy. It advertises itself as "the first oil company to voluntarily introduced gasoline with reduced sulfur... the equivalent of taking 100,000 cars off U.S. roads everyday" (green@work September/October 2001, inside cover).

Several car companies – including Honda, Toyota, Ford, Lexus, and Volkswagen – have been developing cars with improved environmental performance.[1]

A pilot facility operated by Choren Industries in Freiberg, Germany, is producing high-quality synthetic diesel fuel from biomass such as wood scraps. *Courtesy of DaimlerChrysler.*

Honda's and Toyota's hybrid cars have been on the market for some time. Ford released the first hybrid SUV, and other companies have followed suit. For example, DaimlerChrysler's Dodge Ram 2500/3500 Quad Cab pickup truck is a diesel-electric vehicle. The company also has created the Jeep Liberty CRD as well as some diesel vehicles for Europe's large diesel market.

Volkswagen Jetta TDI – 2006 model. *Courtesy of Volkswagen of America.*

Jeep Liberty CRD. *Courtesy of DaimlerChrysler.*

Following Hurricane Katrina and the resulting rise in oil prices in 2005, some automakers have increased their production and hastened the release of hybrid and other more fuel-efficient cars. Meanwhile, U.S. interest in the new generation of cleaner diesels has grown. Although Volkswagen has offered diesel cars in the U.S. for many years, diesel autos began making a return to the U.S. with companies like Ford and DaimlerChrysler, which has released both hybrid and diesel vehicles. The new diesels generally are longer-lived than gasoline engines, have higher torque at lower RPM, and get better fuel economy – generally between 20-40 percent – than their gas-powered counterparts (Mello 2003). Additionally, they can use biodiesel fuel[2] or, with some vehicular modifications, straight vegetable oil (SVO). Depending on their source[3] (i.e., waste oil or virgin oil), biodiesel and SVO offer one part of a larger exit strategy for the dependence on petroleum.

Bill Ford Jr., Ford Motor Co.'s CEO, has suggested that his company is working to create an emission-free vehicle in environmentally friendly facilities. Reflecting the desire for flexibility in the move toward creating a greener industry, he has said, "... the last thing we should ever do is define ourselves as an automaker... In the future, we may be selling mobility, rather than cars" (Winsemius and Guntram 2002, 90).

General Motors' Chairman and CEO, John F. Smith, Jr., has recognized that the automotive industry's future will have to change as land use, infrastructure, and other issues become more apparent (*BusinessWeek* as cited in Winsemius and Guntram 2002). Smith also stated that General Motors' "goal has to be nothing less than an emission-free vehicle that is built-in clean plants, which contribute to the environment" (*Green Futures* as cited in Winsemius and Guntram 2002, 31). Smith has a brief time frame in mind, stating, "and it can happen within my lifetime – hopefully, within my working lifetime" (*Green Futures* as cited in Winsemius and Guntram 2002, 31).

Though it may seem unusual for mainstream corporations to embrace the concept of greening so fully that they begin to re-envision themselves and their products, Ford has explained, "our social obligation is much bigger than just supporting worthy causes. The responsibility to consumers – and to society – of a company our size is defined in very broad terms. It includes anything that impacts [on] people and the quality of their lives" (Winsemius and Guntram 2002, 183). The Ford Motor Company and General Motors have announced that they now require their suppliers to improve their environmental performances, acting in accordance with ISO 14000 standards[4] (Babakri, Bennett, and Franchetti 2003, 749). In addition to improving the environmental performances of their production processes, auto manufacturers today recycle about 75 percent of their scrap vehicles. Ultimately, BMW's goal is to recycle 90 percent of its vehicles (Stead and Stead 1996) while Lexus hopes to recycle 95 percent of its vehicles by 2015 (Lexus, 2005).

Other sectors within the automotive industry also are interested in improving their environmental performances. Visteon, a spin-off from Ford Motor Company and the second-largest automotive supplier in the world, follows eleven principles to reduce the environmental harm associated with its business practices. Peter Pestillo, the company's CEO, has stated, "We ought not to have business initiatives *and* environmental initiatives. We ought to have solid business initiatives that embrace environmental considerations" (Sosnowchik November/December 2001, 10-11).

The automotive industry is not the only industry that is seeking to become greener. Other industries are working either to reduce their environmental impacts or to become ecologically sustainable. For example, Baxter International Inc., a multibillion-dollar medical products company, encourages its employees to undertake volunteer work for environmental and other causes. Furthermore, it has taken steps to ensure the health of its employees. This is important because a number of Baxter facilities are located in countries with limited access to healthcare. When employees get ill, they often go to the company doctor, who is authorized to determine appropriate treatment. In countries like China and India, employee health services also include education on healthy lifestyles. Not only was the company selected as an industry leader by the Dow Jones Sustainability Group Index, but it also has a membership with Ceres[5] and is a pilot member of Global Reporting Initiative (GRI) (Sosnowchik January/February 2002, 18-25).

A member of the wastewater treatment team at Baxter's facility in Halle, Germany, samples wastewater effluent for environmental compliance assurance. *Courtesy of Baxter International Inc.*

Some food manufacturers also have sought to be greener, as evidenced by a plethora of available natural foods products. Some products are created with a cause in mind, such as Ben & Jerry's One Sweet Whirled™ flavor, which was named for the Dave Matthews Band's song "One Sweet World." Ben & Jerry's is working with the Dave Matthews Band and SaveOurEnvironment.org (a coalition of environmental organizations) to encourage the public to pledge to reduce its emissions of carbon dioxide, a major greenhouse gas that contributes to global warming. In addition, proceeds from the sale of One Sweet Whirled™ will support initiatives to end global warming and will be given to the Band's Bama Works Foundation.

Volkswagen's New Beetle – 2006 model.
Courtesy of Volkswagen of America.

Baxter International employees at the company's Haina, Dominican Republic, facility stretch to help prevent ergonomic injuries. *Courtesy of Baxter International Inc.*

Through Ben & Jerry's flavor "One Sweet Whirled," the company encourages the public to reduce its carbon dioxide emissions. *Courtesy of Ben & Jerry's.*

Closing the loop. *Courtesy of Interface Flooring Systems.*

Companies selling greener foods – organic and not genetically modified – are increasingly popular. National companies, such as Whole Foods and Wild Oats, and more regional chains, such as the Southeast's Greenlife Grocery, offer a broad array of greener foods and household items.

Some companies within the flooring industry also have embraced greening. Collins & Aikman, a carpet manufacturer, recycles used carpeting in the production of its new carpet products. Commercial flooring giant Interface, Inc., has developed an aggressive program to achieve ecological sustainability, resulting in cleaner production processes and more eco-friendly products, including carpet tiles. The company states, "Interface continually looks for new technologies to reduce its reliance on nonrenewable materials. In 2004, Interface introduced its first commercial modular carpet made with Polylactic Acid (PLA), a derivative of corn."

Clothing designers also are working to be greener. Famed clothing designer Giorgio Armani has incorporated environmentally preferable hemp[6] into his design palette, stating, "When I discovered how efficient hemp is, it was an easy decision to use it, since it's my belief that clothing should not hurt the environment..." (Boodro 2002, 72-81). The Delano Collection makes clothing – as well as furniture and houseware – from greener materials, including a woman's winter coat made of 100 percent organic wool with bamboo buttons.

One hundred percent organic wool coat. *Photographer Jina Lee. Model Summer Rayne Oakes. Hair/make-up, Oggi. Courtesy of Delano Collection.*

A variety of greener products, including those for babies, are sold at a Whole Foods store. *Courtesy of Whole Foods.*

IKEA, which manufactures furniture for the home, requires all of its stores to reuse, recycle, or create energy from 75 percent of their waste (IKEA 2002). Herman Miller, a company that produces office furnishings, has won several environmental awards over the past decade and was named by *Fortune* magazine as one of America's most admired companies in 1999 (Herman Miller 2002, section 1999, para. 2). Steelcase, a company that makes products for the workplace environment, has produced the Think™ chair. The chair was certified by McDonough Braungart Design Chemistry to be environmentally safe, is 99 percent recyclable, and comprises up to 41 percent recycled materials. Meanwhile, New York-based Scrapile, founded by designers Bart Bettencourt and Carlos Salgado, creates furniture from wood scraps originating from the woodworking industry.

Created for the earth as well as for ergonomic comfort, the Think™ chair was conceived, developed, and produced for maximum sustainability. *Photo by Jeremy Frechette Photography. Courtesy of Steelcase.*

Herman Miller's Celle chair is made of 33 percent recycled content and is 99 percent recyclable. *Courtesy of Herman Miller, Inc.*

Each stage of the Think™ chair's life cycle was considered: raw materials, production, transport, use, and end of life. Pictured here are Niki Bey (conducted the lifecycle assessment of the chair), Jay Bolus (of McDonough Braungart Design Chemistry), and Kirt Hiedmann (the lead engineer). *Photo by Jeremy Frechette Photography. Courtesy of Steelcase.*

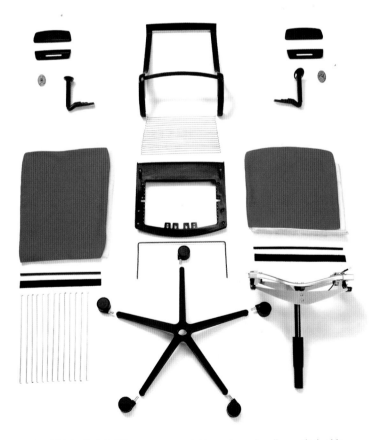

Scrapile crates made from New York woodworking industry scraps. *Courtesy of Scrapile.*

The Think chair is 99 percent recyclable and can be dismantled with simple hand tools into well-labeled components. *Photo by Jeremy Frechette Photography. Courtesy of Steelcase.*

In the architectural arena, companies such as Integrative Design Collaborative, William McDonough + Partners, and the RMI/ENSAR Built Environment team have been at the forefront of redefining how the human-built environment is designed and created. The demand for greener buildings is growing at a steady pace as concerns over high energy costs, ecological degradation, and indoor environmental pollution are viewed as symptoms of poor design that, ultimately, is expensive to maintain and redress. Organizations such as Condé Nast, Herman Miller, Ford Motor Company, Chesapeake Bay Foundation, Gap, and Oberlin College have incorporated green principles into their building designs and renovations.

Herman Miller's Marketplace facility was certified as LEED Gold.
Courtesy of Herman Miller, Inc.

Herman Miller's GreenHouse manufacturing/office complex. Designed by William McDonough + Partners. *Courtesy of Herman Miller, Inc.*

Entrance to the Chesapeake Bay Foundation. *Photo by Loretta Jergensen, Chesapeake Bay Foundation.*

Outside the Chesapeake Bay Foundation. *Photo by Loretta Jergensen, Chesapeake Bay Foundation.*

Another industry adopting greener practices is that of landscape design. With a goal of creating healthier ecosystems, greener landscaping practices include the use of native plants, low-water techniques, and composting. It avoids the use of chemical fertilizers and pesticides because they harm the health of plant and animal communities, including the microflora and microfauna that live in the soil. The Regenesis Group is one company that works with its clients to regenerate healthy ecological functioning during the process of real estate development.

The hotel and tourism industry also has become involved with greening. The Green Hotels Association has member hotels around the world that are working to reduce their environmental impact by saving water, energy, and other resources. For example, Natura Hotels was developed by green-minded entrepreneurs who wanted to start a greener hotel chain. The company's first hotel, located in Victoria, British Columbia, is expected to open in 2008. Some of the hotel's green features will include a LEED[7] platinum building certification; a rooftop park that holds an organic garden, which will provide food for the hotel's restaurant while adding insulation; a renewable energy power plant that will power all of the hotel's needs; plenty of daylighting via a seven-story atrium; a chemical-free laundry and pool; and on-site waste and greywater recycling.

Natura Dockside Urban Resort and Spa, Victoria, British Columbia.
Courtesy of Natura Hotels.

The Raptor Center, part of Holland America Line's Alaska cruise. *Courtesy of Holland America Line.*

Couple traveling on a Holland America Line vessel. *Courtesy of Holland America Line.*

Even luxury travel is becoming greener. For instance, Holland America Line, which complied with standards for waste processing and disposal before they became law, has a "zero discharge" policy in certain areas in which discharge is allowed legally. The company trains every crewmember in environmental issues, undergoes annual environmental audits, and has an extensive recycling program.

Holland America Line vessel in Alaska. *Courtesy of Holland America Line.*

Clearly, the environment is playing an ever-greater role in business practices, and this trend is expected to continue as environmental pressures increase over time (Winsemius and Guntram 2002). Therefore, businesses that hope to exist over the long-term will need to adapt to local, regional, and global ecological opportunities and constraints just as they adapt to those opportunities and constraints within the economic marketplace.

Coca-Cola's CEO Roberto Guizueta has said,

> While we were once perceived as simply providing services, selling products and employing people, business now shares in much of the responsibility for our global quality of life. Successful companies will handle this heightened sense of responsibility quite naturally, if not always immediately. I say this not because successful business leaders are altruistic at heart. I can assure you many are not. I say it because they will demand that their companies will remain intensely focused on the needs of their customers and consumers. (As cited in Winsemius and Guntram 2002, 23)

Nonetheless, the environment is an increasingly central issue to businesses, and some even believe that business will be responsible for finding solutions to the world's environmental problems. Interface's founder and chairman, Ray Anderson, has stated, "Business is the largest, wealthiest, most pervasive institution on Earth, and responsible for most of the damage. It must take the lead in directing the Earth away from collapse, and toward sustainability and restoration" (Winsemius and Guntram 2002, 196). Harry Pearce, General Motors' Vice Chairman, has stated that although everyone is responsible for environmental health, "business must take the lead, because only business has a global reach, the innovative capability, the capital and, most importantly, the market motivation to develop the technologies that will allow the world to truly achieve sustainable development" (Winsemius and Guntram 2002, 195).

Paper made of grass and recycled fiber. *Courtesy of Twisted Limb Paperworks.*

Big companies are not the only ones involved in becoming more environmentally friendly. One small company, Twisted Limb Paperworks, recycles a combination of grocery bags, grass cuttings, junk mail, and office paper to produce its 100 percent-recycled papers. Because all of the papers' colors come from the source materials, no dyes are used. Furthermore, the company provides at least half of its studio's energy using electricity from greener sources, has adults with developmental disabilities do some of the prep work required to make the paper, and gives 10 percent of its annual profits to environmental and community groups.

Paper made with 100 percent recycled fiber. *Courtesy of Twisted Limb Paperworks.*

Antarctic sunset. *Photo by Dave Mobley, Jet Propulsion Laboratory. Courtesy of the National Oceanic and Atmospheric Administration.*

Clif Bar, the maker of energy bars, has worked to create greener products and business practices. For instance, it uses certified organic ingredients in its bars; 100 percent certified organic cotton in all of its promotional tote bags and T-shirts; 100 percent post-consumer-content recycled paper; non-toxic inks and recycled, unbleached papers in its printing; 100 percent recycled paperboard for its cartons, which also were redesigned to reduce 90,000 pounds of shrink wrap annually; and *Native* Energy green tags (renewable energy credits sold by a privately held Native American energy company) to offset the energy it uses in its bakeries and office. Clif Bar also has an Eco Posse to green the company's internal activities, including finding ways to recycle or compost 80 percent of all waste at the company's headquarters. Its staff ecologist focuses on "food, agriculture, and resource use" (Clif Bar 2005). The company intends to move toward zero waste and is committed to seven causes, including working to eliminate the environmental causes of breast cancer.

One of Clif Bar's products. *Courtesy of Clif Bar.*

The organic Z Bar for kids. *Courtesy of Clif Bar.*

Maine-based Planet Dog makes toys and other items for dogs and cats. The founders stated, "We wanted to sort of encapsulate what we thought was special about Ben & Jerry's and Patagonia, pick it up, and drop it right in the pet industry" (CNN, "News Night with Aaron Brown," May 2005). The company's most popular product is a ball that is both durable and easily recyclable, which reduces manufacturing waste. Planet Dog has a philanthropic arm through which it donates proceeds to such organizations as the Susan G. Komen Breast Cancer Foundation.

Planet Dog's Ribbon Buddy dog toy.
Courtesy of Planet Friendly PR.

Emory Knoll Farms provides plants and expertise for extensive green roof systems. This Maryland-based company farms land that has been in its family since 1709. Today, it is guided by the Natural Step principles of sustainability (see Glossary). Much of the land has been set aside to restore native meadow plants and trees in order to recreate habitat for native species. Emory Knoll's buildings are energy- and resource-efficient, and the company is using biodiesel to heat its greenhouses, farm, and personal vehicles. It hopes to be a model for other companies in the nursery trade.

What Is Sustainable?

Although I have defined sustainable, sustainability, and sustainable development in the Glossary of this book, it is worth stating here that I view "green" and "sustainable" as synonymous. Something cannot be green, or environmentally friendly, unless it provides sustenance for ecosystems. Though there are many definitions of the word sustainable, a few guiding questions used to determine if something is sustainable are shown below.

From an ecological perspective, does the product/activity…

> * …benefit numerous species, not just humans, throughout its entire life cycle?
> * …materially give back at least as much it takes throughout its entire life cycle? ("giving back" can be viewed on the scale of the individual organism, species, and ecosystem)

For a product/activity that relies on the use of renewable virgin materials, does it…

> * …give back to the same place(s) from which those materials were taken? If it gives back to the place(s) of material origin, does it do so in a timely manner? (Clearly, sustainability has temporal and spatial components that need to be considered. A more detailed exploration of these issues will be considered in a forthcoming book.)

If the answer is "No" to any of these questions, we know that an activity is not green on one or more temporal or spatial scales. There appears to be some consensus among green business researchers that no company can claim to be ecologically sustainable. Nonetheless, many have made an enormous difference for environmental health simply by reducing their environmental harm and by working to continuously improve their environmental performances. Today's greening activities are important steps in the transition toward sustainable business and industry.

Furthermore, several authors (Rowledge, Barton, and Brady 1999) have suggested that the foundation of sustainability comprises three "pillars" – environment, equity, and economy. These three pillars sometimes have been referred to as the "triple bottom line," indicating that businesses and economies need to broaden their view of their economic "bottom line" to include all three issues. This conceptual triad of sustainability is represented in the figure below.

As important as it is to address environmental, social, and economic issues, the notion of the three pillars of sustainability, or the triple bottom line, is problematic because it seems to imply that these three issues – environment, economy, and equity – have equal standing. Though these three issues are *key* for a healthy society, the ecological reality is that the environment is the context within which all else exists. It has been recognized that "Our industrial economy, indeed any human economy, is contained within and dependent upon the natural world" (Nattrass and Altomare 1999, 4) and that "… the human economy is a fully dependent sub-system of the ecosphere" (Wackernagel and Rees 1996, 4). Though economies and social equity could not occur without ecosystems, the same cannot be said in reverse. The existence of ecosystems depends neither on the existence of human economies nor social equity, although *these two factors do play a role in modern ecological health.* "As a popular saying among ecologists goes, 'Ecosystems support economies, not vice versa'" (Jennings and Zandenbergen 1995, 1015). Therefore, to put economy, social equity, and ecology on the same level as the three necessary elements of ecological sustainability is ecologically inaccurate. Instead, I would suggest that long-term economic health requires social health and equity, both of which require ecological health. As the figure below indicates, the environment is the foundation for society, which creates economies. Although economies are created by societies, they are fully dependent upon the material resources of the environment.

Therefore, this book's relative inattention to the social and general economic aspects of sustainability does not imply that these issues are inconsequential. Rather, it simply indicates my assumption that ecological health is necessary for the long-term existence of healthy societies and economies. It also recognizes the need to limit this book's scope.

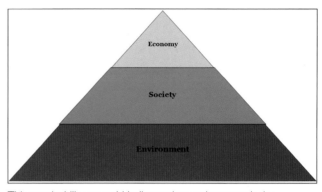

This sustainability pyramid indicates that environment is the foundation of both society and economy. *Townsend 2004.*

The Rise of Green Business

The greening of business and industry has advanced through four major stages in the U.S. These stages, the result of changing political, economic, social, and environmental factors, have been cumulative with each stage building on the previous ones. The first stage began toward the end of the nineteenth century and was characterized by the establishment of basic environmental regulations that typically focused more on human health from industrial activity than on the need to reduce resource use. The second stage began with the creation of environmental laws that tended to focus on pollution prevention. The third stage was characterized largely by the competing circumstances of corporate growth and associated resource use on the one hand and new environmental regulations over hazardous waste concerns and a rising call for corporate environmental accountability on the other. Currently, firms are entering the fourth stage, which is focused primarily on intensive resource efficiency and more stringent pollution prevention. In the final chapter, I suggest that a fifth stage, which I refer to as business ecology but which others may call by different names, will redefine the business-environment relationship entirely and help to define the future of green business.

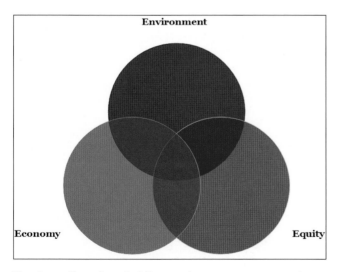

The three pillars of sustainability – environment, economy, and equity. *Townsend 2004.*

The lines separating one stage from another are not clearly defined; instead, they overlap. Nor does greening represent the interests and activities of every company. Though greening is increasing in popularity and sophistication, there are some that, for reasons discussed later, have not responded to environmental concerns.

Businesses' entry into the fourth stage is a fairly recent phenomenon. In the early 1990s, few businesses appeared to be paying much attention to their environmental impacts beyond complying with environmental regulations. Yet, that decade saw a shift in priority, as hazardous waste became only one of many environmental concerns associated with business (and other human) activities. Global climate change, the loss of biological diversity, the destruction of ecosystems, acid rain, the loss of topsoil, and the growing hole in Earth's protective ozone layer all became cause for worldwide concern.

In 1992, the UN hosted the United Nations Conference on Environment and Development (UNCED) – also called the Earth Summit – in Rio de Janeiro to address these and other issues. Representatives from governments and non-governmental organizations (NGOs) met to discuss the need for sustainable development. From this conference emerged Agenda 21, a detailed plan to achieve sustainable development. However, a few years went by before a large number of businesses developed formal environmental strategies. Once the move toward greener businesses began, it took root quickly.

In 1995, Arthur D. Little conducted a study that suggested that only 4 percent of the 187 companies that responded considered environmental issues seriously in their business decisions (Finnegan 1999, 54). Just two years later, however, another study indicated that over 80 percent of Fortune 500 companies had created environmental charters and that most multinational firms had designed environmental strategies in response to stakeholder pressures (Maxwell, Rothenberg, Briscoe, and Marcus 1997). As the decade wore on, environmental issues began to be considered strategically (Dobers and Wolff 1995). In 1998, *Industry Week* magazine conducted a study of 287 businesses and found that 90 percent of them considered the environment in their activities (Finnegan 1999, 54).

Reducing businesses' environmental impacts benefits numerous species. *Photo by David Wiley. Courtesy of the National Oceanic and Atmospheric Administration.*

Some companies found ways to make greening pay off. For the first time, a number of firms began looking beyond compliance as they sought to increase their profits and productivity by creating more re-source-efficient, healthier workplaces while reducing their environmental harm. Additionally, the trend to move "beyond compliance" enabled companies to avoid the costs associated with reacting to changing environmental regulations on timelines that were not their own. As a result, companies that proactively stayed ahead of environmental regulations found that they could 1) avoid the costs of reacting to new regulations, 2) keep ahead of competing companies that do not outpace regulations, and 3) influence future regulations by creating greener technologies and/or processes. Businesses during this stage began to incorporate environmental considerations into business strategy. They also became more proactive, working to identify business opportunities in greening, assess their likely operational impacts on the environment, and decrease waste and pollution ahead of regulations (Berry and Rondinelli 1998).

The Carteret-Craven Electric Cooperative, which provides power to more than 35,000 members in North Carolina, was instrumental in building a wetland needed to restore Jumping Run Creek. The creek drains into the White Oak River Basin, an important area for shellfish. *Courtesy of Carteret-Craven Electric Cooperative.*

Meanwhile, the number of environmental regulations continued to grow. In 1970, there were about 2,000 environmental rules and regulations (Berry and Rondinelli 1998, 39). By 1998, U.S. federal, state, and local governments had created over 100,000 (Berry and Rondinelli 1998, 39).

During this stage, companies also gained an increased understanding of the severe penalties associated with ignoring environmental issues as well as economic and social ones, such as fair trade and workers' rights. Although some companies, such as Dow, 3M, and SC Johnson started environmental initiatives long before they were popular (largely for economic benefit), others, such as Interface, Inc., began implementing greener practices, as sustainability became an increasingly mainstream concept following the Earth Summit.

By the early 1990s, several companies had created waste minimization programs. These included Allied Signal, Amoco, AT&T, Boeing, Chevron, Dow Chemical, General Dynamics, General Electric, IBM, Polaroid, and Xerox (Berry and Rondinelli 1998, 41). Companies began to conduct audits to ensure that they were complying with environmental regulations, and some used these audits and other tools to identify opportunities for environmental improvements (Berry and Rondinelli 1998).

Nonetheless, large industrial accidents and environmentally related human rights issues continued to gain the attention of government, industry, and the public. Royal Dutch/Shell's 1995 crises over the Brent Spar oil platform and the execution of people protesting its Nigerian oil development provide two examples. In April 1998, a tailings reservoir, created by the Swedish-Canadian mining company Boliden, collapsed in Spain. Toxic sludge poured over 4,200 acres of farmland and threatened Donana National Park, one of the largest nature reserves in Europe. Cleanup costs were estimated at $320 million, most of which was not covered by insurance (Winsemius and Guntram 2002).

Large-scale, highly visible events such as these have had a profound impact on many industries and companies worldwide. The company response has been focused mainly on what I refer to as *reduction and replacement strategies* – the reduced use of resources through efficiency and the replacement of harmful substances with less harmful ones. These include using fewer resources and less energy, replacing virgin materials with recycled stock, reducing or preventing pollution at the source, and, even, committing to the concept of zero waste. Some companies became interested in sustainable development or, simply, sustainability, and developed and implemented environmental management systems. Meanwhile, others took steps to understand and improve their environmental performances through environmental audits, benchmarking, and other means. Firms also began to report on social issues and human rights in their sustainability or environmental reports.

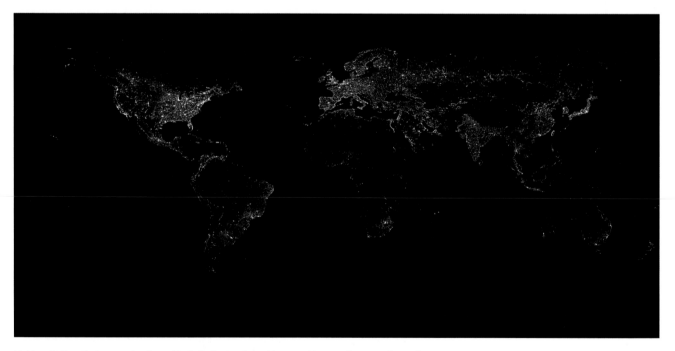

Light pollution that emanates from Earth indicates the widespread human impact of people on the planet. *Courtesy of NASA's Visible Earth team (http://visibleearth.nasa.gov/).*

General Dynamics reduced its hazardous waste emissions by 40 million pounds between 1984 and 1988 (Berry and Rondinelli 1998, 42). Chevron eliminated 60 percent of its hazardous waste emissions between 1987 and 1990, saving the company over $10 million in waste disposal costs (Berry and Rondinelli 1998, 42). Between 1988 and 1993, General Electric reduced its harmful emissions by 90 percent (Berry and Rondinelli 1998, 42). From 1990 to 1995, Xerox eliminated 50 percent of its hazardous waste (Berry and Rondinelli 1998, 42). Scott Paper also worked to reduce, reuse, and recycle waste and to replace less environmentally friendly materials with greener ones (Berry and Rondinelli 1998).

Demand-side management, which emerged from the utility industry, was adopted by some companies as a means of improving their environmental performances. This type of management focuses on customer needs and follows three principles: "1) do not waste product (electricity); 2) sell exactly what the customer demands; and 3) make the customer more efficient in the use of the product" (Berry and Rondinelli 1998, 43). Using this approach, Proctor & Gamble created "highly concen-trated liquid detergents and refill packs," which eliminated the need for over 152,000 tons of packaging in 1995 (Berry and Rondinelli 1998, 43).

A growing number of industry green business best practices were developed, such as those associated with design for environment (DfE) and eco-efficiency. Using DfE practices, Proctor & Gamble set its goal of eliminating waste from certain business areas through better design by 1998 (Berry and Rondinelli 1998, 43). General Motors designed its Saturns for ease of disassembly, enabling about 95 percent of the cars to be recycled; it also built the auto industry's first disassembly plant for cars in Maryland (Berry and Rondinelli 1998, 44).

In 1992, the Laidlaw Corporation and Pitney Bowes developed a joint venture for the disassembly and separation of office equipment, preventing over 870,000 pounds of waste from entering landfills in only four years (Berry and Rondinelli 1998, 43-44). Meanwhile, Dell Computer began using fully recyclable fillings and coatings in its Optiplex computer chassis (Rondinelli 1998, 43).

Eliminating waste removes the need for landfills such as this one in Malta, which emits toxic smoke as other waste burns underground. *Courtesy of Victor Mercieca.*

A new landfill under construction on the island of Malta. *Courtesy of Victor Mercieca.*

During this period, green business authors Stead and Stead (1996) recognized the use of two types of sustainability strategies – process-driven and market-driven ones. Process-driven sustainability strategies are based on resource efficiency. They help to save the company money, often through the redesign of products or processes. Market-driven sustainability strategies provide economic benefits because they occur when the company differentiates its products from those of its competitors. Together, the authors have suggested, these strategies reflect product stewardship.

The fourth stage was characterized by another type of sustainability strategy as well though it was employed far less often. That was what I refer to as a *non-production sustainability strategy*. Such a strategy occurred when a company decided that the existence of one of its products was environmentally harmful and stopped manufacturing it.[8] This strategy is not related to replacing more harmful materials with less harmful ones. Instead, it focuses on ending the manufacture of products that are inherently harmful to the environment, including human health.

By the end of the twentieth and beginning of the twenty-first centuries, many companies had adopted the triple bottom-line concept, which views true sustainability as dependent not only on environmental sustainability but also on social and economic sustainability (Elkington 1998). Still others had adopted corporate codes of conduct, such as the CERES Principles and the Business Charter for Sustainable Development,[9] to guide their actions toward the environment.

Companies also began to examine their reasons for being. After all, conventional thinking dictated that the sole purpose of companies was to earn profits for their founders and shareholders (Milton Friedman as cited in Allenby 1999). Although this view still exists, it has been countered by another – the need for companies to be environmentally and socially responsible. This latter idea has been adopted not only by companies known for selling greener products, such as Patagonia and The Body Shop, but also by more mainstream companies, such as Interface, Inc., and Mitsubishi Corp., which have recognized that environmental health is necessary for business success.

Tachi Kiuchi (1997), Mitsubishi's CEO, has indicated that the economy and environment are not in conflict since economic opportunities arise from being greener. Kiuchi (1997) also has stated that maximizing profits is not the corporation's mission: "We don't run our business to earn profits. We earn profits to run our business" (63). Kiuchi is not alone in believing that businesses can be greener and maximize profits as well. The late David Packard, Hewlett Packard's co-founder, expressed similar sentiments:

Why are we here? I think many people assume, wrongly, that a company exists solely to make money. Money is an important part of a company's existence, if the company is any good. But a result is not a cause. We have to go deeper and find the real reason for our being. As we investigate this, we inevitably come to the conclusion that a group of people get together and exist as an institution that we call a company, so that they are able to accomplish something collectively that they could not accomplish separately – they make a contribution to society, a phrase which sounds trite but is fundamental. (Handy 1998, 70-71)

Furthermore, there was a distinct movement toward greening not just by for-profit businesses but also by other organizations, such as government entities, NGOs, cities, communities, and families. For example, some governments (e.g., Germany, New Zealand, The Netherlands) have begun to change their policies in response to environmental damage. Realizing that they wield enormous economic power, they have instituted greener purchasing policies in their procurement of buildings, office products, company fleets, and other goods, thereby helping both to influence the success of greener products and technologies and to encourage the development of new ones. Governments at all levels – federal, state, and county – have recognized that they have both the opportunity and the obligation to serve as examples to the individuals and businesses within their political borders and to protect, rather than squander, their current and future residents' natural resources.

Children in Mozambique campaign against malaria, which is predicted to increase as climate change intensifies. Businesses are believed to be a major contributor to anthropogenic climate change. *Courtesy of the US Agency for International Development.*

Similarly, some cities, communities, and families have begun to recognize that the choices they make have direct environmental consequences. Individual families and entire communities have begun working to develop greener, more self-sufficient living patterns. This is evidenced by the creation of community-based economies and barter systems, co-housing, and a growing interest in greener building techniques (e.g., straw bale, cob, rammed earth, ecobag[10]/sandbag, isochanvre[11]) and in living "off the grid."[12]

Using natural materials to finish the exterior of the People's Coop in Portland, Oregon. *Courtesy of David Eisenberg.*

Actor and environmentally concerned citizen Woody Harrelson with Manitoba Harvest™ hemp seeds. *Courtesy of Planet Friendly PR.*

Furthermore, growing concerns over increasing energy prices and the dependence on others for energy and other resources have provided additional incentives to decentralize energy production and become materially self-reliant at home and at work. This interest in greener lifestyles has spurred the growth of the multibillion-dollar "lifestyle of health and sustainability" (LOHAS) industry.

Organically grown cotton clothing and sleepwear from Chandler & Greene. *Photos by David Nations. Courtesy of Chandler & Greene.*

Natural dog treats from Blue Dog Bakery. *Courtesy of Planet Friendly PR.*

Guayaki's Yerba Mate, an organic beverage made of ingredients harvested by hand in a Paraguay rainforest. *Courtesy of Planet Friendly PR.*

Loading Yerba Mate ingredients into a truck. *Courtesy of Planet Friendly PR.*

Glee natural chewing gum made of sustainably harvested rainforest chicle. *Courtesy of Verve, Inc.*

One company that is doing well by doing good is T.S. Designs. This North Carolina-based company has committed to sustainability in its mission: "…to build a sustainable company by looking after People, the Planet, and Profits" (T.S. Designs, Sustainability 2005). The company makes shirts from 100 percent-certified organic cotton and water-based inks. It also has invested in solar panels, has a company garden and walking trail on its property, and the owner drives a car that is fueled by vegetable oil and biodiesel. T.S. Designs has won several awards for its environmental commitment, including the Co-Op America Green Leadership Award, Governor's Conservation Achievement Award, Save Our State North Carolina Sustainability Award, N.C. Recycler of the Year, Governor's Award for Excellence in Waste Reduction, and others.

T.S. Designs employee working in the company garden. *Courtesy of T.S. Designs.*

T.S. Designs founder Eric Henry with landscape architect Bonnie Hutchinson on the company's walking trail. *Courtesy of T.S. Designs.*

Several people involved in the greening of business have suggested that business is about to enter a new phase – one that has been referred to by industrialist Stephen Schmidheiny as "a new industrial revolution" (Berry and Rondinelli 1998) and others as "the next industrial revolution" (Anderson 1998; Hawken, Lovins, and Lovins 1999). Characterized by the movement toward zero waste and the further incorporation of systems thinking into company activities, companies will 1) save money because they will experience no waste and 2) reduce their environmental harm because there will be no pollution and fewer demands on natural resources. This period includes the development of business-to-business (B2B), closed-loop relationships, such as those exemplified by eco-industrial parks. This will require companies to move beyond the checklist approach to greening and to think in a more integrative fashion.

Chemist Michael Braungart and architect William McDonough (2002) have contributed significantly to this vision with their concepts of technical and organic nutrients. Technical nutrients are human-engineered materials that cannot be metabolized easily by ecological systems but that can be used and reused in industrial processes. Organic nutrients are those materials that can be metabolized easily by Earth's systems.

Many of today's products, they have suggested, result in a considerable amount of wasted resources. Sometimes, this occurs because products embody both technical and biological nutrients that cannot be separated easily. For example, aseptic packaging is made of an organic nutrient, paper, which can decompose and feed back into ecosystems; however, the packaging also is made of a technical nutrient, a metallic lining, which can be recycled and used in the manufacture of other products. By combining these two materials in a way that makes their separation difficult or costly, their manufacturers have created a waste product that provides neither organic nor technical feedstock.

If such materials were kept separate or were easy to separate, products' technical nutrients could provide "food" for other human manufacturing processes while organic nutrients could be reused by ecological systems (e.g., via composting). This strategy has profound implications not only in how businesses develop and manufacture products, but it also suggests the need for firms' full accountability throughout their products' life cycles. If these changes come to pass, they will provide significant steps in companies' transitions toward ecological sustainability.[13]

As businesses and industries were poised to undergo some fundamental changes, the beginning of the twenty-first century represented a setback as an environmentally regressive administration took power. Though the new government could have played a central role in encouraging and facilitating businesses' ecological responsibility, it relaxed a number of environmental regulations that could have served as both disincentives to free riders and incentives to companies interested in greening.

For example, in August 2003, the administration changed a 1977 Clean Air Act provision that required plant operators to add pollution-reduction equipment when they upgrade their facilities. Strong lobbying by the electricity and oil industries appears to have paid off, as the Environmental Protection Agency (EPA) exempted thousands of older factories (e.g., pulp and paper mills, chemical plants, manufacturers), refineries, and power plants from having to use pollution prevention technologies when upgrading their facilities (The Associated Press 2003). It is too early to determine the specific impacts that this and other environmentally regressive actions will have on the greening of business.

Regardless of the political context, this fourth stage has represented significant progress in the environmental performances, accountability, and transparency of companies that have committed to greening. Yet, as several green business leaders and researchers have noted, today's green business best practices have not resulted in companies that are green. Though a new industrial revolution might be the next step in industry's move toward becoming greener, I contend that companies will need to take a different path than that being discussed at present for sustainability to be possible.

The Purpose of This Book

The purpose of this book is four-fold. First, I want to illustrate just how mainstream business greening has become. A growing number of companies have helped to pave the way by establishing, testing, and modifying green business best practices and determining what has worked and what has not.

Second, I want to explain why many companies are choosing to improve their environmental performances. As stories of greening appear in the media with increasing frequency, many are questioning whether corporate greening activities are out of genuine concern for the environment or whether they are just "greenwash." Though I wish that all companies chose to become greener because it is the right thing to do for the environment, there are several legitimate incentives for greening, and this book explores them.

Third, many companies have heard about and are interested in being greener but do not know where to begin. This book offers a five-part conceptual model to help companies think about what needs to be greened and how to approach reducing the environmental harm associated with each of the firm's five "elements."

Fourth, though it is beyond the scope of this book, I feel I would be remiss if I did not discuss the need to fundamentally alter the nature of business and of greening. As I will discuss later, several individuals have recognized that most of today's best practices are inherently incapable of resulting in companies that are truly green insofar as being environmentally benign or, even, beneficial. I will explain why this is so and provide a brief overview of an alternative concept for the future of green business, which I intend to explore in an upcoming book.

Audience

This book was written for firms that are interested in learning more about greening business and for those that are committed to ecological sustainability but uncertain of how to approach it conceptually and practically. It also might be of use to governments interested in developing effective business-ecological policies. Many of the greening examples that are used come primarily from large companies since much of the available data on green business has focused on large corporations. Moreover, large corporations have access to vast amounts of capital, labor, and other material resources as well as networks of industrial and other relationships. As such, they wield an enormous amount of power. Nonetheless, this book also was written with small and mid-sized enterprises (SMEs) in mind and includes examples of some small and mid-sized companies. Similarly, though most case studies refer to for-profit companies, non-profit businesses have many of the same challenges that for-profits experience when it comes to reducing their environmental impacts. Thus, the intended audience includes non-profit organizations as well.

Clearly, it is not only businesses that need to be environmentally accountable and transparent. Other human organizations, including government entities, communities, and families, need to be environmentally responsible and aware because they also contribute significantly to environmental degradation through their activities. Therefore, this book might be of use to city, state, and national government agencies mandated to become greener; communities that want to become greener; policy-makers interested in developing more comprehensive regulations; and green business consultants and academicians.

To learn about reducing your company's environmental harm in the workplace, you can view the text from my earlier book *The Smart Office* on my web site (http://www.smartoffice.com) at no cost.

Not all companies choose to reduce their environmental harm out of concern for planetary health. *Courtesy of the National Atmospheric and Space Administration's (NASA's) Visible Earth team (http://visibleearth.nasa.gov/) and of Goddard Space Flight Center. Image by Reto Stöckli (land surface, shallow water, clouds). Enhancements by Robert Simmon (ocean color, compositing, 3D globes, animation). Data and technical support: MODIS Land Group; MODIS Science Data Support Team; MODIS Atmosphere Group; MODIS Ocean Group Additional data: USGS EROS Data Center (topography); USGS Terrestrial Remote Sensing Flagstaff Field Center (Antarctica); Defense Meteorological Satellite Program (city lights).*

Chapter 1
The Five Reasons Why Companies Are Greening

This chapter explores the five key reasons why some businesses are choosing to become greener. It offers examples of companies that have chosen to improve their environmental performances for one or more of these reasons. (Be aware that the companies discussed herein were selected as examples and do not necessarily represent the greenest firms in their industries.) Finally, the chapter surveys a few reasons why some companies might not choose to become greener while focusing on one in particular – the lack of green business training in many of today's MBA programs.

Overview

The ecological effects of businesses, industries, and economies have been well documented in the green business (Buccholz 1998), environmental (Brown et al. 2002), and ecological economics literatures (Costanza 1991). Although compelling for some, not all companies choose to become greener for environmental reasons. In fact, the growing body of green business literature suggests that companies become more environmentally friendly for one or more of several reasons.

For instance, Livio D. DeSimone, Chair and CEO of 3M Company, and Frank Popoff (1997), Chairman of Dow Chemical Company, have written that the 1992 Earth Summit in Rio de Janeiro signaled businesses to become greener for ecological, economic, and social reasons. Both men have served as chairs of the World Business Council for Sustainable Development.

Colin Hutchinson (1995), an environmental management consultant, has suggested that businesses are becoming greener due to legislative, social, environmental, and ethical reasons. Klaus North (1992), professor of International Management at Germany's Wiesbaden Business School, has purported that companies become greener following major industrial accidents, pressure from green consumers, the discovery of new markets, pressure from managers' families regarding their company's environmental pollution, competitive disadvantage due to green competitors, and the desire to stay ahead of new environmental regulations. Meanwhile, Pratima Bansal, assistant professor and J.C. Taylor Fellow at the University of Western Ontario's Richard Ivey School of Business, and Kendall Roth (2000), J. Willis Cantey Chair of International Business and Economics at the University of

South Carolina's Darla Moore School of Business, have reported that the green business literature offers regulatory compliance, pressure from stakeholders, competitive advantage, senior management commitment, ethical concerns, and critical events as reasons for greening. Finally, a diverse group comprising author Ernest Callenbach, physicist Fritjof Capra, organizational consultant Lenore Goldman, author and design ecology professor Rudiger Lutz, and geography and environmental history professor Sandra Marburg have explained that companies become greener out of a desire to be ecologically responsible, improve their image, safeguard themselves, comply with legal requirements, increase profits, respond to market pressure, enhance the quality of life, and protect their employees (1995, 6, Figure I).

Together, these motivations for greening a company can be grouped into the following categories:

Environmental Impacts & Values

Environmental impacts – Companies in this category are motivated to become greener due to the potential or real environmental harm that they already cause. For example, a firm might decide to stop producing cancer-causing substances or developing genetically modified seeds that could pollute the genetic code of natural species thereby threatening ecological integrity. Environmental values and impacts are not mutually exclusive categories.

Environmental values – Companies in this category become greener primarily due to their environmental values, such as a belief that all living things, including humans, have the right to a good quality of life and a broad range of evolutionary opportunities through time. Similarly, they might follow the Hippocratic corollary to "do no harm." In the latter case, a company might decide not to develop a particular product or might stop producing an existing product due to its potential to cause harm to its employees, users, and the environment (a non-production sustainability strategy).

Government Regulation

Companies in this category institute greener behaviors in response to current or anticipated regulation. As a result, they might benefit in several ways. For instance, they might achieve or surpass current regulations by avoiding penalties (e.g., fines or lost market share when competitors move ahead of them), get a head start on developing greener technologies, help to shape the direction of greener technologies in their favor, and increase profits through compliance-related innovations.

Economic Opportunities & Disincentives

Companies in this category become greener for the competitive advantage gained by new products, processes, or greening strategies. They also might become greener to avoid the financial burdens associated with non-compliance or the failure to respond to environmental issues.

Organizational Crises

Companies in this category change or develop strategies and/or behaviors following one or more environmental or other crises that result from unethical behaviors, lack of transparency, and so on.

Stakeholder Pressure

Companies in this category respond to pressure from one or more stakeholders (e.g., employees, managers, customers, suppliers, industry, NGOs, shareholders, communities, politicians, regulators, and/or others). Although the environment is a key stakeholder (Callenbach et al. 1992; Bansal and Roth 2000), it is placed in a distinct category (Environmental Values & Impacts) due to its significance in some companies' decisions to improve their environmental performances.

These five reasons are illustrated in the figure below.

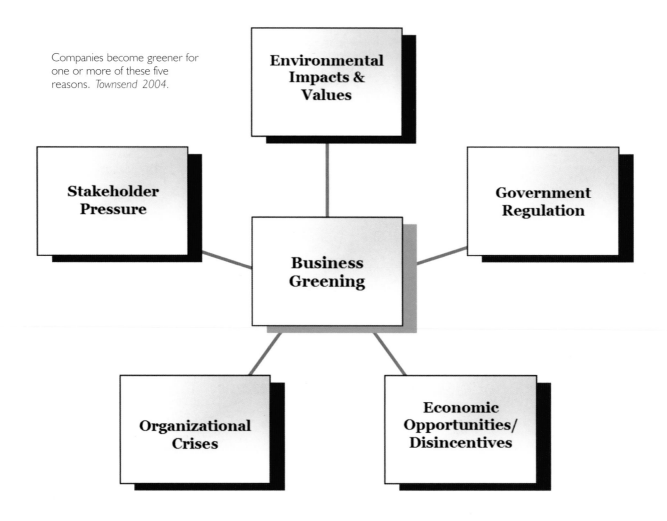

Companies become greener for one or more of these five reasons. *Townsend 2004*.

Of course, companies might decide to become greener not for one but for several of the above reasons. Moreover, they might not include the entire company in their efforts; instead, they might improve the environmental performance of only one or a few things, such as a building, department, activity (e.g., purchasing), or process (e.g., manufacturing).

The relationships among the five categories discussed above and those mentioned by North, Bansal and Roth, DeSimone and Popoff, Callenbach, and Hutchinson are shown in the table below.

Company Motivations for Greening: Proposed Alternative Principles	North (1992)	Bansal & Roth (2000)	DeSimone & Popoff (1997)	Callenbach (1995) (INEM)	Hutchinson (1995)
Environmental Impacts & Values	Pressure from managers' families regarding the company's environmental pollution	Senior management commitment Ethical concerns	Ecological reasons, Social reasons	Sense of ecological responsibility, Quality of life Employee protection	Environmental reasons Social reasons Ethical reasons
Government Regulation (current & anticipated)	Desire to preclude regulation	Regulatory compliance		Legal requirements	Legislative reasons
Economic Opportunities & Disincentives	Discovery of new markets Competitive disadvantage due to green competitors	Competitive advantage	Economic reasons	Profit Market pressure Safeguarding the company	
Organizational Crises	Major industrial accidents	Crisis events			
Stakeholder Pressure	Pressure from green consumers	Pressure from stakeholders		Image	

Though these five categories provide a general outline of the different reasons why businesses become greener, some of the categories are multi-dimensional and contain overlapping components. Thus, they might not perfectly delineate the reasons why companies improve their environmental performances.

For example, a company might decide to become greener due to existing and anticipated government regulations. But why is the company interested in regulatory compliance? One reason might be that the company wishes to be viewed as a good citizen. This might be due to the company's values and to the fact that it wishes to engender the trust of regulators, communities, potential customers, and other stakeholders. Therefore, internal and external stakeholder pressures might provide another incentive for meeting or exceeding compliance. Through compliance, the company also might want to avoid fines, imprisonment, or other penalties associated with regulatory non-compliance. Additionally, by outpacing new regulations, the company might hope to avoid losing time involved with compliance-related activities, thereby staying ahead of competitors and profiting handsomely as a result. Though regulation might be the primary incentive, a bundle of other incentives also can help to motivate a company toward greening.

This is true of the other four greening incentives as well. For instance, Royal Dutch/Shell (discussed later in this chapter) decided to become greener following some organizational crises. Though the company was in compliance with environmental regulations, these crises occurred, in part, due to the company's failure to respond to stakeholder pressures. The company began to take its stakeholders seriously when it felt, perhaps, the economic pain and social stigma associated with boycotts and other stakeholder-driven activities.

Drainage from the Escondida mine in Chile. *Courtesy of NASA's Visible Earth team (http://visibleearth.nasa.gov/) and National Atmospheric and Space Administration GSFC, MITI, ERSDAC, JAROS, and U.S./Japan ASTER Science Team.*

Unlike Royal Dutch/Shell, Suncor (now Suncor Energy, discussed later in this chapter) failed to comply with environmental regulations for a period of time (Rowledge, Barton, and Brady 1999). Its primary incentive to become greener came from stakeholder pressure over its poor environmental performance; however, one of the stakeholders that pressured the company for environmental improvements was its local government, which threatened to close one of the company's core businesses. Therefore, it was a mixture of pressure from certain stakeholders and the right combination of regulatory disincentives that prompted the company to improve its environmental performance.

The company 3M (also discussed later in this chapter) provides another example of mixed incentives for greening. This is a company that instituted resource-efficiency programs back in the 1970s, before most businesses were thinking of efficiency. However, in 2000, 3M announced that it would take one of its multi-million dollar surfactant products off the market because studies had shown it to be in the blood of people around the world. Though the company was operating in compliance with existing environmental regulations, it took the initiative to announce the problem publicly and phase out production. I suggest that the way in which 3M publicly handled the issue helped it to avert a potential organizational crisis. However, the company's incentives are unclear. Was it moved by the threat of impending regulatory action, the existence of internal stakeholder pressure, the desire to preempt external stakeholder pressure, and/or financial disincentives associated with potential loss of value for shareholders and others? Instead, the company's move resulted in the opposite, garnering praise for the company's environmental transparency and a rise in its stock price.

These examples indicate that companies can become green for a number of reasons, and some of these reasons cannot be teased apart easily. Although it is beyond the scope of this book, future researchers might wish to determine with greater precision companies' greening motivations in order to identify leverage points that can hasten organizational greening.

Hutchinson (1995) has proposed that there are several benefits associated with becoming greener just as there are disadvantages associated with *not* greening. For instance, companies that factor the environment into their business activities are more able to meet consumer demand for greener products, improve their reputations because they are environmentally accountable, and reduce their liability risks by using environmentally responsible business practices. They also increase their chances for getting investments from banks; furthermore, if they are added to socially responsible investing (SRI) lists, they will appeal to shareholders who want to invest in greener and more ethical businesses. Companies that integrate the environment into their business activities also tend to gain more market share, save money through resource efficiency, prevent pollution, pay lower insurance premiums, and recycle and reuse waste materials. They also attract and keep staff with similar values by having high workplace standards and engendering loyalty, maintaining a strong competitive edge, creating good community relations, becoming accredited product distributors or suppliers, developing partnerships with others who are becoming greener, and raising their chances for business longevity.

GrandyOats Nat Pierce and Aaron Anker have worked to create a green company. *Courtesy of Planet Friendly PR.*

Conversely, Hutchinson (1995) has explained, companies that do not incorporate environmental issues into their business practices might suffer the consequences in a number of ways. By ignoring the environment, companies are likely to damage their reputations, lose stakeholders' trust, and degrade the health of employees and others as well as incur penalties.

They also might lose business by failing to meet customer demands for greener products. Companies that ignore the environment might find that getting banks and shareholders to invest in them is increasingly difficult. Both share value and market share might fall when competitors gain ecological and related economic advantage. Companies also might lose their competitive edge because of the failure to realign R&D priorities with the market's direction.

Government fines and pressure from both industry and the public to respond to environmental issues are two more problems associated with environmental inaction. As a result of ignoring the environment, companies might pay increased insurance rates or have considerable difficulty becoming insured. Moreover, they might experience trouble finding and keeping good employees when company values do not reflect those of their staff. Firms also might alienate the local community because of their failure to work with it. All of these consequences make the company's long-term survival uncertain as it fails to adapt to a changing world in which environmental health becomes an increasing priority.

The table on the following page illustrates the connections between Hutchinson's (1995) benefits and costs associated with either greening or not greening, respectively, and the five reasons for greening ("Proposed Alternative Greening Responses" in the table on the following page).

Both the benefits of greening and the harm that can result from failing to implement greener measures can serve as *positive incentives* and *negative incentives*, respectively. Thus, the motivating factors that cause a company to improve its environmental performance might be positive and/or negative.

George Washington University's Mark Starik and Western Illinois University's Gordon Rands (1995) have explored the factors motivating companies either to respond or not to respond to environmental issues and concerns. Referring to these motivating factors as feedback, they explain that feedback either moves companies toward ecological sustainability (pro-sustainability) or away from it (anti-sustainability). They have developed a typology of four business responses to the environment – positive/pro-sustainability feedback, negative/pro-sustainability feedback, positive/anti-sustainability feedback, and negative/anti-sustainability feedback.

Positive incentives are represented by positive/pro-sustainability feedback, such as environmental awards, that indicates that the business should continue its greener behaviors. *Negative incentives* are represented by negative/pro-sustainability feedback, such as consumer boycotts, that signals businesses to "decrease or reverse" those organizational practices that are ecologically unsustainable (Starik and Rands 1995, 914). There also are positive and negative *disincentives* to greening, which are discussed in this chapter's last section on why some businesses do not improve their environmental performances.

The following five sections will discuss in more detail each of the five proposed motivations for greening business.

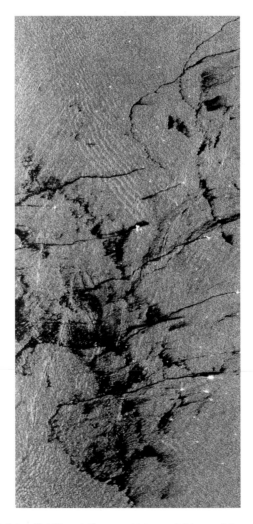

Oil slicks off drilling platforms, which are visible as white spots. *Courtesy of the National Atmospheric and Space Administration's Visible Earth team (http://visibleearth.nasa.gov/) and the National Atmospheric and Space Administration Jet Propulsion Laboratory.*

Responding to Environmental Issues:

Topic	Incorporating environmental issues into business results in….	Failing to respond to environmental issues results in….	Proposed Alternative Greening Responses
Consumer Demand	Increased business because green products meet customer demand	Lost business because of failure to meet shifting customer needs	Economic Opportunities & Disincentives
Risks	Reduced government and legal risks from efficient use of resources and environmentally accountable business practices	Damaged credibility when accidents occur that affect environmental health; this means poor public image and confidence and might be costly	
Investment	Increased investment from banks and shareholders; inclusion on ethical and environmental investment lists	Difficulty in raising money from shareholders and banks as company share value diminishes	
Efficiency	Gain in market share with more efficient products and processes	Lost market share as streamlined, efficient competitors outperform you	
Insurance	Lower insurance premiums	Higher insurance which reflects the high costs of environmental cleanup some environmental risks may not be insurable	
Competitive Edge	Ability to keep ahead of mainstream businesses; may be on environmentally accredited distributor and supplier lists for products and services	Inability to compete effectively when R&D and company priorities are not environmentally responsible	
Green Claims	Good reputation	Bad reputation for falsely touting company or products as environmentally responsible	Economic Opportunities & Disincentives, Stakeholder Pressure
Community	Develop cooperative, positive relationships with local community	Damaged credibility with local community, which hurts business	
Employees	Retention of good employees, whose environmental values and priorities are similar to those of the company	Lost staff to companies who reflect their own values	
Company Longevity	Better chances of survival through shared vision (stakeholder alignment), efficient resource use, lower risks, and useful, responsible products	Struggle to survive over time due to waste, loss of competitive edge, costs of environmental cleanup	
Pollution	Stronger economy through pollution prevention and decreased waste	Government penalties (e.g., fines, jail time), consumer backlash, and pressure from industry to clean up	Economic Opportunities Organizational Crises, Government Regulation (current & anticipated)

(Adapted from Hutchinson 1995, 115-117)

Environmental Impacts & Values

Some firms improve their environmental performances out of concern for their potential or real environmental impacts. Firms also might become greener as a result of environmental values, such as a reverence for all life or a Hippocratic desire to do no harm. This section explores how the environmental impacts *and* values of three companies – Patagonia, Chouinard Equipment, and Interface – became the driving force behind the companies' efforts toward ecological sustainability.

Patagonia & Chouinard Equipment

DeSimone and Popoff have suggested that the 1992 UNCED Earth Summit was the "wake-up call" for businesses to pay attention to their impacts on Earth's ecosystems (1997, xix). However, some businesses began long before that. Patagonia and its parent company Chouinard Equipment are two such businesses.

Patagonia is a California-based business that designs and supplies outdoor clothing. Though it first created its market niche by designing high-quality, technical clothing for those involved in such sports as biking, kayaking, surfing, skiing, rock climbing, ice climbing, and fishing, the company now also caters to other customers who enjoy the outdoors but do not require clothing that meets the same rigorous specifications.

Patagonia is a privately held company. It is one of several subsidiaries of the Lost Arrow Corporation, which was established in 1984. The other subsidiaries include Black Diamond (originally Chouinard Equipment), Patagonia Mail Order, and Great Pacific Ironworks. With 900 employees, Patagonia's 1998 sales were U.S. $165 million (Rowledge, Barton, and Brady 1999, 95).

The seeds of Patagonia's environmental commitment were sown long before the company was formed. In 1957, founder Yvon Chouinard was a young mountain climber who could not find a pair of climbing pitons that he liked. Those available were made of soft metal that bent during use. A self-taught blacksmith, he decided to forge his own pitons and sold them to his friends and other climbers as well. Shortly thereafter, Chouinard began to produce pitons. By the mid-1960s, he had found a business partner in fellow climber Tom Frost and was producing climbing hardware under the name Chouinard Equipment. Chouinard's company worked to redesign much of the equipment used in climbing in order to ensure that it met the rigors of the sport. By 1970, the company was the world's biggest supplier of climbing equipment, including pitons.

Despite their success, however, Chouinard and Frost came to believe that their business had become "an environmental villain" (Patagonia 1998, 3). As climbing increased in popularity worldwide and piton use skyrocketed on many well-traveled climbing routes, Chouinard began to see the cumulative damage that hammering pitons into rock crevices and, then, removing them was having on mountain faces. One summer, after climbing El Capitan along a degraded route that had been pristine just a few years prior, Chouinard returned home "in disgust" (Patagonia 1998, 3). He and Frost decided to phase out the production of pitons and develop aluminum chocks instead. At the time, few climbers knew about chocks or how to use them; however, because they were wedged into the rock face by hand, they left little trace of climbers' journeys (Patagonia 1998).

Chouinard and Frost realized that they not only needed to provide a more environmentally friendly product but also to educate a generation of climbers about the environmental harm associated with pitons and the advantages of using chocks. The company's 1972 catalogue discussed the environmental damage that pitons caused and offered a 14-page essay that explained how to use chocks for "clean climbing" (Rowledge, Barton, and Brady 1999). Within a few months, piton demand had dropped not only for Chouinard Equipment but also across the entire industry. Meanwhile, chocks could not be made quickly enough to fill the company's growing orders.

In addition to producing equipment, Chouinard began to expand into "soft" goods. Though the profit on climbing hardware was small, there was great profit potential in clothing for climbers and other outdoor enthusiasts. In the mid-1970s, the company moved into the soft goods market; however, the quality of some rugby shirts that Chouinard Equipment purchased for sale was inconsistent, and this caused tension between the partners with regard to the direction of the company. By the end of 1975, Chouinard and Frost had ended their partnership.

Chouinard continued to sell soft goods under the name Patagonia so that the apparel side of the business would not damage the reputation of the hardware side. In 1979, Patagonia Clothing Corporation was formed, and, in 1984, it simply became Patagonia, Inc. Like his first company, Chouinard's Patagonia was created around the enjoyment of the outdoors. Many of its practices reflect a clear concern for environmental health. These include hiring employees who are active in the outdoors, paying employees while they intern at environmental organizations, and encouraging employees to volunteer for environmental organizations on company time. They also include a Tithing Program through which money is given annually to small grassroots environmental organizations.

Moreover, despite the fact that its own market research indicates that only about 20 percent of its customers care about the impact of their purchases on the environment (Rowledge, Barton, and Brady 1999, 98), Patagonia has made environmental commitments due primarily to the internal environmental concerns and values of management and staff throughout the organization. This concern for the environment started at the top with Chouinard, who has worked to create a company that is environmentally friendly. Chouinard has stated,

> We believe quality is not something you can do piecemeal. Either you believe in quality, or you don't. Either it surfaces everywhere and you commit to it everywhere, or you don't. There is no gray area here…. It's all linked: Quality product, quality customer service, quality workplace, quality of life for your employees, even quality of life for all living things on this planet. If you miss any one piece, there is a good chance you'll miss it all. (As cited in Rowledge, Barton, and Brady 1999, 99)

One study conducted by *The Economist* supports Chouinard's sentiment that business and environmental quality are found together. Those firms that are the best managed also have the strongest environmental records; meanwhile, companies that are managed poorly have poor environmental records (as cited in North 1992).

Like Chouinard Equipment, Patagonia has sought to learn about its environmental impacts and improve them. For example, when it learned of the environmental damage associated with growing cotton using conventional, non-organic methods, Patagonia switched to 100 percent organic cotton for all of its cotton products. Additionally, when the company learned about the environmental impacts of using conventional fleece, which is made of polyester from crude oil, it developed a synthetic fleece – "Synchilla" – made of recycled milk bottles.

Shelled Synchilla Jacket. *Courtesy of Patagonia.*

The company has stated that it wants to help solve "the environmental crisis" – in part, by sharing its knowledge of organic cotton, renewable energy, and other issues with its millions of customers. The company has stated, "We have built an audience. We do feel great urgency that as a society we can't continue on the high consumptive pathway we're on. We need leadership to find a different way of being" (as cited in Rowledge, Barton, and Brady 1999, 106).

Patagonia has worked hard to build a company that reflects the environmental concerns and values of its founders and employees. In a market that is highly competitive and with products that can be difficult to differentiate among manufacturers, Patagonia has distinguished itself largely by its commitment to the environment and social equity, which is an essential part of its founder's commitment to "do the right thing."

Interface, Inc.

Interface, Inc., is the world's largest producer of carpet tiles and floor coverings. Founded in 1973, this Atlanta, Georgia-based company had net sales of $881.7 million in 2004, an increase of over $100 million in 2003 (Interface, Inc. 2005, 1). In 1997 and 1998, *Fortune* magazine named it one of the nation's 100 best companies for which to work (Interface, Recognitions and Awards 2003).

In 1994, Ray Anderson,[1] Interface's founder and then-CEO, began to consider his company's environmental impacts when he was asked to give a kick-off speech about his environmental vision. The speech was for Interface's research division, which had created a new task force to handle the growing number of requests from customers who wanted to know about the company's environmental policies. This task force was made of representatives from all of Interface's businesses. Its purpose was to develop a worldwide response to customers' questions regarding the company's environmental stance. The research division had invited Anderson to give the opening speech to the task force outlining the company's environmental vision; however, Anderson had none (Ray C. Anderson 1998). In the company's – and the world's – first public environmental sustainability report, Anderson explained, "Frankly, I didn't have a vision, except "comply, comply, comply…." (Interface, Inc. 1997, 1). He went on to explain that though he had heard the term "sustainable development," he did not know what it meant. Anderson reports that he "sweated for three weeks" over the kick-off speech (Interface, Inc. 1997, 1). Then, someone sent him a copy of Paul Hawken's *The Ecology of Commerce*, which Anderson has said changed his life: "It was an epiphany…. In preparing that kick-off speech, I went beyond mere compliance in a heartbeat" (Interface, Inc. 1997, 1).

Anderson gave the task force an environmental vision – "to make Interface the first name in industrial ecology worldwide through actions, not words" (Interface 1997, 2). He told the task force "to convert Interface to a restorative enterprise; first by reaching sustainability in our practices, and then becoming truly restorative – a company returning more than we take – by helping others reach sustainability" (Interface 1997, 2).

Once Anderson committed his company to sustainability, he sought to follow through. Interface hired consultants to help it identify its current environmental impacts, set goals for improvement, and develop strategies to achieve those goals. Anderson has served as Co-Chair of the President's Council on Sustainable Development, given numerous talks, and authored a book on corporate environmental sustainability. He has stated that he wants Interface to lead the world's sustainability efforts, explaining that the company's employees, vendors, and customers share the dream of creating a "company that will grow by cleaning up the world, not by polluting or degrading it" (Interface 1997, 2).

Interface has committed publicly to the goal of sustainability and, in 2004, celebrated 10 years of progress. It counts its top ten achievements during that decade as:

1. Cutting greenhouse gas emissions by 46 percent
2. Using renewable energy to meet 12 percent of its total energy needs
3. Launching the carpet industry's first 100 percent post-consumer/post-industrial polyester
4. Offsetting the carbon emissions from some carpet products and from company cars
5. Working to eliminate waste, successfully reducing its landfill waste by 65 percent as well as its water and energy use
6. Introducing the carpet industry's first recycled vinyl backing to keep vinyl out of landfills
7. Gaining Scientific Certification Systems' Environmentally Preferable Product certification for modular and broadloom carpets
8. Using the concept of biomimicry to create nature-inspired products
9. Actively participating in sustainability initiatives
10. Using a corn-based polymer to make residential carpet (Interface 2004)

Ray Anderson, Interface founder and board chairman. *Courtesy of Interface Flooring Systems.*

Interface provides an important example of a company that is working toward ecological sustainability. That is because it was one of the first mainstream, multinational companies to adopt the concept of sustainable development and begin to change its production processes and products with that goal in mind. Additionally, at the time that Interface released its *Sustainability Report* in 1997, few companies had disclosed so much information about the amount of natural resources they extracted and produced as well as the waste that they were creating to make everyday products. This helped to establish the growing trend in environmental reporting and transparency.

Note: The examples of Chouinard Equipment, Patagonia, and Interface raise two important points that are worth mentioning here. The first is that, regardless of the motivation for greening, *there is no substitute for a sincere greening commitment among senior management*. Although green business is replete with stories about staff heroes and heroines who have sought to make their workplaces greener, such efforts, while essential, will be limited without the support of top management. For a company to become green throughout, that goal must be embraced and practiced by all senior managers, who set the example for the rest of the firm. Each of the three companies highlighted here was able to commit to ecological sustainability because its founder and CEO committed to it both personally and professionally.

The second point is that the *timing* of greening is likely to have profound economic ramifications. For example, if a company is committed to environmental health from its inception and is built on and grows up around environmental values, it is likely to be aware of and more readily able to respond to environmental issues that arise over time. Chouinard Equipment and, later, Patagonia, were created by people with a strong environmental ethic and concerns over their companies' environmental impacts. The companies responded proactively when they discovered some of the ways in which they harmed the environment.

Meanwhile, a business that is built around compliance as its only concern is likely to find that responding to environmental regulations as they arise is far more expensive – economically and ecologically (though ecological costs typically are externalized) – than integrating environmental thinking into the very fabric of the company from its inception. For example, Interface's commitment to ecological sustainability occurred after the company already had caused extensive environmental damage. The process of re-envisioning the company, retraining employees, and redesigning products and processes with sustainability in mind would have been far less costly if sustainability had been the seed from which the company had emerged.

Interface products with GlasBac RE contain at least 55 percent total recycled content. *Courtesy of Interface Flooring Systems.*

Government Regulation

Though some companies are inspired to become greener out of concern for their environmental impacts and personally held values, government regulation serves as the primary impetus for others. Government regulations have played a significant role in greening because companies have had to respond to several environmental laws, including the Clean Air Act; Clean Water Act; Emergency Planning and Community Right to Know Act; Comprehensive Environmental Responsibility, Cleanup, and Liability Act; Federal Insecticide, Fungicide, and Rodenticide Act; Resource Conservation and Recovery Act; Safe Drinking Water Act; Toxic Substances Control Act; and Superfund Amendments and Reauthorization Act. Companies that depend on the marine environment also have had to respond to a host of laws and conventions, including the United Nations Convention on the Law of the Sea, the Convention on the Prevention of Marine Pollution by Dumping Wastes and Other Matter (also known as the London Convention), the Convention on Fishing and Conservation of Living Resources of the High Seas, and the International Convention for the Prevention of Pollution from Ships (MARPOL).

Compliance with government regulations can be costly. One study indicated that by the mid-1990s, U.S. companies were spending over $125 billion every year in order to meet increasing environmental regulations and pay fines for non-compliance, an amount totaling more than 2 percent of the GNP (Chinander 2001, 276). The estimated cost to companies for compliance with the 1990 Clean Air Act amendments, alone, ranged from $4-7 billion (Chinander 2001, 276). Between October 1992 and September 2003, in order to comply with new standards for clean air, industry and local and state governments spent $23-26 billion to retrofit facilities and plants and make other changes (Pianin 2003).

Though some have complained about these costs, a study by the Office of Management and Budget has reported that the *savings* resulting from the social and health benefits of enforcing tough clean air laws are five to seven times greater than their costs (Pianin 2003). This is due to a lower need for hospitalization as well as fewer premature deaths, emergency room visits, and lost workdays (Pianin 2003). In the decade from October 1992 to September 2002, savings from better air quality totaled $120-$193 billion (Pianin 2003).

Pollution from chemical plants such as this one in Louisiana can cause a wide array of human and environmental health problems. *Photo by Stephen C. Kowal.*

Old barrels left to decay and leak in an unlined landfill surrounded by farmland. *Townsend.*

Some companies and industries also have additional costs associated with lobbying to defeat or gut existing regulations. One journalist suggested, "Since corporate America increasingly treasures a green image, it no longer openly fights environmental initiatives, though its heft behind the scenes is considerable (Motavalli 2001, 33). For example, one electronic firm's internal memo, which was reported to have been leaked to the media in 2000, described the company's work to "cripple" attempts to pass laws requiring electronics to be recycled (Motavalli 2001, 29). Similarly, the beverage industry is said to lobby heavily against bottle bills, which would require beverage producers to be responsible for bottles at the end of their useful lives (Motavalli 2001). Though lobbying against regulation might benefit companies in the short term, it is likely to harm them over time because lobbying against environmental issues might indicate to stakeholders that companies do not care about the environment. Moreover, such lobbying can help to polarize peoples' positions and lead to a harder environmental fight later (Winsemius and Guntram 2002).

Recognizing the burden that some companies feel from environmental regulation, the U.S. government has developed voluntary programs – like WasteWi$e and Energy Star – in order to help businesses to achieve regulatory compliance through innovation. Such assistance has become particularly important since heightened regulatory enforcement has become a real concern for some business managers, who can be held personally accountable – fined or jailed, for instance – for their companies' environmental violations.

The development and enforcement of environmental regulations have been crucial, as regulations have forced businesses to alter their approaches to the environment. Clearly, regulation has played a critical role in reducing environmental harm and has been particularly necessary for those companies known as free riders – those that continually take advantage of a situation. In spite of the apparent necessity of regulations, however, there are mixed views on the utility of regulations to achieve sustainability. For instance, some have suggested that it is unclear whether environmental regulation serves as an incentive or disincentive for U.S. companies to become as environmentally friendly as possible (Sharfman, Meo, and Ellington 2000). This is because, while some research has indicated that government regulation inhibits technological innovation, other studies have shown that companies need more regulation in order to develop more sustainable technologies (Sharfman, Meo, and Ellington 2000). Pieter Winsemius, environmental consultant and past Environment Minister for The Netherlands, and Ulrich Guntram, COO of AXA Art Insurance and past management consultant (2002), have noted that environmental regulation and legislation do not always produce the desired results. Though this may be true, some have acknowledged the need for well-crafted regulations that facilitate corporate innovation and economic benefit (DeSimone and Popoff 1997; McDonough and Braungart 2002).

One of the factors determining whether a regulation might inspire or deter the development of sustainable technologies and processes is the *type* of regulation proposed. Regulations can be divided into two types – prescriptive and performance-based. Prescriptive ("command and control") regulations are fairly rigid in that they prescribe the use of a specific technology or process in order to address an environmental problem. The vast majority of environmental regulations to which companies must respond are prescriptive regulations. Conversely, performance-based regulations require that a goal be met while allowing some flexibility in how that goal is achieved.

Because they demand the use of a particular product or process, prescriptive regulations have their drawbacks. To begin with, they can be expensive for companies to implement. For example, DuPont's past-CEO, Edgar Woolard, has stated that his company's voluntary waste reduction efforts cost about three times less than those associated with government regulations (Winsemius and Guntram 2002). Additionally, prescriptive regulations might inhibit the development of better solutions than those required by a particular regulation. This is because companies and industries typically know far more about their businesses than do regulators and, theoretically, could design a solution that exceeds regulatory goals while providing additional environmental and economic advantages.

Thus, the flexibility of performance-based environmental regulations might provide an impetus for creative, innovative solutions developed by businesses. There is a greater likelihood that industries and businesses can develop far more economical and, perhaps, more ecologically beneficial solutions with performance-based regulations than with prescriptive regulations. Additionally, performance-based regulations, which do not require technological and process conformance, leave room for more traditional, greener technologies and processes; this can serve to move the focus away from increasingly higher tech solutions to those that simply make sense.

Companies can benefit from performance-based regulations in many ways. For instance, consider a company given a specific pollution reduction goal. By redesigning manufacturing or other processes, a company might develop a means to prevent pollution rather than merely capture it through costly end-of-the-pipe solutions. The development of performance-based regulations can enable a company to satisfy regulators in a way that provides the greatest win-win situation (DeSimone and Popoff 1997). One way in which companies can encourage the development of more performance-based regulations is to become involved in the development of regulations by sharing their own expertise and visions with regulators and policy-makers (Winsemius and Guntram 2002).

Companies have found several ways to benefit from the existence of regulations, regardless of whether they are prescriptive or performance-based. For example, firms that stay ahead of new regulations can take more time to develop and implement greener changes before regulatory compliance is required. Additionally, they can gain competitive advantage by developing solutions to certain environmental problems. This occurred in the 1990s when DuPont encouraged the EPA to abbreviate its timetable for phasing out chlorofluorocarbons (CFCs), which are substances that destroy Earth's protective ozone layer. Because it already had developed an alternative to CFCs, the company was ahead of its competitors when the EPA decided to shorten its timetable by five years (Winsemius and Guntram 2002).

Companies also can help to shape upcoming regulations by setting new standards for innovative technologies and processes, placing their competitors at a severe disadvantage as a result. For example, a company might develop a new process or technology that is such an improvement over the industry standard that the government will require all companies in its industry to use it, giving its creator a distinct competitive advantage. Sweden's Svenska Statoil did this when it began recycling vapors at all of its gas stations. The government later made this practice mandatory (Winsemius and Guntram 2002). Finally, by going beyond regulatory compliance, firms can avoid government fines and other penalties that are associated with the failure to achieve compliance.

The issue of environmental regulation as an incentive or deterrent to the development of the greenest technologies and processes is likely to escalate in the future. However, North (1992) has suggested that environmental regulations might play an important role in determining which companies will be the most successful in the global green market, stating that businesses from the most stringent legislative countries might be the best prepared. For example, from an environmental perspective, many German companies outperform other companies around the world. In part, this is due to Germany's adoption of some of the world's most stringent environmental regulations in the 1990s, which have prompted companies to change many of their business practices. Michael Porter, who teaches at Harvard Business School, has noted, "I found that the nations with the most rigorous [environmental standards] requirements often lead in exports of affected products…. The strongest proof that environmental protection does not hamper competitiveness is the economic performance of nations with the strictest laws" (as cited in Schmidheiny 1992, 4).

Germanys' greener business legislation began in 1991 with the German Packaging Legislation (*Verpackungsverordnung*). About one-half (by volume) and one-third (by weight) of the country's waste is made of packaging waste (Motavalli 2001). Short on landfill space, the government decided to tackle packaging by implementing a law requiring manufacturers to take their packaging back after use. The law requires German companies to accept and recycle discarded packaging materials from their customers until it is no longer technically feasible to do so (Stead and Stead 1996).

This German Packaging Legislation required a two-phase implementation strategy. During the first phase, an infrastructure was developed that would allow customers to discard their unwanted packaging and companies to retrieve and process it. The second phase involved the Ministry of the Environment, which was responsible for setting quotas and targets for packaging retrieval and reuse (Stead and Stead 1996). The Duales System Deutschland (DSD), a new non-profit organization supported by the packaging industry, is responsible for coordinating and implementing this legislation – in part through the establishment of the "green dot" system by which packaging is identified as being recyclable or not.

In its first four years, this program reduced packaging use by one million tons. Manufacturers eliminated unnecessary packaging (e.g., boxes within boxes), made packaging lighter, and sold some products in concentrated forms that provided more service with less packaging (Motavalli 2001). In fact, the program was so successful that other countries followed Germany's lead. In 1994, fifteen European Union (EU) member states adopted less stringent versions of the German legislation, and Japan, Taiwan, Korea, and others are creating their own packaging regulations (Motavalli 2001).

In 1994, the German government went further. It passed the Closed Substance Cycle and Waste Management Act (*Kreislaufwirtschafts und Abfallgesetz*), requiring manufacturers in several industries to take back their products when customers are done using them. Like the German Packaging Legislation, this law shifts the burden of waste from individual customers and the government directly onto product manufacturers. It takes a much broader view of waste, which is seen as anything that is not associated with the intended purpose of a product but that results from materials processing, product manufacture, or con-

sumption (Stead and Stead 1996). This law indicates that the responsibility for a manufacturer's products no longer ends at the point of sale. Instead, companies are responsible for the products and associated waste throughout their products' life cycles.

Since the Closed Substance Cycle and Waste Management Act went into affect in 1996, companies have responded by redesigning manufacturing processes and products, making products easier to take apart and reuse, recycle, or dispose of individual components appropriately. This has resulted in fundamental changes in German industry and provided a greener model for countries around the world (Stead and Stead 1996).

In 1997, Italy began requiring refrigerator manufacturers to take their products back at the end of their useful lives. In 1999, Holland adopted legislation requiring all manufacturers of appliances, computers, and other equipment to take back their products when consumers are done with them. That same year, Norway adopted similar regulations, and Japan followed suit in 2001.

Take-back legislation, which shifts the burden of waste costs from the public (through taxes) to the manufacturers, also can be used for large items, such as cars. For example, the EU hoped to recycle 80 percent of unwanted cars, referred to as "end-of-life vehicles," by 2005 (Motavalli 2001). Under that legislation, car owners would be required to receive a certificate showing that their cars were recycled legally.

Even some local governments are working to reduce their waste – or eliminate it. In 1998, the U.S. city of Seattle, Washington, adopted the goal of "zero waste" in its waste management plan.

The city of Seattle, Washington, has made significant strides in becoming a greener city. *Courtesy of the U.S. Department of Energy's Energy Efficiency and Renewable Energy division.*

Both Seattle and San Jose, California, have reduced their waste by about 65 percent (Motavalli 2001). One North Carolina town and two California counties also have adopted zero waste goals.

The movement toward having companies become responsible for their products throughout their life cycles is known as extended producer responsibility (EPR). This has become a primary incentive behind the growing trend to sell services (e.g., the *use* of a carpet or computer) through product leasing rather than the products themselves. This ensures that the company is responsible for its products from manufacture to reuse, recycling, or disposal. It also removes the burden of disposal from the customer, who might not wish to throw away unwanted products but cannot make use of them anymore, and from the government, which pays (with taxpayer money) for waste removal and other services. Moreover, its helps to close the product loop and ensure an end user for products. This can reduce the demand for virgin materials and result in significant energy savings. For example, making aluminum from recycled aluminum rather than virgin bauxite uses 95 percent less energy (Brown et al. 2002, 66).

Other programs that are retrieving used products have begun to emerge. For example, in 2000, Minnesota's governor Jesse Ventura announced that Sony Corporation would take back all of Minnesotans' outdated Sony products (Motavalli 2001). This program spread to five other states the following year.

Suncor Energy

More than a decade ago, Suncor (now Suncor Energy) was faced with the prospect of failure. The Alberta, Canada-based oil and gas company was known for its poor environmental performance. It sometimes was cited for failing to comply with environmental regulations, and local community members complained about environmental damage caused by the company. Meanwhile, oil extraction costs were high, and the company struggled to remain viable. Employees were laid off, and morale was low.

Then, Alberta's provincial government warned Suncor that it would lose its key Oil Sands operations unless it made significant environmental improvements. Suncor has three autonomous business units of which the Oil Sands are one. Located near Fort McMurray, Alberta, Suncor's Oil Sands unit mines bi-

Aluminum contains a high degree of embodied energy, making it an ideal product for recycling. *Courtesy of the U.S. Department of Energy's Energy Efficiency and Renewable Energy division.*

tumen, a petroleum derivative, and refines it for diesel fuel and feedstock for refineries.

Faced with increasing pressure from the local community and a government ultimatum, Suncor hired a new CEO, Richard George, in 1991 and began an impressive transformation. It began to incorporate environmental issues into its decision-making processes, integrating them with both economic and social issues. It also sought to integrate the concept of sustainability into its thinking and established its goal of becoming an environmentally sustainable energy company.

In the past, the company's attitude toward stakeholders had been either adversarial or disregarding (Rowledge, Barton, and Brady 1999). The idea of involving stakeholders was looked upon with "indifference, ignorance, and, in some cases, fear" (Rowledge, Barton, and Brady 1999, 73). However, by the mid-1990s, the company sought to take a proactive stance toward its stakeholders by developing a team that was devoted to stakeholder relations.

This new approach was based on the idea of principle-based leadership, something in which the entire company was being trained. Principle-based leadership was developed by Steven Covey, the author of *Seven Habits of Highly Effective People* (Rowledge, Barton, and Brady 1999). It reflects the need for companies to develop strong corporate identities by recognizing and focusing on their values and beliefs. By establishing a strong corporate identify that is based on values and beliefs shared by the company's employees and managers, the company can move forward with the support of its staff, which works together toward a common purpose and goals.

Working with stakeholders, the company compiled a list of principles that define its rules of stakeholder engagement. These principles include such things as providing stakeholders with accurate, timely information, respecting stakeholders' cultures and values, and involving stakeholders early in any process (Suncor Energy 2001). By taking such steps, Suncor began to establish trust as it worked with members of local aboriginal communities as well as other stakeholders, such as environmental regulators.

Suncor began to elicit feedback from its employees, local communities, and other stakeholders regarding new development projects and its plans for growth. The company has benefited financially as a result. For instance, when Suncor wanted to start a new project,

the Steepbank Mine at Oil Sands, it developed an environmental impact assessment[2] to determine the project's likely effects on air, water, land, and local communities' economic and social well-being (Rowledge, Barton, and Brady 1999, 76). Working with stakeholders throughout the process to balance its development with environmental needs, the company was able to gain approval for the project without a public hearing. This enabled Suncor to begin development two years earlier than anticipated and begin earning income from its petroleum development (Rowledge, Barton, and Brady 1999, 76). The company has used stakeholder processes in other projects as well.

In 1998, with the Environmental Defense Fund's help, Suncor Energy worked with Niagara Mohawk in New York to establish the first international greenhouse gas emissions trade (Winsemius and Guntram 2002). Richard George has been outspoken with regard to the company's need to reduce its greenhouse gas emissions, acknowledging the scientific consensus on climate change to the Vancouver Board of Trade on the first day of the Kyoto Summit on Climate Change (Rowledge, Barton, and Brady 1999). In 1999, Suncor Energy was one of the first companies selected for the Dow Jones Sustainability Index. In 2003, it was listed as one of Canada's fifty best corporate citizens, ranking third (Suncor Energy, Social Responsibility, para. 4). By 2003, the company's share value had risen by 1,100 percent since the company became publicly traded in 1992 (Suncor Energy, About Suncor, para. 6).

Today, Suncor is considered a leader in the energy industry with a goal of becoming a sustainable energy company. Though its mission is to develop hydrocarbon resources for today's energy requirements, Suncor recognizes the need to develop renewable energy for the future. It committed to invest $100 million in renewable energy projects by the end of 2005 (Suncor Energy, Renewable energy sources, para. 1). It also launched the $22 million SunBridge Wind Power Project in Saskatchewan and received approval for a $48 million wind power project in Alberta (Suncor Energy, Renewable energy sources, para. 1-2). Together, these two wind projects will provide about 15 percent of Canada's wind energy and result in about 115,000 tons of carbon dioxide emission reductions each year (Suncor Energy, Renewable energy sources, para. 2).

Economic Opportunities & Disincentives

Although some companies might commit to greening for environmental reasons and others might be spurred on by regulation, other firms decide to improve their environmental performances in order to gain economic benefits or avoid penalties. Companies can benefit from competitive advantages that are gained when they develop new products, processes, or greening strategies, all of which are positive incentives. They also can avoid the financial burdens associated with non-compliance or the failure to respond to environmental issues, which serve as negative incentives. By becoming greener, companies can benefit from improvements in sales through better brand images, a loyal customer base, price premiums for higher quality products, and new market, business, and product opportunities. One example is Estee Lauder's 1997 acquisition of the natural body care products company Aveda. Leonard Lauder, Estee Lauder's chairman and CEO, stated, "It's a perfect fit for us. It's part of an overall strategy to plug in to where the market is growing and where the market opportunities are" (Parker-Pope 1997, 1).

Typically, firms that become greener for financial reasons focus on greening their products and services and/or their facilities. This section discusses both greening strategies.

Greener Products & Services

Some companies have sought to make or save money through greener products and services. Greener products generally have one or more environmentally preferable characteristics. For example, they might be made of renewable or recycled materials. They also might be resource-efficient during manufacture and use, non-toxic throughout their life cycles, appropriately durable, and biodegradable or recyclable.

Companies can make or save money with greener products and services in several ways. For instance, they can 1) tap into green markets by developing greener products or services or making existing products and services greener, 2) develop greener production processes, and/or 3) reduce their risk and liability associated with non-green products. Each of these is discussed below.

Tapping into Green Markets

In 1985, only .5 percent of new products were touted to be green (Stead and Stead 1996, 164). By 1990, about 25 percent of new household-related products were marketed with some green claim while about 70 percent of marketers claimed that their products' packaging was more environmentally friendly (Stead and Stead 1996, 164). In 1991, about 13.4 percent of all new products (not just household products) were touted as having green features (Stead and Stead 1996, 164). Those numbers reflect only the beginning of the move toward creating greener products.

Green products and services represent what some believe to be an enormous business opportunity. In the early 1990s, Arthur D. Little estimated that the worldwide market for green products and services was $280 billion and predicted that this number would double by the end of the decade (Menon and Menon 1997, 2). By 2000, the LOHAS industry had U.S. sales of more than $226.8 billion (Cotlier 2001, 6) and more than twice that much worldwide. Companies have responded to this market opportunity both by developing new greener products and services and by improving the environmental performances of existing products and services.

New Products and Services – Companies have used innovation to help fill the niche for greener products. It is worth mentioning that some "new" products actually are old ones that have reemerged as their environmental benefits have been realized. Green roofs and living walls are two examples in the building industry.

Existing Products and Services – Companies also have worked to make existing products greener by ensuring that they have one or more green qualities, such as being made of renewable or recycled products or being recyclable or biodegradable. For example, Herman Miller designed its Aeron chair to be made mostly of recycled materials and "sparing of natural resources, durable and repairable, designed for disassembly and recycling" (Herman Miller, Inc. 2003, Aeron Chairs, "Design Story" section, para. 6). The company's Mirra chair is 96 percent recyclable (Herman Miller, Inc. 2003, Mirra Chairs, "Earth Friendly" section, para. 1).

Herman Miller's Mirra chair. *Courtesy of Herman Miller, Inc.*

Some products commonly identified as greener command a premium price. For example, the company Tom's of Maine, with toothpaste and other products at prices 20-50 percent higher than competing brands, has found success in touting its environmental and social responsibility (Ottman, Environmental branding 1998, 8). So have other companies, including Body Shop, a UK-based company that sells cosmetics and body care products (Wheeler and Sillanpaa 1997). Electrolux also has gained price advantages with its greener products, experiencing a 3.5 percent higher-than-average profit margin with its products that had the best environmental performance (Rowledge, Barton, and Brady 1999, 27).

Environmental preferability also might help to differentiate a company's products and services from those of its competitors, giving it a distinct competitive advantage (Winsemius and Guntram 2002; North 1992; DeSimone and Popoff 1997; Stead and Stead 1996). In highly competitive markets, such differentiation can be essential because a company's environmental performance might be the main factor that truly distinguishes the firm from others and determines whether or not it succeeds. For example, one of Patagonia's managers has indicated that the company's environmental commitment might be what separates the company from its competitors in what is otherwise a very competitive industry (Rowledge, Barton, and Brady 1999). Though the company's managers and staff cite their environmental commitment and desire to do the right thing as their incentives for sustainability, products that reflect that commitment might be just what give the company an advantage over some of its competition.

Developing Greener Production Processes

Companies also can benefit financially from greening by altering their manufacturing processes. Improvements in production can result in better processes, less waste, improvements in supply chain management, and lower operating costs. Furthermore, such changes can save money by reducing the overall use of materials and even eliminating the need for certain materials. When fewer materials are required, the need for storage tends to decrease, thereby reducing another operating cost (Winsemius and Guntram 2002). Recycling materials decreases the need for the procurement of raw materials, which provides additional savings and further reduces environmental harm.

Scrapile collects scraps from the New York area woodworking industry and designs beautiful furnishings. *Courtesy of Scrapile.*

Companies often find that technical improvements to their products or processes decrease other operational costs as well, such as those associated with compliance (Winsemius and Guntram 2002). This can help companies to save money, stay ahead of environmental regulations, and shape future environmental regulations.

3M: Minnesota Mining & Manufacturing Company (3M) has experienced significant financial benefits from making environmental improvements to its manufacturing processes. This is due largely to the company's formal environmental policy, which was established in 1975 – long before most other companies had formal environmental policies (3M, 3M's Environmental Tradition, para. 1 2003). 3M's policy called for the company to take responsibility for its own environmental problems by conserving natural resources, preventing pollution, and creating products with minimal environmental impacts (3M, 3M's Environmental Tradition, para. 4 2003). That same year, 3M developed its Pollution Prevention Pays (3P) program. The 3P program was created with the idea that preventing pollution is more effective and less costly than controlling it. Predicated on employee awareness and innovation, the program's success relies on employees to develop innovative solutions to environmental problems by identifying opportunities for reducing or eliminating pollution and waste. Today, the company envisions itself as helping society move toward sustainable development through eco-efficiency.

Since the inception of the 3P program in 1975, the company has prevented the emission of 474,000 tons of sludge and solid waste, 3.7 billion gallons of wastewater, 234,000 tons of air pollutants, and 31,000 tons of water pollutants (DeSimone and Popoff 1997, 2). As a result, it has saved the company more than

$750 million in first-year savings alone (DeSimone and Popoff 2000, 2). Between 2000 and 2002, 3M improved its energy efficiency by 10 percent, reduced its waste by 12 percent, reduced its volatile organic compound (VOC) emissions by 25 percent, and reduced its Toxics Release Inventory emissions by 38 percent (3M, Environmental Highlights 2003).

Caveat: Do all companies that implement greener production processes benefit financially? Much of the literature on the economic benefits of implementing green best practices suggests that they do. Through programs like 3M's Pollution Prevention Pays (3P), Chevron's Save Money and Reduce Toxins (SMART), and Dow's Waste Reduction Always Pays (WRAP), these companies have been touted as economic beneficiaries of strong environmental management strategies.

Yet, Rutgers Business School professor Petra Christmann (2000) has suggested that by studying the companies that have benefited economically from the implementation of best practices while ignoring those that have not presents a skewed picture. Moreover, Andrew King (1995) of Dartmouth's Tuck School of Business has asserted that the body of green business data is small and spans only a brief period, making identifying successful sustainability strategies difficult.

Christmann (2000) conducted a survey of eighty-eight chemical companies to test a series of hypotheses. Her research focused on best practices associated with production processes (rather than products). That is because previous research has indicated that a company must implement technologies for preventing pollution before it can successfully differentiate its products and undertake product stewardship (Hart as cited in Christmann 2000). Christmann's (2000) research results indicated that companies need "complementary assets" in place in order for pollution prevention and other process-related best practices to pay off. For instance, companies that want economic benefit from greening their production processes need to have the skills and capabilities in place to innovate and implement greener processes.

Similarly, Stefan Schaltegger, of the University of Lüneburg's (Germany) Centre for Sustainable Management, and Terje Synnestvedt, of the Norwegian School of Management's Department of Economics, have expressed that "superiority in environmental performance does not necessarily lead to competitive advantages" (2002, 342). They have suggested that economic benefits resulting from improved environmental performance depend on external and internal variables, both of which are affected by management. Therefore, environmental management is extremely important in the success of greening (Schaltegger and Synnestvedt 2002). Winsemius and Guntram (2002) have stated that before firms pursue an integrated response, they must ensure that all functional skills and supporting systems are in place.

Reducing Risk & Liability

Not only can companies make or save money by tapping into green markets and improving the environmental performance of production – they also can find savings in the reduced risks and liability that are associated with greener products and services. Greener products and services are healthier for the environment, employees, users, and others throughout their life cycles.

Greener Facilities

Though some businesses have chosen to develop greener products and services for economic profit and savings, others have developed greener facilities. Greener facilities are resource-efficient, seeking to reduce their use of energy, water, and other resources and saving money as a result. They also are healthy because they have a high level of comfort, natural light, and clean air and water. They contain few to no toxins, such as radon or the myriad of toxic substances commonly found in building, cleaning, and office products. As a result, companies benefit from the increased profits and savings that are associated with better employee performance, fewer sick days taken, and higher employee morale, satisfaction, and retention.

In greening facilities for financial benefit, companies typically focus on improved energy efficiency (while sometimes ignoring the use of water and other resources) and, to a lesser extent, creating a healthy environment for staff. This section explores the financial benefits gained by energy efficiency and creating healthier facilities.

Creating More Energy-Efficient Facilities

Energy often comprises a significant portion of business expenditures. However, several companies have found ways to reduce their energy costs through efficiency. As a result, some have discovered that energy-efficient building initiatives often provide far higher returns on investment (ROI) than those gained from conventional investments, such as stocks and bonds.

Companies can create more energy-efficient facilities and reduce their facility-related energy bills through energy upgrades, lighting retrofits, day lighting, and other measures. For instance, companies that undertake an ordinary, comprehensive energy upgrade can reduce their energy use by half. Not only do resulting energy bills drop by about $1/\text{ft}^2$, but a mere 5 percent rise in employee productivity from increased comfort associated with better heating, cooling, and lighting systems can result in an added annual gain in profits of over $10/\text{ft}^2$ (Romm 1999, 5). That helps to explain why a comprehensive energy upgrade that results in better employee comfort typically yields a 33-50 percent ROI (Romm 1999, 5).

A family takes a break on harvest day on an organic cherry farm. *Courtesy of Food for Thought.*

Clif Bar employees are encouraged to work out at the company gym. *Courtesy of Clif Bar.*

Studies at Carnegie-Mellon University have shown that even simple improvements in lighting design can have a large impact on a company's energy costs. Lighting improvements in a 100,000ft^2 workplace with 500 employees can cost $370,000 up front while saving $680,000 in reduced energy and operating costs. These savings are impressive but hardly compare to the $14.6 million-worth of increased productivity that typically occurs as a result of good lighting design (Romm 1999, 79). Romm has reported that by undertaking a comprehensive energy upgrade, companies could save about $1 per square foot every year, enjoy a two- to three-year payback, and get a 33-50 percent return on investment (1999, 5).

Some of the simplest resource-efficient measures are those that cost little or nothing. For example, turning off lights and office equipment whenever they are not in use can lead to significant energy and cost savings. Turning computers off when they are not in use can reduce their energy consumption by 75 percent while turning off copiers at night and during weekends reduces their energy demand by about 65 percent (U.S. Department of Energy 1996, section Small Steps Equal Big Savings, para. 1). Installing and using sensors and timers to turn off lighting and equipment, respectively, also can result in significant energy savings. By educating employees about the importance of these simple activities, companies are saving energy, cutting costs, and reducing carbon dioxide emissions.

Companies also can replace old office equipment with more efficient equipment. In U.S. commercial buildings, which house many of today's large businesses, office equipment consumes an enormous amount of electricity each year – 30 billion kilowatt-hours (U.S. Department of Energy 1996, para. 1). This represents about 5 percent of the total amount of energy that is used commercially in the United States and costs businesses a total of $2.1 billion every year in electric bills (U.S. Department of Energy 1996, para. 1). According to the American Council for an Energy-Efficient Economy, office equipment is the fastest-growing consumer of electricity (1996 1). Additionally, because office equipment emits heat, it creates a greater demand for cooling in buildings. Taking the need for additional cooling into account, office equipment really consumes about 40 billion kilowatt-hours of electricity every year (U.S. Department of Energy 1996, para. 1).

The U.S. Department of Energy (1996) has estimated that if U.S. companies switched to office equipment that was certified by the U.S. Environmental Protection Agency's Energy Star Program,[3] they could save

enough energy every year to feed the annual energy use of three New England states – Vermont, New Hampshire, and Maine. This would reduce current carbon dioxide emissions by an amount equivalent to removing five million cars from the roads; additionally, it would save businesses approximately $1.7 billion (U.S. Department of Energy 1996, para. 2).

Energy Efficiency, Global Warming, and the Insurance Industry: Reducing energy use through energy-efficient measures not only helps the company financially, but it also helps to reduce the firm's contribution to global warming. Reducing the risk of global warming through such efficiency has profound implications. The U.S. Environmental Protection Agency (EPA) has reported that energy efficiency not only saves companies money, but it also helps to slow global warming and its associated costs. The Agency has suggested that industry can be a leader in reducing global warming by increasing efficiency and developing cost-effective tools that reduce energy use. Through increased efficiency, companies can gain a competitive edge over their less environmentally proactive competitors (U.S. EPA 2001, "Global Warming – Industry," para. 1).

News reports of a heat wave in Great Britain on August 5, 2003, offered an indication of some of the expenses that could be associated with global warming. Through the combination of lost productivity and increased absenteeism, each day during a heat wave costs (in British pounds) Great Britain the following:

* 80 degrees Fahrenheit (26.6 degrees Celsius): *38 million pounds*
* 90 degrees Fahrenheit (32 degrees Celsius): *132 million pounds*
* 100 degrees Fahrenheit (37.7 Celsius): *280 million pounds* (Newsworld International news broadcast, August 5, 2003)

One industry that is affected strongly by global warming and other types of environmental degradation is the insurance industry. Due to several years of extreme weather, this industry has already lost "tens of billions of dollars" (U.S. EPA 2001, "Global Warming – The Insurance Industry," para. 1). This loss promises to grow as climate change and related irregular weather patterns become more prevalent, human populations increase in size, and people continue to build in high-risk areas. In the meantime, insurance costs are likely to continue to rise in response. As a result, insurance companies are likely to become increasingly interested in the reduction of anthropogenic

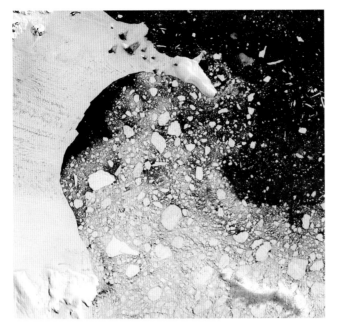

Antarctica's 600-foot-thick Larsen Ice Shelf broke apart in 2002 following rising temperatures that have been associated with climate change. *Courtesy of the National Atmospheric and Space Administration Earth Observatory.*

greenhouse gas emissions via energy efficiency, renewable energy, and other measures.

Several companies of all types and sizes have incorporated energy efficiency measures into their business practices and experienced substantial cost savings as a result. In fact, some companies have been improving their environmental performances for many years. The examples discussed here are IBM, American Express, and the Way Station, all of which indicate that greening is a good idea that has been around for some time.

IBM: IBM provides one example of a company that has reduced its costs through energy efficiency. The company estimated that in 1991 it saved $17.8 million worldwide simply by encouraging employees to turn off unused equipment and lights (U.S. Department of Energy 1996, section Small Steps Equal Big Savings, para. 3). This savings was accomplished not by employing costly technologies but merely by raising staff awareness. The company's proactive stance on energy-efficiency reduced its carbon dioxide emissions by 210,000 tons (190,000 metric tons), which was equivalent to removing 50,000 cars from the road (U.S. Department of Energy 1996, section Small Steps Equal Big Savings, para. 3). As a result, IBM gained significant savings, might have enhanced its public image, and reduced its environmental damage by using less energy.

American Express & Consolidated Edison Company: Similarly, American Express has benefited from energy-efficient activities. The New York City utility Consolidated Edison Company worked with American Express to inform its 10,000 New York em-

Hurricane Wilma, October 20, 2005. *Courtesy of the National Oceanic and Atmospheric Administration.*

ployees to turn off their computers nightly and on weekends. Not only did this reduce the company's power demand and resulting environmental degradation, but it also reduced the company's expenses significantly. If every employee responded, this single action was estimated to save the company $730,000 each year (U.S. Department of Energy 1996, section Small Steps Equal Big Savings, para. 2).

Way Station: The Way Station, Inc., is a treatment and rehabilitation facility that was created for people with long-term mental illness. Designed by the ENSAR Group of Boulder, Colorado, this 30,000 square-foot facility opened in 1991 as a healthy, efficient place for its inhabitants and users. The facility was recognized by the American Institute of Architects (AIA) as one of the top five most energy-efficient buildings in the United States, using only one-third of what it would have used had it been built using conventional techniques (Way Station, 1). Energy expert Amory Lovins has suggested that the building's reduced energy use will prevent the emissions of 4,800 tons of carbon dioxide and 42 tons of sulfur dioxide over twenty years (Way Station, 2). The building also relies heavily on daylight, which contributes to the health of the place, reduces energy use, and reduces the need for cooling.

The Way Station was designed with the health of its residents and employees in mind. As such, it was furnished using paints and fabrics that are non-toxic or have low toxicity. Ceramic tile was used in place of unhealthy vinyl tile, and the cleaning materials and floor wax are safe for the building's users. The building is well ventilated to ensure fresh air and has good indoor air quality due to adequate ventilation, non-toxic products, and plants, which help to remove pollutants from the air. It has an open design, passive solar features, greenhouse and atrium plants, and lighting changes that occur throughout the day according to the sun's angle. According to Tena Meadows O'Rear, the facility's Chief Operating Officer, "Our members deal with a lot of restriction, depression, and mental walls in their lives. It makes a tremendous difference being in a building that embraces the natural world and feels expansive and sunny" (Thayer 1994, 24).

National Audubon Society: In the 1980s, the National Audubon Society had outgrown its New York headquarters and decided to relocate. The organization wanted to make its new space an environmentally responsible one. Moreover, it wanted to prove that any company could create an efficient, non-toxic workplace using off-the-shelf products without spending more money.

It purchased an existing 98,000 square foot building in downtown Manhattan. Dubbed "Audubon House," the building was gutted, and the original materials were reused or recycled, keeping in place 300 tons of steel, 9,000 tons of masonry, and 560 tons of concrete (National Audubon Society, "Resource Conservation and Recycling" section, para. 1). The renovation was completed in 1992. Financed partially through tax-free bonds, the purchase cost was $10 million, and the cost of renovation was $14 million (National Audubon Society 2003, "Biography" section, para. 2). There was an additional $2 million in soft costs (Rocky Mountain Institute 1998, 439). The cost of development was $122 per square foot, well within the market range of $120-128 per square foot (Rocky Mountain Institute 1998, 439; National Audubon Society 2003, "Key Statistics" section, para. 1). By renovating an existing building, Audubon saved 27 percent in construction costs (Rocky Mountain Institute 1998, 439).

The resulting retrofit made Audubon House 62 percent more energy-efficient than a conventional office building would have been (Rocky Mountain Institute 1998, 439). Due to energy efficiency, the organization saves $100,000 each year in operating costs (Rocky Mountain Institute 1998, 439). Motion sensors with manual buttons were installed in each room to control the lights, and zone sensors were placed in open areas. Long, rectangular pendant fixtures were hung from the ceilings, reflecting light off the ceilings and shining it in all directions. General Electric T-8 bulbs were used, which dim as the sensors detect sunlight. Audubon's lighting, alone, has reduced the organization's lighting and saved the organization at least $60,000 annually over conventional lighting (Rocky Mountain Institute 1998, 439). Task lighting (arranged specifically for the tasks at hand) was used to minimize waste from unnecessary, general lighting. The need for electric lighting was reduced by 75 percent (Rocky Mountain Institute 1998, 439). Because of the efficiency of the building's lighting system, Audubon's electricity bills were reduced by $60,000 (Rocky Mountain Institute 1998, 439).

The gas-powered heater/chiller heats and cools with natural gas and uses no chlorofluorocarbons (CFCs); it also does not emit sulfur dioxide and emits 60 percent less nitrogen oxides than conventional units (National Audubon Society 2003, "Key Statistics" section, para. 1). When installed, the unit was only one of about three in New York City. The heater/chiller is relatively small and sits on the top floor of Audubon's offices. It results in cleaner air that is circulated six times every hour (the heater/chiller has the capacity to exchange the air up to eighteen times per hour) (National Audubon Society 2003, "Healthy Indoor Environment" section, para. 9). Most offices only circulate their air about four times each hour.

With utility rebates, the building's green design features provided a payback period of three years (Rocky Mountain Institute 1998, 439).

Other Companies That Save Money through Efficiency: Several other companies have benefited from efficiency as well. For instance, with the help of the Environmental Protection Agency, **Boeing** reduced its lighting energy use by up to 90 percent (Romm 1999, 47). The lighting retrofit paid for itself in two years, a 53 percent return on investment (Romm 1999, 47). Reduced glare and greater lighting comfort helped the employees to work more productively and create fewer defects (Romm 1999).

In the 1980s, Ron Perkins, **Compaq Computer's** facilities manager, reduced the company's energy use, saving it about $1 million a year (Romm 1999, 102). Compaq's changes were designed to remove the blockages to worker productivity through increased daylighting and other activities. In 1985, alone, productivity rose by 55 percent (Romm 1999, 103).

Comstock's ten-story building was designed and constructed within eighteen months, cost $500,000 less than was budgeted for, and operates at half the cost of one of the company's other, less-efficient buildings (Romm 1999, 75).

Since 1982, in its Louisiana Division, **Dow Chemical** has held an annual energy-saving contest for employees. Over 700 employee ideas have been implemented, saving the division over $110 million (Romm 1999, 12).

Using energy-efficient measures to reduce operating costs, **Kraft General Foods** avoided closing its Framingham, Illinois, plant and laying off 200 employees. Through an energy retrofit, Kraft was able to keep a plant open, reduce its energy use by one third, and increase employee productivity by 10 percent (Romm 1999, 176-177).

Lockheed-Martin had a $50-million engineering design and development facility, Building 157, constructed in Sunnyvale, California. Completed in 1983, the building's energy-efficient features saved the company $500,000 each year (Romm 1999, 93). While the lighting design cost an extra $2 million, Lockheed claimed that the productivity gains in the first year offset the extra cost (Romm 1999, 94). The considerable amount of daylighting reduced the need for artificial lighting. As a result, the company's lighting bill costs three-quarters less than it would have in a conventionally constructed building. In addition, employee productivity went up 15 percent, and absenteeism dropped by 15 percent (Romm 1999, 94). In just one year, the drop in absenteeism, alone, recouped the extra $2 million that Lockheed-Martin had paid for its new energy system.

VeriFone, which makes phone credit card verification systems, built a greener building for its headquarters in Costa Mesa, California. The building experienced a 60 percent decrease in its energy use, a 45 percent drop in absenteeism, and a 5+ percent increase in productivity (Romm 1999, 5).

Creating Healthier Facilities

As important as energy efficiency is, it is only one characteristic of greener facilities. Though many companies have sought to save money through energy efficiency, others, like the Way Station and Audubon Society, also have incorporated health considerations into their facilities. Creating healthy facilities extends far beyond the design or renovation of a building to include its entire life cycle. Just as good design and construction are important, so are greener operations and maintenance and greener procurement and use.

Healthy buildings are important because many furnishings and other office materials contain numerous toxins. The glues used to hold together pressed wood furniture and building materials, adhere laminated surfaces to furniture, and keep floors and carpets in place often are toxic (Townsend 1997). Paints, particularly those that are oil-based, often are another source of toxins in the workplace (Townsend 1997). The toxins emitted from carpets, furniture, and plastics through "offgassing" can create a variety of health problems in anyone exposed to them (Matthews 1992; Townsend 1997). These toxins, combined with poor ventilation, can sicken a company's staff as well as its cleaning crew.

Between home and work, most people spend up to 90 percent of their time indoors and in cars, stores, and other synthetic environments (US EPA, Region 6 2003, para. 1; CDC 1998, para. 2). These artificial spaces often are full of unhealthy chemicals, electrical equipment, and poor lighting design. The US EPA has suggested that the top indoor air quality health risks are due to secondhand smoke, radon, organic compounds, and biological pollutants (CDC 1998, para. 2). As a result, many building owners and occupants experience a variety of problems at work that can result in sickness and sensory deprivation. These include air pollution; asbestos; poorly designed lighting; carbon monoxide; dry, overheated, or uniform environments; electro-magnetic fields (EMFs); eye strain;

formaldehyde; metals; microorganisms (molds, mildew); noise; organochlorines; ozone; poor smells; radon; stress; uncomfortable workstation design; and water pollution (Townsend 1997).

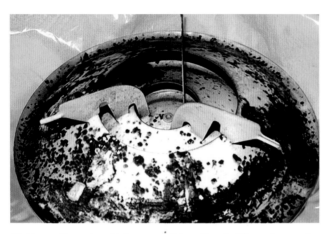

Mold growth, such as that seen on this ceiling air diffuser, is one of many substances that can pollute the indoor environment. *Courtesy of the Environmental Protection Agency.*

Though some air pollutants are found indoors in concentrations two to five times greater than outdoors, indoor air pollution can be over 100 times greater than that found outdoors (US EPA, Region 6 2003, para. 1). Long-term exposure to pollutants can cause serious health problems, something with which many people have to come to terms. Over the past few decades, the use of synthetic building materials and furnishings, fabrics, and cleaning chemicals, as well as dust, bacteria, and fungi, have contributed to dangerous conditions for those who work or live in these environments.

Between 1965 and 1982, more than four million new chemical compounds were created, and up to 6,000 new compounds have been created every week since 1982 (Wilson 1993, 1). The National Institute of Occupational Safety and Health (NIOSH) has files on more than 100,000 of these chemical compounds (Wilson 1993, 1). Meanwhile, the EPA has files on about 65,000 toxic chemicals and receives requests to register about 1,500 new compounds every year (Matthews 1992, 6; Wilson 1993, 1). The National Academy of Sciences has suggested that as much as 15 percent of the human population in the United States might be particularly sensitive to chemicals, and that number is expected increase to 60 percent sometime during the next generation (Wilson 1993, 3). Cynthia Wilson (1993), the Executive Director of the non-profit Chemical Injury Information Network, has asserted, "According to the National Research Council, no toxicity data are available for over 39,000 commercially used chemicals" (2).

An industry has grown up around indoor pollution, as illustrated by this individual doing mold remediation. *Courtesy of the Environmental Protection Agency.*

The IXTOC I oil spill of 1979 saw 140 million gallons of oil enter Mexico's Bay of Campeche. Accidents such as these can cause widespread exposure to toxins via air and water. *Courtesy of the National Oceanic and Atmospheric Administration.*

Wilson (1993) has estimated that there are at least 16,250,000 chemical injury victims with 375,000 new ones reported annually (2). Meanwhile, NIOSH has suggested that there are as many as 25 million chemical injury victims (Wilson 1993, 2). The National Cancer Institute (NCI) has estimated that up to 98 percent of all cancers may be associated with chemical exposures (Wilson 1993, 2). Additionally, the NCI has estimated that three out of ten people in the U.S. can expect to contract some form of cancer in their lifetimes (Wilson 1993, 2).

Exposure to chemicals can occur in many ways. For example, in some buildings, the air intake (which is supposed to bring in fresher outdoor air) is placed by the loading dock. As a result, fumes from delivery trucks and other vehicles are left to circulate within the buildings. The average, resting adult requires 8,640 liters of fresh air every day (Matthews 1992, 5), thereby giving pollutants an easy entry into the body.

Yet, toxicity is not the only health problem present in the workplace. Poorly designed lighting is another. It can result in eyestrain, headaches, and higher-than-average work errors, which reduce workplace productivity. Too much or too little light — or lighting that is not designed for the tasks at hand — actually can impair worker vision or make it difficult for employees to do their jobs correctly.

The costs of an unhealthy workplace can be tremendous. The use of unhealthy furnishings, paints, supplies, and poor lighting has cost many firms more than just the purchase price of those materials — it has cost them in health care expenses, sick leave, and decreased productivity. Over the life of the building, this can result in significant costs as discomfort,[4] indoor

pollutants, poor lighting, and other problems can compromise the health and productivity of staff. As a result, businesses and the insurance industry pay an enormous amount for the unintended consequences of "sick buildings." According to the World Health Organization, sick building syndrome occurs in about 30 percent of new and newly renovated buildings (Kustin 1999, 131).

Each year in the United States, colds and other respiratory ailments result in approximately 160 million sick days being taken at work as well as 300 million days of restricted activity in the workplace (Lawrence Berkeley Labs, "Improved Indoor Air," para. 7). This costs companies about $64 billion each year – $35 billion every year in lost work and $29 billion for health care (Lawrence Berkeley Labs, "Improved Indoor Air," para. 7). By improving indoor environmental quality, it is estimated that the U.S. can save the following amounts every year:

* $6 to $19 billion – due to decreased respiratory disease
* $1 to $4 billion – due to decreased asthma/allergies
* $10 to $20 billion – due to decreased sick building syndrome
* $12 billion or more (estimated) – due to increased staff productivity (LBL, "Improved Indoor Air," para. 4)

This indicates just how costly many facilities are for the companies that own them or lease space in them, for the health of those who work in them, for the insurance industry, and for insured individuals who pay higher premiums and co-pays.

Healthier facilities are more pleasant places in which to work, and they also can save money. Companies with healthy facilities might experience improved employee morale and productivity while work defects and absenteeism fall. Hawken, Lovins, and Lovins (1999) have explained that this is due to greater comfort, which results in reduced stress, greater productivity, higher sales, and better quality work.

Therefore, investments in healthier facilities often provide unexpected returns for these and other reasons. These returns often far exceed the savings achieved through resource efficiency measures. This is due, in part, to the fact that most companies exist in unhealthy facilities and might assume that employee illness, low morale, and reduced productivity are normal. Though they might be normal, they are not always necessary.

Durst Organization: Several companies, both for-profit and not-for-profit, have recognized the importance of creating healthy workplaces. For instance, the Durst Organization's forty-eight-story office tower, the first office building to be constructed in mid-Manhattan in a decade, was designed to be healthy and efficient. Douglas Durst, the company's president, has stated, "Being environmentally responsible is part of our lifestyle. We were pleased to learn that the economics made sense as well" (Holusha 1996, para. 9).

The company anticipates considerable energy savings and a rise in productivity. Its tenant guidelines specify the use of healthier materials and good indoor air quality. Condé Nast, the travel magazine publisher, is Durst's anchor tenant and plans to do its part to maintain high indoor air quality, focusing primarily on adhesives, carpeting, paint, and wall coverings, all of which can cause poor indoor air quality.

National Audubon Society: Audubon House also provides a good example of a non- or low-toxic workplace. Although some of the new products' initial costs were higher than the cost of conventional products, Audubon required that they pay for themselves within five years. The materials used (furniture, carpets, etc.) had little or no toxicity. For example, the organization used mahogany tables certified by the Rainforest Alliance as sustainably harvested and containing no polyurethane (a hazard to those applying it). It also used only low-VOC paints. Additionally, it had 100 percent virgin wool carpets made without chemicals or dyes installed (wool carpet lasts much longer than does synthetic carpet, so the carpeting will not need to be replaced as quickly). It used natural carpet padding made of jute fibers encased in recycled paper. The carpets and pads were tacked to the floor, avoiding the chemical offgassing that would have occurred had they been glued. GTE floor tiles were made of recycled glass left over from light bulb manufacture. Much harder than most, the tiles will not need to be replaced as often as standard floor tiles. In addi-

tion, they are impregnated with color and are non-porous, will not scratch, and do not need waxing. Although their initial cost was higher, the tiles require less care and last longer than most.

All materials brought into the building, from file folders and stationery to food packaging, meet strict purchasing guidelines specifying that they must contain recycled material and must be recyclable/compostable. The building's air intake is located on the roof where the air is cleaner rather than over the loading dock where some buildings' intake vents are placed. The Audubon system filters out 80 percent of the particles that move through the air intake, which is twice that required by the New York City building code. The non-toxic insulation materials include Homasote™ (recycled newspapers mixed with water and compressed with heat) used under the floors, multiple layers of fiberglass on the roof, and six inches of Air-krete™5 in the walls (National Audubon Society 2003).

The staff enjoys Audubon House so much that it comes to work earlier, keeps the desks neater (which are cleaned with citrus oil rather than toxic cleaners), and stays later. Elizabeth Hax of Audubon's Membership Department, has stated, "I love coming here to work every day. I love knowing that I'm not breathing crud" (Rocky Mountain Institute 1998, 352).

Children's Museum of Pittsburgh: The Children's Museum of Pittsburgh was one of the first LEED-certified children's museums in the U.S. The museum has several green features, including a high amount of recycled content, no-irrigation landscaping, low-VOC materials, and easy access to public transportation. In addition, about 80 percent of the wood used in the new construction was from certified sustainable sources, more than half of the materials were locally made or harvested, and much of the building waste was salvaged by local companies (Children's Museum of Pittsburgh 2005).

Brooklyn Children's Museum: The Brooklyn Children's Museum also has focused on being greener. The Museum will be one of the first "green" children's museum in the country and the first green museum in New York. Undergoing an expansion that is slated to open in 2007, the Museum will have several green features. For instance, it will encourage greener commuting by providing secure bike racks for staff and public use; shower facilities for staff bike and foot commuters; and city signage to encourage commutes via mass transit, bike, bus, subway, and train. It also will sort and recycle waste on site and compost food waste.

Furthermore, materials with little to no offgassing and high levels of renewable or recycled content will be used. These might include bamboo, cork, rubber, linoleum, and greener carpet. The Museum will have a geothermal heating and cooling system, and spent condenser water will be recycled or used for irrigation. Photovoltaics will produce about 2.5 percent of the museum's energy, and state-of-the-art carbon dioxide, occupancy, and daylight sensors will ensure a healthier, more resource-efficient building. Enhanced insulation and low-emissivity windows will help to reduce energy use, and low-flow faucets and waterless urinals will reduce the building's water use. The Museum anticipates saving about $103,000/year from energy-efficient technologies and is expected to achieve a LEED Silver rating by the U.S. Green Building Council. Landscaping will facilitate natural water retention and the flow of run-off to planted areas.

Meanwhile, the Museum's programs and exhibits will teach visitors about energy efficiency and environmental conservation. These will include interactive exhibits and signs that highlight the building's high performance features; an Energy Garden that will demonstrate how the Museum harvests its solar power; Energy Exploration areas that will show how the Museum uses water from deep in the earth to heat and cool the building and how the heat and light sensors work; and renewable resources education that explains, for example, that the bamboo flooring was selected for its durability and rapid growth. Additionally, the Museum will establish a Center for Biodiversity Research and Information.

The Children's Museum of Pittsburgh has several green features. *Courtesy of Children's Museum of Pittsburgh.*

The Children's Museum of Pittsburgh's "Backyard Wall" was made of construction debris. *Courtesy of Children's Museum of Pittsburgh.*

This bathroom sign at the Children's Museum of Pittsburgh leads visitors to the restrooms where there are dual-flush toilets, low-flow urinals, and aerators on all faucets. *Courtesy of Children's Museum of Pittsburgh.*

Organizational Crises

Company crises also provide incentives for greening as companies must work to regain ground lost as a result of environmental accidents or crises. This section discusses one company – Royal Dutch/Shell – that experienced two environmental crises in the same year and sought to become greener as a result. It also provides a brief example of a company – 3M – that might have averted a crisis by handling its environmental harm proactively.

Royal Dutch/Shell

In 1995, Royal Dutch/Shell underwent a major crisis for two reasons. That year, Shell UK planned to dispose of an enormous, 14,000 ton oil loading and storage platform (named the Brent Spar) by sinking it in the North Sea. In May, however, Greenpeace organized opposition to the company's plan. As a result, Shell received a considerable amount of negative press coverage as well as pressure to rescind its plan from the public, environmental groups, and the heads of several European governments. The British government, which had approved the plan, was lambasted by both Greenpeace and the media.

Shell believed that it had done everything right, from complying with environmental laws to undertaking a cost-benefit analysis and following scientific advice, which suggested that sinking the platform was the best environmental option (Winsemius and Guntram 2002). Yet, from a public relations point of view, the decision was a disaster. The company was unable to convince any countries around the North Sea that sinking the platform was the best option from an environmental point of view.

A consumer boycott that began in Germany cost the company about five million pounds weekly in lost sales. The boycott struck the company hardest in Germany where ninety million people recycle their garbage and might not have been able to rationalize the disposal of such an enormous product (Livesey 2001). As a result of the negative feedback, Shell had to find an alternative way to dispose of the Brent Spar onshore. Ultimately, the Brent Spar was dismantled, cleaned, and reused, a process that cost forty-one million pounds – twice as much as the disposal would have cost (Livesey 2001, 80).

Royal Dutch/Shell was not the only company affected by this incident. The negative press and the public pressure and scrutiny affected the entire oil industry. The eleven countries that make up the OSPAR (Oslo and Paris) Commission, an oil industry committee, established a short-term moratorium on the off-shore disposal of oil rigs until they could meet regarding a permanent ban. They also sought to revise the London Convention (previously the Convention on the Prevention of Marine Pollution by Dumping of Wastes and Other Matter) in order to place a permanent, worldwide ban on the offshore disposal of oil rigs.

That same year, Royal Dutch/Shell suffered an even greater blow as a result of its environmental and human rights policies. Shell had created a joint venture with the Nigerian government through a company called Shell Petroleum Development Company of Nigeria. This company was Nigeria's biggest oil producer, providing 90 percent of Nigeria's foreign exchange currency from taxes and royalties, 80 percent of the country's federal revenues, and approximately 14 percent of the Shell Group's entire global oil production (Livesey 2001, 71).

About 80 percent of Shell's Nigerian oil came from the Niger Delta, which is home to such cultures as the Ogoni people. The Ogoni people and others had been severely affected by Shell's activities in Nigeria due to oil spills, the open-air burning of gas byproducts, and other events. In 1993, an organization known as the Movement for the Survival of the Ogoni People led a large, nonviolent protest against Shell and the other oil companies that operated in their region. As a result, Shell closed its operations in the region. In response, the Nigerian government blamed the Ogoni organization for Shell's withdrawal. It tried and executed nine Nigerian Ogoni environmental activists, including well-known writer Ken Saro-Wiwa, who had spearheaded the movement against Shell's business activities in Nigeria (Livesey 2001).

The company was criticized heavily for its business activities in Nigeria and its part in the execution, although the company claims to have tried to discuss the matter with the government (Livesey 2001). Nonetheless, Shell came under heavy public scrutiny and criticism for failing to stop the executions. As a result, Shell Group, the company's global conglomeration, changed its corporate structure, incremental management programs, and policies on human rights and the environment. Transparency, communication, and attention to stakeholders have become fairly new values in the company's culture. As Shell has described it, the ways in which it once made decisions and carried them out has changed from a "decide, announce, deliver" process to a "dialogue, decide, deliver" process (Livesey 2001, 80).

Coming out of these two events, Shell was forced to reexamine its business practices and environmental policies. The company adopted a new policy of openness and transparency in 1995 (Livesey 2001).

Since then, Shell Nigeria has developed plans for environmental tracking and reporting. The company also has committed to upgrade its facilities and reduce the ways in which it harms the environment and human health in the region.

Sharon Livesey (2001), of Fordham's College of Business and Graduate School of Business, has explained that Shell's environmental and human rights crises were not the same types of crises as the Bhopal, Chernobyl, and *Valdez* crises. Instead, Shell was conducting business as usual but was criticized heavily because, without realizing it, the context in which the firm operated had changed to value corporate caring and communication.

3M

Some crises do not receive as much attention as Royal Dutch/Shell's; nonetheless, they might serve as catalysts toward better environmental behavior. One example of this occurred at 3M.

On May 16, 2000, 3M issued a press release stating its intention to phase out the production of perfluorooctanyl, a chemical used in some surfactants and repellents. Dr. Charles Reich, the Executive Vice President of the company's Specialty Material Markets division, stated, "While this chemistry has been used effectively for more than forty years and our products are safe, our decision to phase out production is based on our principles of responsible environmental management" (3M 2000, 1). It had been producing PFOS and potential metabolic precursors since 1948 (3M 1999, 3).

The day that the 3M press release was issued, the EPA released an internal memo discussing the health risks associated with using perfluorooctanyl sulfonate. The memo stated, "Following negotiations with EPA, 3M Corporation today announced that it will voluntarily phase out perfluorooctanyl sulfonate (PFOS) chemistry…." (Auer 2000, 1). It went on to report that 3M had supplied data to the EPA indicating that PFOS are environmentally persistent, bioaccumulative, and might cause harm over time (Auer 2000, 1).

Perfluorooctanyl is the common name for perfluorooctane sulfonic acid (PFOS), which is one of many types of sulfonated perfluorochemicals (PFCs) (Auer 2000, 1). Sulfonated perfluorochemicals can break down into PFOS (Auer 2000, 1). 3M is the only company in the U.S. that manufactures these chemicals, which are used in a number of applications, including stain resistant products, floor polishes, cleaning products, pesticides, and others. Familiar products containing PFOS include Post It™ notes, new clothing (particularly water-resistant articles), Tyvek™, and blue ice; similarly, the packaging used for microwave popcorn, fast food, pizza, bakery products, beverages, candy, and cookies might contain PFOS (Battelle 1999, 8).

According to the EPA memo, PFOS has been found in the blood of employees who manufacture the products at parts-per-million levels and in other individuals at parts-per-billion levels. In fact, it has been found in wildlife throughout the United States, particularly in fish-eating birds in Canada, Japan, Italy, and Korea, although PFOS have been found as far away as the Polar Regions. Additionally, PFOS has been found in human blood banks and in the blood of lab rats; the rats' exposure has been traced to fishmeal in their rat chow. This information, available to 3M in the 1970s, spurred the company to launch further studies into the effects of PFOS.

Charles Auer, the EPA's Director of Chemical Control Division Office of Pollution Prevention and Toxics, reported that PFOS "caused postnatal deaths (and other developmental effects) in offspring in a two-generation reproductive effects rate study" (2000, 2). "At higher doses," he continued, "*all* progeny in first generation died…." and "many of the progeny from the *second* generation died. It is very unusual to see such second generation effects" (2000, 2). PFOS is highly accumulative in humans as well.

With the blood data and rat study, the EPA requested that 3M provide detailed information on the risks associated with PFOS. The company complied and ultimately decided to leave the world market for this product "based on concerns about the widespread presence and longer term risks presented by PFOS" (Auer 2000, 3).

Products containing the chemical contributed almost $16 billion, or 2 percent, to the company's annual sales. These products included many Scotchgard™ products, including grease- and oil-resistant coatings for paper packaging; foams used to put out fires; water, oil, and soil repellants; and others. The company reported that it would phase out these products largely by the end of 2000. Reich stated, "Our decision anticipates increasing attention to the appropriate use and management of persistent materials" (3M 2000, 1). He stated that the company is "reallocating resources" in order to speed innovation of more sustainable products and technologies (3M 2000, 1). Livio DeSimone, 3M's chairman and CEO, stated, "Our growth engines are more powerful than ever and we're confident in our ability to continue delivering on expectations" (3M 2000, 1). 3M also plans to stop producing perfluorooctanoic acid (PFOA), a related chemical used as a solvent, as it also presents health risks (Auer 2000, 3).

3M's decision to phase out its production of those products voluntarily enhanced the company's image, and its stock price went up nearly 5 percent on the day that it made its announcement (Winsemius and Guntram 2002). The fact that 3M voluntarily reported this problem and stopped producing a lucrative product indicated to many that the company cares about the environmental and the health effects of its products and that it is environmentally transparent.

Had the company not voluntarily reported this problem and it had been discovered and made public first, it is likely that the public's view of 3M would have been quite different. Then-EPA Administrator Carol Browner announced, "Today's phase out announcement by 3M will ensure that future exposure to these chemicals will be eliminated, and public health and the environment will be protected" (US EPA, Press Statement 2000, 1). The way in which 3M handled this matter might have helped the firm to avert a crisis.

Nonetheless, there has been some speculation that the company was not as forthcoming as it appeared. In 1999, the 3M Medical Department compiled a report "to summarize the data related to the biological effects of perfluorooctane sulfonate (PFOS)" and to share "current thinking on human health risk related to PFOS" and "information about future study plans" (1999, 3). It stated that, for more than twenty years, 3M has conducted "medical surveillance" on 3M employees who were exposed to PFOS (3M 1999, 3). PFOS is absorbed easily by mouth and distributed through the blood serum and liver and is not metabolized but slowly exits the body. "In three retirees," it reported, "the half-life in human sera ranges from 1100 to 1500 days" (3M 1999, 4).

Exposure in rat studies has resulted in "GI toxicity, hematological abnormalities, weight loss, convulsions, tremors, and death" (3M 1999, 4). Furthermore, the report stated, "Monkeys show anorexia, emesis, diarrhea, hypoactivity and at higher doses prostration, convulsions and death. Atrophy of exocrine cells in salivary glands and the pancreas, and lipid depletion in the adrenals is found at high doses in the monkey" (3M 2000, 4). This indicates that 3M was long aware of the health risks associated with a product that it continued to manufacture. Research into the effects of perfluorochemicals is ongoing.[6]

Stakeholder Pressure

In addition to the four reasons already discussed, businesses become greener in response to stakeholder pressure. The environment, also a stakeholder, is placed in a distinct category (Environmental Concerns and Values) because of its prominence in some companies' decisions to become greener.

Pressure from regulators, communities, employees, NGOs, industry, customers, suppliers, shareholders, politicians, and/or others can play a crucial role in influencing a company's decisions to become greener. That is because businesses need stakeholder support in order to survive. The remainder of this section explores one company – Mitsubishi – and its decision to improve its environmental behaviors as a result of stakeholder pressure.

Mitsubishi

In 1998, following five years of often intense negotiations, two companies within the Mitsubishi Corporation – Mitsubishi Motor Sales of America (MMSA) and Mitsubishi Electric of America (MEA) – came to an agreement with the environmental group Rainforest Action Network (RAN). RAN had protested the Mitsubishi Corporation's business practices, especially the company's logging in tropical forests, and had begun a boycott of Mitsubishi Corp. and its many affiliates eight years prior. The agreement signaled the end of RAN's boycotts against MMSA and MEA, though RAN stated that it would continue to boycott the Corporation's forestry group, banking unit, and heavy industry unit. The Mitsubishi Corporation's American arm, which also was involved in negotiations, left the talks before any agreement was reached. Freelance journalist Peter Asmus (1998) has reported that this incident has put tremendous strain on the relationships between both the Mitsubishi Corporation and the MMSA and MEA.

Mitsubishi Corp. is not one company but many that share a common name and are related through stock ownership and board membership. However, the Mitsubishi companies act as separate business entities that are independent of one another. Therefore, MEA and MMSA "were dismayed" to find that they were among those being boycotted for Mitsubishi Corporation's non-sustainable logging practices in old-growth forests (Asmus 1998, 51).

Winsemius and Guntram (2002) have discussed this problem of association, which is not unique to Mitsubishi. They have explored the trouble of "major differences in environmental responses within large companies which, apart from increasing exposure to external criticism, also raise questions with regard to the internal conditions for change" (Winsemius and Guntram 2002, 98-99). The authors have suggested that such questions include "How can top management be clear and consistent in its communication when the message differs among its businesses?" and "How can it maintain credibility within its middle echelons if coworkers are confronted with variations in environmental aspirations when they're transferred from unit to unit?" (Winsemius and Guntram 2002, 99).

Tachi Kiuchi, who once ran MEA and is managing director of Mitsubishi Electric Corporation, expressed his belief that the boycott was poorly informed. "We have no timber holdings. We make no forest products," he said (Asmus 1998, 54). He stated that MEA has been separate from Mitsubishi Corporation since 1946: "not subsidiaries, not divisions – separate" (Asmus 1998, 54). Yet, he saw an opportunity in the boycotts. Because the Mitsubishi companies shared a name, people often assumed that they were part of one large company. Rather than try to set the record straight, Kiuchi decided that it would be easier to try to solve the problem.

MEA and MMSA wished to end the boycott and began negotiating with RAN by 1992. Negotiations lasted several years because both sides (MMSA and MEA on the one hand and RAN on the other) were not getting what they wanted. RAN wanted to reduce the companies' environmental impacts, and the companies wanted a framework to tie it together. Then, MEA and MMSA discovered and adopted The Natural Step (refer to the Glossary) as their sustainability framework. "MEA had a number of initiatives designed to reduce our impact on the environment, but we were searching for a framework to tie it all together," Kiuchi has noted. "When we were introduced to The Natural Step we realized that we had found our framework!" (Asmus 1998, 54). Since then, MEA has developed a joint venture with the Japanese government to establish dozens of product take-back centers, created product analysis software, developed a Design for Environment program, integrated its quality and environmental management programs, and won environmental awards (Asmus 1998).

Kiuchi visited the Malaysian rainforest and states that he "learned that saving the environment is an opportunity to pursue business opportunities that use creativity and technology to substitute for trees, for resources of any kind" (Asmus 1998, 55). Upon his return, he asked Amory Lovins of Rocky Mountain Institute to put together a global team to study business opportunities to save forests (Asmus 1998). Lovins' Systems Group on Forests released several reports in response.

Though Mitsubishi has suggested that the boycott's impact was not great, some company officials apparently stated that the company's image was harmed as a result (McCoy 1998, 1). In fact, the company lost one $137 million San Francisco airport contract following the lobbying by RAN and others (McCoy 1998, 1).

In the end, MMSA and MEA committed to end their use of products (e.g., packaging, paper) made from wood that is taken from either rare or old growth forests. This commitment was set to begin in April 1998. The companies also committed to a longer term phase-out of all wood products, agreeing to use paper and other products made of non-wood fibers, such as waste materials or agricultural products (e.g., kenaf) (McCoy 1998). Furthermore, the companies agreed to donate some profits for forest restoration and to help indigenous communities, some of which were affected by Mitsubishi's logging operations. John Savage, the executive vice president of Mitsubishi Electric, stated, "Global companies increasingly are realizing that we have a responsibility to the ecosystems in which we do business" (McCoy 1998, 1).

Meanwhile, RAN has pressured retailers, including the Home Depot, to stop buying wood from old growth forests. Home Depot has stated that it is actively working to determine the sources of its wood; however, with over 50,000 wood products purchased from about 5,000 producers, the company has experienced some challenges (Lazaroff 1998, 9.A). Levi Strauss, Nike, Kinko's, 3M, and the two U.S. Mitsubishi affiliates discussed above have signed RAN's pledge to end their purchase of old growth wood (Lazaroff 1998, 9.A).

Key Factors Determining a Company's Reasons for Greening

Thus far, this chapter has explored some of the motivations for company greening – environmental impacts and values, regulatory compliance, economic incentives and disincentives, organizational crises, and stakeholder pressures. However, it has not addressed some of the underlying factors that might lead to such motivations. Though it is beyond the scope of this book to discuss the "motivations behind the motivations" in depth, it is worth mentioning one study that addressed this issue.

Bansal and Roth (2000) conducted research that provides additional insights into how different companies approach greening. They have suggested that while some research cites environmental regulation, stakeholder pressures, ethical concerns, critical events, and other reasons as incentives for greening, such reasons do not provide a means for predicting which companies are likely to become greener and what incentives are the most likely to stimulate company greening. Furthermore, they do not explain why some companies fail to become more environmentally friendly.

As a result, Bansal and Roth sought to identify specific motivating factors behind companies' decisions to become greener – what they have referred to as "the antecedent conditions of corporate ecological responsiveness" (2000, 717). The authors have defined corporate ecological responsiveness "as a set of corporate initiatives aimed at mitigating a firm's impact on the natural environment" (Bansal and Roth 2000, 717).

After studying fifty-three auto manufacturing, food, retail, oil, and other companies in Japan and the UK, the authors concluded that companies become greener ("embrace ecologically responsive initiatives") for three reasons, which they refer to as legitimation, competitiveness, and ecological responsibility (2000, 717).

Legitimation refers to a company's desire to improve its activities "within an established set of regulations, norms, values, or beliefs" (Bansal and Roth 2000, 726). Its greening activities might include a focus on regulatory compliance, the creation of an environmental manager position or environmental committee, the establishment of relationships with environmental advocates, the creation of an emergency response system, and environmental audits.

The companies most concerned with legitimation were those that belonged to industries characterized by "high field cohesion" (Bansal and Roth 2000). This means that they have tight networks of relationships within their industries. For example, the oil companies that took part in Bansal and Roth's study were less motivated by competing with one another for stellar environmental performance or products than they were in maintaining their industry relationships and conforming with industry norms, complying with regulation, and gaining the acceptance of stakeholders, including the public.

The study indicated that industry associations could be used to increase companies' commitments to become greener. However, to be effective, such associations would need to encourage collaborative research efforts among their membership as well as their members' voluntary disclosure of their environmental impacts. These two changes, alone, would help to introduce environmental issues and priorities into industries characterized by high field cohesion (Bansal and Roth 2000).

Competitiveness refers to a company's desire "to improve long-term profitability" (Bansal and Roth 2000, 724). Companies that become greener in order to compete with one another more effectively might focus on improvements in energy and waste management, source reductions, ecolabeling and green marketing, and the creation of green products (Bansal and Roth 2000).

Those companies most interested in competitive greening belonged to those industries in which environmental impacts were more certain and obvious and resulted in strong public emotion. Such firms tended to compete for green market share in those areas in which their ecological impacts were most noticeable. For such companies, reducing toxic emissions might be a greater company priority than reducing a company's effects on climate change.

Motivating such companies to improve their environmental performances in areas that are less apparent might be a challenge. However, new and better research on those issues over which there is considerable debate might help to increase the clarity of issues and encourage companies to respond to their impacts on environmental health (Bansal and Roth 2000).

Ecological responsibility refers to the company's concern over "its social obligations and values" (Bansal and Roth 2000, 728). Companies that become greener in order to be more ecologically responsible might focus on greening previously developed land, using recycled paper and more environmentally friendly office products, developing less profitable but greener products, donating to local community and environmental groups, and recycling office paper and other materials.

The companies that demonstrated ecological responsibility were those in which employees and/or management held strong environmental values and had the power to act on those values. Individual employees played important roles, helping to champion or prioritize environmental issues for the company. Meanwhile, individual managers had the power to incorporate their values into company goals and operations. Bansal and Roth (2000) have suggested that such individual values could be increased through training staff about the ecological impacts of company activities.

Although Bansal's and Roth's (2000) sample was small (only fifty-three firms), this research could help researchers to predict if certain businesses might choose to improve their environmental performances and how they might go about improving those performances based on their industrial contexts.

Why Some Businesses Do Not Go Green

Though an increasing number of companies are committing to the goal of environmental sustainability or, at least, working to reduce their environmental harm, not all businesses are going greener. Given the apparent benefits of greening, why have some businesses failed to commit to greening? This section briefly explores a few reasons why companies might not be committed to changing their environmental relationships and, then, focuses on one in particular – the lack of green business training in today's business schools.

At the beginning of this chapter, I explored some of the positive and negative incentives for greening, such as Starik's and Rands' (1995) positive and negative pro-sustainability feedback. This section discusses some of the positive and negative *disincentives* to greening – those factors that help to prevent companies from improving their environmental performances. These include Starik's and Rands' (1995) positive/anti-sustainability feedback and negative/anti-sustainability feedback.

Positive/anti-sustainability feedback provides cues to the company that its non-sustainable behaviors are appropriate or acceptable. For example, a firm that fails to comply with environmental regulations because they are not enforced (positive/anti-sustainability feedback) is subject to positive disincentives. When a business is penalized for its attempts at sustainability, such as incurring high costs for environmentally proactive efforts, it receives negative/anti-sustainability feedback. This can serve as a negative disincentive for greening.

Sanjay Sharma (2000), Professor and Director of Wilfrid Laurier University's Centre for Responsible Organizations, has explained that there are three attributes that help to determine whether a manager views environmental issues as a threat or opportunity. These are "negative or positive emotional associations, loss or gain considerations, and a sense of the issues as uncontrollable or controllable" (Sharma 2000, 684). Madhu Khanna, of the University of Illinois' Department of Agricultural & Consumer Economics, and Wilma Rose Quimio Anton (2002), of the University of Central Florida's Department of Economics, also have discussed whether companies are driven to become greener because of perceived threats or opportunities.

Auden Schendler (2001) has suggested that most of the corporate sustainability literature focuses on green business successes while ignoring failures, which have the potential to provide important lessons in busi-

nesses' movement toward ecological sustainability. Schendler (2001), the Aspen Skiing Company's (ASC's) Director of Environmental Affairs, has written of some of his challenges to improve his company's environmental performance.

The ASC is recognized as the world's most environmentally responsible ski resort (Schendler 2001). Yet, Schendler (2001) has asserted that while resource efficiency and other greening activities might make financial sense, corporate politics often interfere. He has recounted a story in which energy-efficient lighting was installed at one of the company's restaurants. The restaurant manager did not like to look of the compact fluorescent bulbs, so he removed them and threw them away (Schendler 2001). Schendler has explained that most greening successes typically are "messy, hard-fought battles fraught with complications and often on the edge of failure" (2001, 294). He has stated that sustainability will occur only with grit and cash incentives if they are available (Schendler 2001).

However, the failure to green can occur for other reasons as well. Bob Doppelt, Director of the University of Oregon's Resource Innovations Group, has identified "seven sustainability blunders," including 1) "patriarchal thinking that leads to a false sense of security," 2) a "siloed approach to environmental and socioeconomic issues," 3) "no clear vision of sustainability," 4) "confusion over cause and effect," 5) a "lack of information," 6) "insufficient mechanisms for learning," and 7) the "failure to institutionalize sustainability" (2003, 37).

Poor management is one reason behind the failure to become greener. Additionally, even in well-managed businesses, not all senior managers share the personal values and proactive attitudes of Patagonia's founder Yvon Chouinard's, Aveda's founder Horst M. Rechelbacher (refer to Aveda Corporation, Horst Rechelbacher, Aveda Founder 2003), Interface's Ray Anderson, and Body Shop's founders Anita and Gordon Roddick (refer to Roddick 2000).

Additionally, it is likely that many managers are not aware of the full extent of the environmental harm that their companies cause; if they are, they might be uncertain about how to resolve the problem.

Hutchinson (1995) has expressed the need to manage organizational change when greening a firm. Winsemius and Guntram (2002) have purported that managing change is one of the greatest challenges in environmental management. In fact, some companies experience a resistance to change and find that the most difficult part of greening a company is greening its people. Jack Welch once stated, "Get all the facts out…. When everybody gets the same facts, they'll generally come to the same conclusion. Only after everyone agrees on the reality and resistance is lowered can you begin to get buy-in to the needed change" (*Fortune* as cited in Winsemius and Guntram 2002, 178).

Winsemius and Guntram (2002) have identified five barriers to change that companies might face internally, and these can be applied to the firms' transition to sustainability. They are 1) ineffective organizational structures and compliance-related management systems, 2) a short-range vision that misses environmental trends and realities, 3) the perception that current and future environmental issues are growing burdens rather than opportunities for innovation and business success, 4) a failure to understand environmental regulatory, NGO, and other third-party issues of focus (the same could be said of third-party perceptions as well), and 5) uneasy employees whose roles in greening are crucial.

Additionally, firms might believe that the health of the environment and either the economy or their own businesses are inherently at odds with one another. In this instance, a company that wants to be ecologically sustainable might realize that its primary mission harms local and global ecological systems and that, no matter how much progress it makes to improve its environmental performance, it cannot be environmentally benign or restorative. This realization might discourage a company from identifying ways to improve its environmental performance.

Even those companies with the highest opportunities for successful greening – those with buy-in from senior management, access to resources, and a positive attitude – may never get there because those who want the company to become green might not understand what it means to be green or the level of commitment required of them. This can be overcome when the company has the will, or intention, to commit to sustainability and all that it entails and, then, by increasing the environmental awareness and attitudes of all staff throughout the company and working with staff throughout the organization to develop greening strategies.

Another challenge to creating ecologically integrated companies is the fact that firms exist in a larger context of non-sustainable human activity. For example, some companies have pointed to the lack of true-cost pricing within companies, industries, and economies as one disincentive to greening. The incorporation of environmental costs that currently are externalized would help to level the playing field and create an incentive for companies to go green. Helmut Maucher, the CEO of Nestlé, has stated that putting a price on the natural resources that many of us assume to be free will be the most efficient way to allocate those resources (Winsemius and Guntram 2002). Yet, current economic practices continue to externalize environmental costs as both global and regional economies fail to account for the "services" that ecosystems provide naturally. Additionally, even if the entire staff of a company is ecologically aware and makes responsible decisions regarding the environment, it might be difficult for the company to be green unless its suppliers are green and there is consumer demand for greener products and services.

Anita Roddick. *Photo by Joel Anderson. Courtesy of Anita Roddick.*

Mollusks like this one found in the Gulf of Mexico provide many ecosystem services, such as cleaning water. *Townsend.*

Some business greening efforts might also be stifled by the fact that firms' customers and other important stakeholders are not green or environmentally astute. The Business Council for Sustainable Development (now the World Business Council for Sustainable Development), which has as its members the heads of many multinational corporations, acknowledged the need for "substantial efforts in education and training, to increase awareness and encourage changes in lifestyles toward more sustainable forms of consumption" (Schmidheiny 1992, xiii). Additionally, ecosystem managers, who are instrumental in developing policies and setting resource acquisition limits, will need to undergo some significant shifts in their thinking and approaches. The University of Nevada's population and conservation biologist Peter Brussard, conservation biologist J. Michael Reed of Tufts' Department of Biology, and C. Richard Tracy of the University of Nevada's Department of Biology and Director of Biological Resources Research Center (1998) have explained, "Ecosystem management will require radically new approaches for management agencies if it is adopted seriously rather than just used as a catchy new term for business as usual" (1998, 13). Carl Folke and Johan Colding of the Beijer International Institute of Ecological Economics and Fikret Berkes of the University of Manitoba's Natural Resources Institute (1998) have explained that "conventional scientific and technological approaches to resource and ecosystem management are not always working, and may indeed make the problem worse" – perhaps due, in part, to a "focus on the wrong kinds of sustainability" (1998, 414).

Even those businesses that are interested in becoming more environmentally friendly might be overwhelmed by the breadth of tools and activities associated with greening. As a result, they might find it difficult to know where or how to begin. Moreover, they might not know what criteria to use in greening their activities and products and how to assess greening to determine if their efforts have been successful. Furthermore, there are risks associated with being a green business pioneer.

Starik and Rands have suggested the following reasons why some businesses do not seek to work toward ecological sustainability:

> First, dramatic negative impacts on natural systems are relatively recent, and our understanding of the bases, severity, and scope of these impacts is still limited. Second, appreciation of the benefits derived from healthy, diverse ecological systems is underdeveloped. Third, there is insufficient public understanding of both ecological principles and the urgency of bringing humanity's collective behavior into congruence with these principles. Fourth, reversing these impacts and approaching sustainability requires substantial change, much of it antithetical to short-term economic self-interest. Finally, a lack of understanding exists about what practices are required at various levels to act in a sustainable manner. (1995, 911)

The remainder of this section will address one of the most fundamental reasons that some companies do not become greener – the failure of many business schools to provide adequate (if any) green business training. Those schools that do provide training in business greening do not require that their students take any environmental science courses; as a result, it is possible to graduate as a "green" business student without understanding anything about how environmental systems work.

Lack of Green Business Training

Every year, about 200,000 undergraduate, 100,000 masters, and 1,000 doctoral business students graduate from colleges and universities across the United States (World Resources Institute and the Aspen Institute for Social Innovation through Business 2001, 4). Meanwhile, many business leaders have expressed a need for employees skilled in green business; however, they have reported that they have a difficult time finding even entry-level employees who are adequately trained (Bunch 1999). That is because many business schools do not incorporate environmental concerns, approaches, and tools into their curricula. Moreover, in their campus recruiting, many companies do not actively seek out students who are trained in environmental stewardship (WRI and Aspen ISIB 2001). This could portend severe problems as businesses and their future business leaders are increasingly faced with resource depletion and calls for increased accountability.

Though a growing number of business programs are beginning to address green business to some degree, most do so by offering green business courses as electives or green business opportunities via voluntary extracurricular activities (WRI and Aspen ISIB 2001). Though such courses and activities are important, they tend to reflect the individual commitment of a few faculty members rather than the backing of entire business programs.

Few schools integrate environmental issues into their curricula (WRI and Aspen ISIB 2001). Yet, just as businesses need to integrate the environment into all of their decisions and activities in order to improve their environmental performances, so do business schools need to integrate environmental thinking and teaching into the most fundamental aspects of all that they teach. Accounting, finance, marketing, and all other business-related fields need to assimilate environmental issues, approaches, and tools into their programs if students are to be adequately trained as future business leaders in a world increasingly eager for a sustainability compass and green leadership. Instead, however, even in the academic arena, environmental issues still tend to be viewed as a constraint rather than an opportunity for competition and growth.

Richard Bunch (1999) has suggested that environmental management programs offered at business schools typically face several challenges. First, business instructors' often lack general environmental knowledge and strategies. The slow growth of educational materials in this area also makes teaching about the environment in a business curriculum challenging. Furthermore, many of the professors interested in environmental issues are in the earlier parts of their careers and may face older professional ideologies within their departments that do not recognize or value green business and its necessary place at the foundation of any business education. Additionally, there is a low demand for environmental knowledge and skills by incoming students and by some of the businesses that hire those students. Even students with environmental interests might take fewer environmental courses if they feel that a course in marketing, for instance, would make them more competitive in the job market. Finally, there is a general lack of knowledge regarding both the environmental impacts of business and appropriate business responses to environmental issues.

One survey (Benton and Cottle as cited in Neuvelt 1999) indicated that managers prefer environmental professionals with environmentally related scientific or technical training over those with a Masters of Business Administration (MBA) degree. MBA graduates were appealing only if they had the necessary scientific or technical backgrounds. In fact, 33 percent of 1,200 environmental professionals surveyed stated that the MBA was neither advantageous nor disadvantageous in hiring, and 9 percent suggested that it was actually a disadvantage (Benton and Cottle as cited in Neuvelt 1999, 411).

When the World Resources Institute (WRI) and the Aspen Institute for Social Innovation through Business (Aspen ISIB) met with business executives in 2001, they worked together to develop a list of recommendations to help MBA programs better prepare their students. These recommendations are shown below:

* "Develop business school cases with measurable examples of success through sustainability
* Look to international development banks and financial institutions for globalization programs, seminars, cases, and course content
* Accelerate integration of stewardship training into the core curriculum through modules within required courses
* Bring consumer activists, institutional shareholders, socially responsible investors, and industry and NGO representatives into the classroom to work on projects with MBA teams
* Provide role-playing opportunities and consulting experiences that require students to make decisions in scenarios where the population is impoverished, the government is corrupt, and there is no electricity or clean water
* Help students to learn how to manage human and environmental disasters
* Conduct research on different cultures and customs" (World Resources Institute and the Aspect Institute for Social Innovation through Business 2001, 8)

The WRI and Aspen ISIB (2001) have reported that the cutting-edge green business programs already do these things.

This report did not discuss the need for ecological literacy among business students. After all, how can one ensure that a company is green if one does not

Montreat College students learn about the natural environment and how it functions. *Courtesy of Brad Daniel.*

understand how ecosystems function? Though green business courses are in the minority, few, if any, business schools require their students to take courses in the environmental sciences, such as ecology or biology. This means that the world's future business leaders, who may be largely responsible for decisions regarding resource use and ecosystem health, might be unqualified to make such decisions – even with green business training. With so many companies committing to ecological sustainability, how will future, ecologically illiterate business leaders be able to determine how to attain or maintain sustainability – let alone accurately assess their companies' environmental performances beyond quantifying resource use and emissions?

Clearly, business schools can play an important part in educating future businesspersons in greening the companies for which they work. One of the challenges that lies ahead is the development of curricula that will prepare business persons to make the transition from the current business paradigm to an ecologically based one.

Summary

This chapter explored the five key reasons that businesses seek to improve their environmental performances. They might do so for one or more reasons, including environmental impacts and values, economic opportunities and disincentives, government regulations, organizational crises, and stakeholder pressures. Each of these provides a range of both positive and negative incentives for greening, including the positive and negative pro-sustainability feedback reported by Starik and Rands (1995).

Underlying these five reasons are contextual factors that help to determine what a company's environmental response is likely to be. Bansal and Roth (2000) have reported that companies take one of three different approaches to greening – legitimation, competitiveness, and ecological responsibility. These approaches are determined largely by the industry within which the company is embedded.

The chapter also explored some of the reasons why firms might choose *not* to become greener. It explained that companies might respond to positive and/or negative disincentives to greening, including the positive and negative anti-sustainability feedback that Starik and Rands (1995) have suggested. One fundamental obstacle to sustainable businesses is the lack of green business training in business schools. Though progress is being made, both green business considerations and ecological knowledge need to be fully integrated into business school curricula.

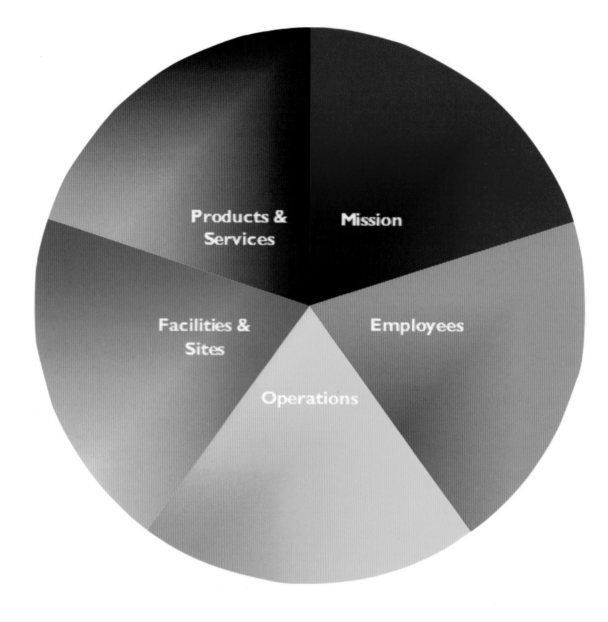

The five elements of greening business. *Townsend*.

Chapter 2
The Need to Standardize
What Companies Green

This chapter explores what companies green. It suggests that greening is not standardized and that most companies focus only on a few areas in their efforts to improve their environmental performances. As a result, most greening efforts are not comprehensive. This chapter suggests that companies can be divided into five elements for greening – their missions, employees, operations, facilities and sites, and products and services. In order to become ecologically sustainable, firms will need to green each of these elements completely.

Overview

The activities required for greening a business are necessarily broad in scope. That is because there are many elements that should be greened if the company wishes to achieve and, then, maintain ecological sustainability. This chapter suggests that in order to develop a green company, greening must focus on the entire business throughout its existence. Here, the company is divided into five segments, or elements, which are intended to represent the entire organization. They are as follows:

* Mission
* Employees
* Operations
* Facilities and sites
* Products and/or services

The figure below illustrates these five elements.

This section explores the need to standardize what it is that companies green. Such standardization is important for businesspersons, academicians, policymakers, customers, and others who might wish for a clear and consistent understanding of what is meant by "green business." It also identifies some of the fields that contribute to current green business best practices.

The growing body of literature on green business and environmental management provides helpful examples of companies that have improved their environmental performances through various methods. Yet, what is greened varies from business to business. Greening approaches and tools differ considerably and frequently fail to address the entire firm for several reasons. As a result, even today's green business best

practices do not result in companies that are truly green (Rowledge, Barton, and Brady 1999; Stead and Stead 1996).

There are several reasons for this. In part, the failure of best practices to result in green businesses occurs because greening activities tend to encompass a fairly narrow scope, focusing primarily on reducing a company's environmental harm through reduction and replacement strategies, such as waste reduction and resource efficiency. This is achieved primarily through environmental improvements in production and, to a lesser extent, aligning staff and company values and training employees to enhance the company's environmental performance (Rowledge, Barton, and Brady 1999; DeSimone and Popoff 1997). Many firms still give little thought to the company's mission, non-production-related operations, and facilities and site. For example, much of the environmental management literature focuses on the need to enhance the efficiency of energy/resource use in production and throughout product life cycles (Rowledge, Barton, and Brady 1999; DeSimone and Popoff 1997). Still other literature discusses the need to ensure solid leadership in greening efforts (North 1992; Chinander 2001). Yet, creating – or recreating – a green business requires a broader focus.

Lorinda R. Rowledge (co-founder of EKOS International), Russell S. Barton (co-founder of EKOS International), and Kevin Brady (Director of Five Winds International) (1999) have identified some of the activities that businesses have undertaken in response to the call for sustainability. Note that these activities focus almost exclusively on production and product-related issues. The activities include eliminating waste and toxic emissions; getting more out of resources;

reducing materials use; using greener processes and technologies; manufacturing greener products; being more energy-efficient; ensuring that production is socially and environmentally responsible; exhibiting transparency in all environmental and social impacts; designing for environment, disassembly, recyclability, and repairability; creating products that are more durable, flexible, and functional; and taking proactive steps to be responsible for products and services throughout their lives (Rowledge, Barton, and Brady 1999).

DeSimone and Popoff (1997) have written that there are five indicators of a company's good environmental performance: employee health and safety, high-quality facility management and housekeeping, commitment to ensuring that products are safely handled throughout their lives, emergency preparedness, and long-term focus beyond compliance (107). This list does not explore the firm's need to align its mission with its sustainability goals nor does it address issues related to operations, such as green investing, transportation, and so forth.

The failure to address businesses in their entirety reduces the chance that companies will be fully green because firms are likely to overlook opportunities or synergies among company departments, processes, and other activities. As a result, piecemeal greening activities will be more costly than if the company was approached as a whole. Moreover, there is a need to standardize the scope of greening if the term "green business" is to regain and maintain both conceptual and practical integrity.

Caveat: The five elements are intended to help a company think about what it is that needs to be greened. As with any model that seeks to reflect some aspect of the world, there is no hard line that separates all of the elements from one another. Thus, *there might be some overlap among the five elements*. For example, a company might not know whether the procurement of materials for a manufacturing process falls under Operations or Production (both discussed in later chapters). Does the procurement of office supplies fall under Operations while the procurement of manufacturing materials falls under Production? There is no hard and fast rule. The important thing is that all types of procurement are considered – regardless of category/categories. Therefore, this conceptual model should be viewed simply as a tool to help companies to organize their thinking about what needs to be greened. Companies will need to tailor it to their requirements and use it in ways that are meaningful to them.

Fields That Inform Business Greening

Though many environmental management books discuss the importance of working toward sustainability and suggest ways to achieve it, they typically focus only on one or two areas, such as greening products and manufacturing processes (often in order to achieve or surpass regulatory compliance), increasing energy efficiency of company facilities, or, less often, greening leadership and employees. Few companies try to green all five of these elements; those that do might only carry out partial greening activities. For example, though Patagonia's founders were committed to environmental health and the company has a made environmental improvements in all five elements of the company, it has acknowledged only partial greening success (Patagonia 1998).

It is not that best practices for greening the five elements of a company have not been developed. They have – although most will lead to green improvements rather than ecological sustainability. However, today's green best practices are spread out across numerous fields and can be difficult to identify. The figure below indicates some of these fields and the business elements that they address.

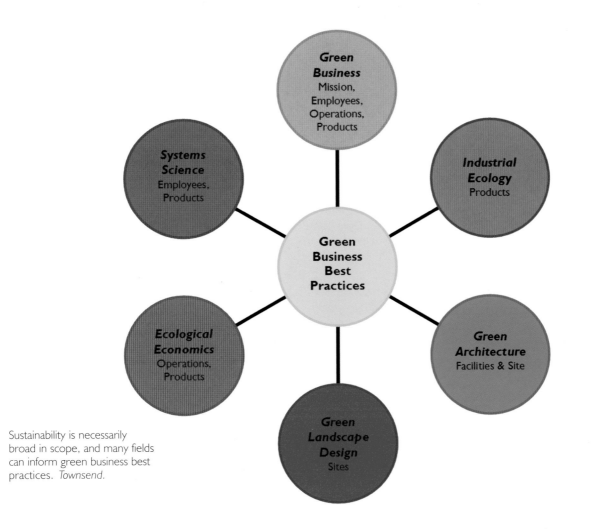

A firm that wishes to be greener might have to consult several sources as sustainability is inherently multi-disciplinary and transdisciplinary (Frankel 1998; Gladwin et al. 1995). This helps to explain why moving businesses toward that goal can be so difficult. For example, books and articles on environmental management, organizational learning, and managing organizational change can provide a company with information on greening its mission, employees, and a variety of other aspects. Research on social and environmentally responsible investing, environmental accounting and finance, green procurement, and greener transportation might prove helpful in greening company operations. A firm also might look into green architecture, building, landscape architecture, and ecological regeneration for information on facilities and sites. Meanwhile, industrial ecology, design for environment, environmental design, and other topics provide information on products and services.

Clearly, this book cannot explore the vast expanse of literature that is reflected in each of these elements. However, it addresses both the need to improve a company's environmental performance in each of the five elements as well as some of the activities that are used toward that end.

Case Study

The following five chapters will explore what it means to green a company's mission, employees, operations, facilities and sites, and products and services. Each of these five sections is organized in a similar fashion. First, I will discuss the importance of greening the particular element at hand. Next, I will examine some of the activities that might occur in greening that element. Finally, I will provide examples of how one company – Patagonia – has improved the environmental performances in the context of each particular element. I chose Patagonia because 1) information on its environmental performance was easily available online and 2) the company has made strides in greening each of its five elements. For examples of how other companies have greened each of their five elements, you can visit the Internet at http://www.smartoffice.com.

Whether intentional or not, the mission statement indicates a
company's place in the natural world. Will it work in tandem
with nature or ignore natural laws? *Townsend.*

Chapter 3
Greening Your Mission

This chapter discusses the need for companies to green their missions. It explores two methods of doing this – greening the company's primary mission statement and creating a separate environmental mission statement.

The Importance of Greening Your Mission

In greening any business, a company first needs to assess its mission, or purpose. The mission is important for all types and sizes of organizations – even firms with only one employee (Jenkins, 2005). Mission statements are important for several reasons, some of which are outlined below.

First, the mission statement can help to establish a company's identity and focus. It reflects the company's intention in the world and helps to set its vision, values, culture, goals, and activities. In many ways, it provides a compass for all that the company is and does.

The company's mission also is important in helping to differentiate the company's products, services, or practices, thereby providing a means of attracting customers that share similar values. For a company that wishes to be ecologically sustainable, the mission clearly states the company's intended and real contributions not only to society but also to the natural world. If a company is transparent in its mission and its behaviors are consistent with its stated mission, this can help to establish the trust and loyalty of customers.

Moreover, the mission is important because it makes a statement to current employees at all levels regarding the fundamental purpose and priorities of the company. It also can help to attract employees whose values coincide with and support the company's (Aveda, Employment, para. 1). This, in turn, can help

to facilitate the alignment of vision and values within an organization and help the organization to meet its goals more effectively.

Additionally, the company mission also sends a signal to governments and industries regarding the direction in which the business is heading. In response, industry associations, government regulators, NGOs, and other stakeholders can find ways to help the business achieve its goals of caring for the environment, achieving social equity, and working on other key issues.

Furthermore, the mission is key because it helps to determine what the company's environmental impacts might be. For example, a company that exists to make paper from trees can cause significant ecological damage by destroying forest ecosystems, soil health, and the ecological integrity of nearby streams and rivers through siltation. Even those paper companies that try to be more responsible by owning forests and replanting areas after cutting them can cause environmental harm by using heavy equipment that damages soil communities and by planting genetically engineered tree species. Unfortunately, "tree farms" are not the same as forests; they simply have neither the degree of biological complexity nor the same types and numbers of ecological niches and services that natural forests provide. Understanding this, the company interested in sustainability might choose to make paper from something other than trees.

Company management and staff can look to their experiences in beautiful outdoor settings to inspire green company missions. *Townsend.*

Although it might enjoy improvements in its environmental performance, a company's corporate mission may preclude it from achieving ecological sustainability. For instance, a company in the business of extracting a non-renewable resource cannot be sustainable. Thus, if sustainability is one of the company's goals or its primary goal, the company will need to eliminate any inherent contradictions between its mission and its activities.

Typically, the mission is a brief statement that explicates the company's core reason for being, or purpose. According to the late Peter Drucker's Leader to Leader Institute, the company mission is not a simple slogan – it "is a precise statement of purpose" that is short enough to fit onto a t-shirt (2005, para. 1) so that all staff, including managers, know and understand it.

Those who write the mission statement should, at the very least, be agreed on the company's goals, intended results, and primary customers. They also should work with all employees to cultivate buy-in and ensure that they have not left out any important aspects of the work that they do or the goal(s) toward which they are working.

How to Green the Mission

There are two main ways in which businesses incorporate environmental priorities into their missions – through company mission statements and through separate environmental mission statements. Each of these is discussed below.

Mission – A mission statement should reflect the company's purpose for existence. The company's mission can set the direction of business-ecological relationships. To develop a green mission, companies need to merge ecologically sustainable values into the company's mission statement. Mission statements that are brief and meaningful can help to ground staff in the company's new direction (Hutchinson 1995). When they understand the fundamental purpose of the company, employees will be better able to identify their roles in working toward its success.

Environmental mission – An environmental mission statement should reflect a company's environmental priorities and policies. Environmental mission statements are fairly new and were developed as a way to indicate a company's commitment to environmental responsibility. However, if a company's mission is inherently nonsustainable, the firm cannot be green regardless of the values reflected in its environmental mission.

Though most firms do not change their mission statements often, they should be reviewed every year or so to ensure that they continue to be aligned with the company's core business (Jenkins, 2005). Revisiting the mission is necessary whenever a company's fundamental purpose shifts (Hutchinson 1995). This will help to refocus employees and send a signal to suppliers, customers, and other stakeholders that the company's purpose has changed.

Company management and staff might reflect on their outdoor experiences – particularly solo time spent in the wilderness – to redefine the company's mission. *Townsend*.

Case Study: Patagonia

Patagonia's mission statement, which it refers to as its "purpose," is a clear example of a statement with the environment at its core: "Patagonia exists as a business to inspire and implement solutions to the environmental crisis" (Patagonia 1998, 29). This statement of purpose is brief and direct enough to be memorized easily by employees and to serve as a focal point for the company. It also sends a clear signal to other stakeholders, such as customers and suppliers, regarding the company's values and priorities.

In its publication, *Defining Quality: A Brief Description of How We Got Here*, Patagonia (1998) explained that its mission says nothing about profits or products. The company exists not to make profits, it has stated; instead, its role is to help lead the way in solving the world's environmental problems. Its profits, it has reported, are merely a measure of its performance.

Mission-related Activities

There are several steps that companies wishing to develop sustainable missions might take. These include:

* Review the firm's current mission statement to determine if it reflects the company's values.

* If it does not, communicate with employees and customers to identify their environmental values and concerns.

* Develop innovative and flexible ways to align company and stakeholder values.

* Talk with ecologists or other environmental experts to get a sense of the company's environmental and social impacts and ways in which the company might become ecologically sustainable.

* Work with staff to envision or re-envision what the company might be and do if it was environmentally friendly.

* If necessary, review several greener mission statements and identify those that might provide helpful insights or models.

Summary

This chapter indicated that missions are important for companies of all sizes and types. This is true for several reasons, including the fact that the mission provides a compass for company activities, helps to differentiate the company and its products/services from competitors, sets a good example for other companies to emulate, and helps to establish trust and loyalty of employees and customers.

It also suggested that there are two types of mission – the company mission and an environmental mission. Companies that are interested in moving toward sustainability might want to incorporate green values and goals into their mission statements, thereby sending a clear signal to all stakeholders and strengthening the alignment of values and goals within the company.

Chapter 4
Greening Your Employees

This chapter examines the need to green employees. It discusses employee greening beginning with the hiring process and suggests some qualities to look for in job candidates. It also considers the importance of strong leadership in the greening process.

The Importance of Greening Employees

No green mission or vision can succeed without the commitment and consistent effort of employees at all levels – particularly management (Callenbach et al. 1993; Winsemius and Guntram 2002). The mission is critical to establishing the company's internal compass, priorities, and goals; however, in order for that compass to be followed, those priorities carried forward, those goals met, and the greening efforts sustained, all employees need to integrate green thinking into their everyday activities. Thus, greening employees is necessary for the success of greening any company, regardless of its size.

Cradle to Cradle™ Design training program run by McDonough Braungart Design Chemistry and held in Charlottesville, Virginia. *Courtesy of McDonough Braungart Design Chemistry.*

How Employee Hiring & Retention Affect Greening

Business managers are beginning to understand how important it is to have staff with environmental values that are aligned with those of the firm. Companies are finding that if they show a sincere, consistent commitment to environmental and social issues, they will have a better chance of attracting employees with similar values and retaining current employees who share those values. As a result, finding environmentally aware employees is easier, and employee retention rises. When employees work for a company in which they can take pride, it can help to inspire loyalty and personal commitment to helping that organization succeed. Conversely, polluting companies sometimes have difficulty hiring top-notch employees and retaining staff (North 1992). In addition, the high costs often associated with poor environmental practices also can eat into a company's profits and result in layoffs. (North 1992).

Qualities Needed for Greening

To be successful in their greening activities, companies need their employees, including managers, to share certain characteristics. For example, employees need a combination of commitment and skill (North 1992). Companies are more likely to be successful in their greening efforts if their employees truly care about the environment because employee creativity and innovation will be driven by personal values and commitment. In addition to commitment, companies need to ensure that their employees have relevant skills that enable them to carry out any new tasks that are required (e.g., new routines, changes in manufacturing processes).

Employees need to be environmentally aware, inspired, and empowered (Callenbach et al. 1993). They must understand the connection between improved environmental performance and environmental quality. Employees need to be allowed to align their personal values with those of the company and be inspired to help the company improve its relationships with the environment. Employees also need to be empowered to act on their values and know that the company will support them.

Additionally, employees need to have an accurate, detailed idea of the relationship between their workplace activities and environmental health or harm. Only when they can create a linkage in their minds between their actions and the environment will they be able to understand how to make better decisions and enhance the company's environmental performance. This is especially important because employees might not always be able to perceive the environmental changes that result from their decisions and activities because they occur over a period of time, across geographic distances, or on scales too great or small to perceive. As a result, companies need to educate and train their employees in order to enhance their environmental performances (Chinander 2001).

Furthermore, accountability is an important employee quality that helps to determine greening success (Chinander 2001). The more a company holds its employees accountable for their personal environmental performances, the greater its overall environmental performance is likely to be (Chinander 2001).

Winsemius and Guntram (2002) have asserted that "will, skill, and thrill" are necessary qualities if employees are expected to carry out the company's green mission and strategy. Will refers to the desire and commitment that employees have to improve their companies and their own professional environmental performances. Skill is important as employees are asked to think and behave differently than they ever have, considering the company's full environmental impacts and identifying solutions that they can implement as individual employees. Finally, thrill refers to the motivation and excitement that helps to drive employees who are committed to the company's journey as well as its end goals.

Interface associate demonstrating reduced waste due to patented technology that reduces production order overruns. *Courtesy of Interface Flooring Systems.*

Interface's Xtreme Green Team – Melissa Vernon, Manager of Sustainable Strategy; Jeff Cotton, Manager of Environmental Policy; Jim Hartzfeld, VP of Sustainable Strategy. *Courtesy of Interface Flooring Systems.*

Others discuss the importance of environmental awareness and strong values. Strong values are based on an understanding of the ways in which systems function, and are reflected in the values of relationship, interconnectedness, wholeness, partnership, and others (Callenbach et al. 1993). Jean Garner Stead and W. Edward Stead (1996), Professors of Management at East Tennessee State University, have contended that environmental ethics are important and suggested that values such as wholeness, spiritual fulfillment, quality, smallness, community, and posterity need to become incorporated into businesses.

Meanwhile, Hutchinson has suggested that the values required to create a sustainable business include peace, justice, honesty, respect, democracy, spiritual understanding, modified free market economies, and freedom of speech (1995, 80). In addition to values, Hutchinson has explained that those who work for companies also need a new set of accurate beliefs about the world around them. These beliefs relate to the size and resources of the planet as well as the harm that can be done by human (including business) activity.

Another quality that has been mentioned by several environmental management authors (Callenbach et all 1993; Hutchinson 1995; Winsemius and Guntram 2002) is the ability of an organization to learn. The importance of the learning organization is discussed by a growing number of authors, including Peter Senge (1990), Arie de Geus (1997), and Callenbach et al. (1993). It is based on the understanding that companies are living systems that are made of people and built on their values, beliefs, ideas, and efforts. It will be important for companies that are becoming greener to view themselves as learning organizations so that the lessons that they can gather and from which they can learn are not lost along the way. Companies that are successful at organizational learning might find themselves at an advantage in developing and evaluating greening strategies (Dobers and Wolff 1995).

Clearly, many of the qualities thought to be important in greening overlap considerably – commitment and will, thrill and inspiration, action and empowerment, environmental awareness and ecological knowledge, and organizational learning and skill. This simply indicates that many people who are involved in the greening of business recognize the need for employees to commit to greening, to be environmentally aware, to be ecologically knowledgeable, to receive adequate training, and to be empowered to act and learn. As important as these qualities are, successful company greening that is sustained over time depends not on the heroism of the few but on the involvement of everyone – and on good leadership.

The Importance of Good Leadership

The same qualities that are required for employees also are required of the company's leaders. However, if a company's plans to improve its environmental performance are to be successful, the onus is on leaders to communicate clearly, effectively, and regularly with staff on a number of issues. For instance, managers will need to explain in great detail the company's mission and vision and why the company is moving toward sustainability. They also will need to discuss how individual employees' decisions and activities make a difference with regard to environmental health.

Managers will need to help employees align the company's environmental values with their own, thereby making greening personal. A sense of personal accountability can send a much-needed signal to employees that positive environmental actions are a company priority.

The company's managers will need to discuss the firm's long-term and short-term goals with employees as well as the time frames for meeting those goals. Managers also should explain company strategies to achieve those goals and how the job of each employee fits into those strategies so that all employees understand the ecological relevance of what they do. To the best of its ability, the company's management will need to discuss the sorts of changes that employees can expect in their own jobs and across the organization as a whole.

Managers will need to share environmental information with employees. This can include the results of environmental audits, inspections, reports regarding the company's compliance with environment regulations, and assessments for monitoring chemicals either inside or outside of company facilities. In essence, a company's staff is entitled to know the direction in which the company is asking it to go as well as the firm's current environmental impacts (North 1992).

Because greening requires the mutual cooperation of employees and management, both will need to develop a dialogue of honesty and mutual trust. This can be done by communicating honestly and fully every step of the way in order to maintain trust and commitment throughout the entire organization. Additionally, the company needs to be able to communicate its environmental values and align its system of incentives and disincentives with those values (Chinander 2001).

T.S. Designs' president Eric Henry stands by his company's solar panels while his car's fuel tank is filled with biodiesel fuel. *Courtesy of T.S. Designs.*

84

Management will need to discuss progress and setbacks openly with employees so that employees feel as though they are part of the company and not merely being used as a means to the company's end. Employees also will need to receive clear, consistent, and timely feedback – both positive and negative – regarding their personal environmental performances. However, management needs to be aware that any negative feedback must be given strategically and with sensitivity; otherwise, it might serve as a disincentive for employees to undertake greening efforts wholeheartedly and with confidence.

A company's managers will need to ensure that even those who are not central to the organization's functions but who still play important roles, such as cleaning staff and maintenance personnel, are involved. Even if such positions are outsourced to another company, maintenance personnel will need to understand the company's greening values and adhere to its behaviors. Otherwise, these persons could jeopardize the organization's greening success even if the greening goals are fairly modest. Examples of companies that separate their trash at source for recycling only to discover that cleaning crews have thrown it all into the same dumpster have left some employees feeling as though they have wasted their efforts to recycle. Furthermore, maintenance staff might use toxic cleaning supplies in a workplace that prides itself on being healthy and non-toxic. Such small negative experiences can cause employees' greening motivation to drop because they feel as though their greener actions have been for naught. Thus, it is important that companies remain vigilant in communicating their greening interests, commitments, and methods to all employees and sub-contractors because all employees are responsible for a company's greening success.

The company's managers, particularly the more visible ones at the top, need to ensure that their own environmental values and behaviors are consistent with the company's. Businesses that wish to ensure systemic greening cannot do so without consistent support and proactive examples from management at all levels, particularly senior management. Without strong green leadership, a company might make incremental greening progress but is unlikely to achieve lasting success. Thus, green leadership by example is imperative from the senior management level through all levels of management. It cannot be stressed enough that the company's president, CEO, and other upper echelon staff need to show real leadership to experience greening success.

Solar panels at T.S. Designs, a company that has been recognized as an environmental leader. *Courtesy of T.S. Designs.*

T.S. Designs' company garden. *Courtesy of T.S. Designs.*

Gary Erickson, Clif Bar's founder and owner. *Courtesy of Clif Bar.*

Without strong leadership commitment and action, employees receive mixed signals, which implies that the company's greening commitment is inconsistent at best. Many companies' environmental decisions reflect significant ambiguity or uncertainty, indicating that environmental health is not a high priority (Chinander 2001). As a result, staff might receive mixed signals from management when managers espouse environmental values and policies without actually carrying them out.

One study of the variables that affect a person's environmental actions indicated that environmental action has a strong situational element (Corraliza and Berenguer 2000). This means that if, for example, a company's management states that it is interested in sustainability but fails to green its environmental performance, employees might get mixed signals and respond with uncertainty. Additionally, if employees feel unsupported or threatened in any way for carrying out environmental directives, they may not carry them out.

The same study indicated that when employees are environmentally proactive in their personal lives and their situations facilitate environmentally proactive behaviors, their workplace actions are likely to be environmentally proactive; however, if they personally tend toward a low degree of environmentally proactive behaviors and their situations make positive environmental actions difficult, then they are unlikely to be environmentally proactive (Corraliza and Berenguer 2000). Moreover, if there is a high degree of conflict between their personal disposition and their situational variables – such as either a proactive personal attitude coupled with a situation in which environmental action is difficult or a personal disinterest in the environment coupled with a situation that facilitates environmental action – it is difficult to predict what an employee's environmental actions might be (Corraliza and Berenguer 2000). Thus, a company's environmental actions are most likely to be environmentally proactive if both its staff and situational variables support such behavior.

Finally, managers need to ensure that greening is incorporated throughout the entire organization. Otherwise, if greening efforts are haphazard and leadership is weak, any greening activities that succeed will be due to individual heroes and heroines who take it upon themselves to help green the company in any way that they can find because it matters to them. Though these people are extremely important to the organization's greening efforts, it is unfair and unsustainable to place the burden of the firm's greening success squarely on them.

Other Stakeholders

It is important for businesses to communicate their environmental goals and intentions to other stakeholders as well in order to be as transparent as possible and gain added support. Of course, some of the most important stakeholders are the company's employees. Others include its board of directors, trade unions, suppliers, retailers, customers, community, media, industry, government, and environmental organizations. Such communication *followed by consistent action* helps to build trust, open dialogue, allow access and disclosure, and, ultimately, reduce environmental harm.

Businesses might want to keep in mind that when they need to choose between disclosing their environmental impacts and keeping this information to themselves, they often benefit from disclosure. When a company is fully transparent and openly working toward constant improvement, it indicates that it is honest and making an effort to improve. By avoiding disclosure, it might appear as though a company is hiding something. The former helps to build trust among multiple stakeholders while the latter works to damage it.

Managing Change

Sustainability as a corporate goal requires companies to step away from the traditional corporate path and become pioneers in redeveloping human enterprise. Thus, the corporate road to sustainability includes many unknowns along the way and requires companies to be open, transparent, flexible, and cooperative both internally and externally. As a result, companies that pursue ecological sustainability will need to facilitate and manage change.

For the sake of convenience, I divide change into three types – technical, relational, and content. Each of these areas can lead to profound changes in relationships within the company and between the company and its suppliers, customers, other companies, industries, and, ultimately, ecosystems.

Technical change refers to changes in such things as organizational structure and manufacturing processes. For instance, companies might find that if they are to work effectively toward sustainability they will need to transition from having hierarchical, vertical organizational structures to more horizontal, empowering ones. This will affect how employees and management perceive one another, how they communicate, and how much empowerment employees are allowed as the company takes on environmental values that its employees enthusiastically share and can

advance through their individual actions. Meanwhile, maintaining old organizational structures might keep people in old patterns of behavior and impede proactive change. This might be quite a challenge for companies that are used to operating in a very different way. This sentiment was reflected by Levi Strauss' Chairman Robert Hass, who once said, "There's a whole range of behaviours that were functional in the old hierarchical organization that are dead wrong in the flatter, more responsive organization that we're seeking to become" (Winsemius and Guntram 2002, 210). Furthermore, the more complex an organization's structure is, the more difficult it might be to manage (Steger, 1996). This also can interfere with company greening.

Relational change refers to the changes in relationship that managers and staff will have to forge both internally and between the organization and its stakeholders with regard to the firm's greening commitment. Winsemius and Guntram (2002) have proposed using questionnaires and interviews to survey employees both vertically and horizontally throughout the firm to identify staff perceptions of environmental issues and current attitudes and practices. It is important to ensure that all management, staff, and functions are represented. This also can help to identify key staff that can help to move greening forward.

The authors also have suggested that there are four primary instruments that management can use to facilitate change. They are: inspire, anchor, steer, and reward. *Inspiration* must be given to maintain and build the thrill that employees feel with regard to the company's vision and journey toward sustainability. It can come through several means, including information with regard to an environmental problem or opportunities for greening, communication about the vision and the mental model that the organization would like its members to adopt, and/or a challenge to change in a way that will fulfill the employees' personal needs. The will of employees to follow through with the company's vision and plans must be *anchored* in appropriate and supportive organizational structures and management systems. In addition, the existence of green training or coaching and green facilities can help to anchor company staff. *Steering* consists of such activities as developing targets, supporting employees with needed resources for change, and providing a management example of environmental and professional excellence. Rewards, which can include such things as measurements of progress, counseling and support, and recognition of progress, help to maintain the company's green momentum.

Content change has to do with information; it refers to ecological and other types of knowledge that employees, including management, will need during the company's transition to sustainability. It is not uncommon for companies to hold training sessions for both new and existing employees. If environmental concerns are to be integrated throughout every aspect of the organization, the company needs to ensure that its training materials reflect its environmental priorities. Training can be held on a number of topics, including environment audits and management, company incentives for innovative ideas, the importance of environmental and social responsibility in the workplace, the costs associated with unhealthy and inefficient workplaces, incorporating environmental externalities into the company's accounting systems, communicating environmental concerns and ideas effectively, exploring the importance of a systems approach for greening the company, discussing environmental legislation and its effect on the company, and so on (North 1992). Of course, all staff should receive the same general training on the company's environmental values and strategies; additional environmental training can be tailored to meet the specific needs of staff that fill particular functions (e.g., facilities managers, accountants, procurement specialists, human resources personnel, materials engineers, product designers).

Staff should be encouraged to participate fully in the development of new training that focuses on enhancing their environmental awareness and any skills that they will need in order to complete their work successfully. Additionally, staff at all levels should be encouraged to participate in local environmental activities in order to reflect the company's genuine commitment to environmental health and to enhance the staff's ecological awareness and understanding of community perspectives. Unions also should be included in designing and implementing new workplace environmental policies and programs that are going to affect their members' work.

There also needs to be a venue through which staff can share concerns, interests, and suggestions with regard to the company's environmental programs and other related issues. The staff needs to feel safe in approaching management and making such suggestions because the company should not expect its employees to buy into its environmental goals and values without respecting theirs. Employees should know what the proper channel is for whistle blowing – for instance, a department that they can go to if they observe a person or division not abiding by the company's environmental goals. This is important because comprehensive company greening depends on the efforts of every staff member, and it is unfair for a few employees to prevent the entire company from achieving its goals when others work so hard to actualize them.

Staff can be encouraged to find ways to reduce environmental harm and should have incentives to improve products, processes, and other aspects of the company's environmental performance. Employees should understand that though the changes required for greening might make for organizational, departmental, or personal uncertainty at times, the employees are helping to shape the direction of their organization, redefining its environmental performance, and contributing to environmental health.

It is important for the company to realize that its top management will need support as well because the company is undergoing such profound change at so many levels – in terms of its values, vision, and specific goals as well as changes to the organizational structure and the resulting changes in relationships with employees. For the early greening pioneers, this can create feelings of anxiety as management and other staff members feel as though they and their company are taking risks by forging their own path while leaving much of the corporate world behind.

Interface employees work together to create a sustainable company. *Courtesy of Interface Flooring Systems.*

Case Study: Patagonia

As with any company, Patagonia's success depends largely on its employees. Unlike many companies, however, Patagonia has developed a different sort of relationship with many of its employees and has won awards as one of the country's best companies to work for by both *Fortune* and *Working Mother* magazines. This is due, in part, to the company's attempt to ensure that its environmental and social values and those of its employees are aligned. Dave Olsen, the company's past President and CEO, explained that he worked to create a culture for the company that every employee could embrace. That includes encouraging risk-taking, flexibility, curiosity, and mutual support across the board (Rowledge, Barton, and Brady 1999).

Ensuring that its employees care about the impacts of the products that they make and sell is a requirement for Patagonia. One way this occurs is through the company's hiring process. Patagonia not only encourages its employees to be active outdoors; passion for an outdoor activity or sport is one of its key hiring criteria. The company believes that such commitment is a top company priority that cannot be taught while technical skills can.

Moreover, the company pays its employees to work for any nonprofit environmental organization for up to two months. This internship program provides a good opportunity for the company to connect with environmental organizations and for its employees to learn more about and become active in trying to solve environmental issues, reflecting the company's mission. Employees return with new skills and enthusiasm about the environment. Ron Hunter, an Associate in Patagonia's Environmental Programs, has commented on the firm's environmental internship program: "We consider it an absolute success when someone comes back and then leaves the company because they feel they have to follow their passion. We may lose an employee, but we gain a full-time conservationist" (Patagonia, Enviro Internship, para. 5, 2003). Nearly one out of five employees have taken part in this internship program.

As a result of its own qualities and activities, Patagonia experiences high employee retention and loyalty. Terri Wolfe, the director of Patagonia's Human Resources, suggests that the company's culture is not just linked to but is entirely dependent on Patagonia's business mission.

Employee-related Activities

In summary, greening employees comprises several activities, including the following:

* Ensure that all employees at every level are clear on the company's environmental policies.
* Survey employees to find out what their attitudes are toward greening.
* Make greening personal. That means that in order for greening to be optimal, to the greatest extent possible, employees need to understand the connections between their everyday activities and the environmental impacts that result.
* Hold regular meetings as a company or within departments to encourage proactive environmental behaviors as well as the sharing of company inefficiencies, opportunities for improvement, and the development of solutions.
* Have management set a good environmental example.
* Make it clear to potential employees that environmental health is a key business priority and requirement for the company's success.
* Attract environmentally aware employees by developing a reputation for environmental excellence.
* Require new hires to be environmentally knowledgeable.
* Train new and existing staff in environmental awareness and proactivity.

Summary

This chapter discussed the importance of greening employees. It suggested that no business could become sustainable without employee commitment and action. In order to achieve this, companies can work with current employees to align company and staff values. Companies also can focus on hiring employees who are environmentally committed.

Strong leadership is another factor necessary for greening. Though greening the staff is important, it is imperative that senior management believes in greening and sets an example for all that its own commitment to greening is real. Because greening might require the company to undergo technical, relational, or content changes, both senior management and employees need to find means of supporting one another as such marked change can represent risk and cause feelings of fear and insecurity. However, as greening activities become increasingly mainstream, companies will have less to fear and more to look forward to as green becomes the norm.

Lil Diaper Depot spokesmodel with a basket of organic cotton diapers. *Courtesy of Lil Diaper Depot.*

Chapter 5
Greening Your Operations

This chapter touches upon a few of the areas involved in greener operations. It provides some tips on greening areas as diverse as accounting and food services and offers examples of what some companies have done to improve their operations.

The Importance of Greening Operations

Operations comprise a broad variety of activities that support the everyday functioning of the company. These activities, which can fall under the purview of several departments, can have far-reaching effects on the health not only of the local but also of the global environment and, as a result, on the health and well-being of humans and other species. As such, it is important that businesses green those operations that are conducted in-house or ensure that those that are sub-contracted out meet their green criteria. Again, greening must be an integral part of the organization's thinking and action for it to succeed. The following list indicates a few of the activities that are included under Operations:

* Accounting
* Daycare/childcare
* Employee commuting & business travel
* Food services
* Fleet
* Hiring
* Investing
* Lobbying
* Marketing
* Printing and graphics
* Procurement (unrelated to Facilities & Sites and Products & Services)
* Public relations
* Recycling

Each of these topics is quite broad, and this is by no means a complete list. This section will provide an overview of some of the issues that need to be considered in each of the topics listed above.

Accounting

Accounting is a fundamental part of a company's activities and an area in which greening often is overlooked. Broader in scope than standard business accounting, green accounting also considers, to the greatest extent possible, externalized costs that often are ignored. These include the ecological and social costs of business, such as those associated with the life cycle of a product – the environmental degradation that results from the extraction of raw materials, the energy used and the environmental impacts that result from using the product, and the environmental impacts associated with product recycling and, ultimately, disposal.

Daycare/childcare

Daycare or childcare services are provided by many companies for their employees. Because children's bodies can be particularly sensitive to chemicals, it is necessary to ensure that daycare or childcare facilities are healthy. In general, children's bodies are more sensitive to environmental toxins than are adults' bodies. Toxins can enter the body through inhalation, ingestion, and/or absorption. With their smaller bodies and higher metabolisms, children often breathe more air than adults do. Because of this, chemicals – from pesticides, building materials, furnishings, and other ordinary products – can pose a health risk (e.g., neurological, brain, respiratory, kidney). Additionally, radon and electromagnetic fields are linked to an increased incidence of childhood cancers.

When providing daycare or childcare, not only should a company ensure that the area is made of nontoxic materials, such as those discussed in the chapter on facilities and sites, but it also will want to provide nontoxic toys and art supplies as well as organic foods and beverages.

Many plastic toys contain vinyl plastic, which is highly toxic and has been linked to lung disease and cancer, or polyvinylchloride, which has been associated with cancers, mutations, and birth defects.

Employee Commuting & Business Travel

Because toxins can be particularly harmful to children, organic cotton blankets such as these by Lil Diaper Depot are a healthy alternative. *Courtesy of Lil Diaper Depot.*

Natural and organic baby body care products provide healthier choices to parents who want to ensure their children's safety. *Courtesy of Lil Diaper Depot.*

Employee commuting and *business travel* provide examples of company operations that can result in severe ecological damage. As it occurs today, such travel typically relies on airplanes, cars, buses, or trains that run on petroleum-based products, thereby resulting in increased air pollution. This pollution includes the release of carbon dioxide, which contributes to climate change, as well as the release of other pollutants, which can result in respiratory and other human health problems. With the recent surge of oil prices and the benefits associated with energy self-reliance, companies around the world have ever-greater incentives to provide greener employee commuting and business travel options.

The U.S. Department of Transportation estimates that there are about 220 million gasoline-powered vehicles in United States (U.S. Energy Information Agency 2005). These vehicles use more than 200 million gallons of gasoline every day, which is the equivalent of about fifty-five barrels every second (Anzovin 1993). The increased popularity and use of SUVs has resulted in a greater amount of fuel use. For example, the U.S. EPA's *Fuel Economy Guide* (www.fueleconomy.gov) shows the 2006 Dodge Durango FFV (two- and four-wheel drive) as getting about nine mpg in city driving and eleven miles per gallon (mpg) on the highway. Meanwhile, the Honda Insight gets an estimated sixty mpg in the city and sixty-six mpg on the highway. For every five mpg a car gains in fuel economy, a car's lifetime output of greenhouse gases drops by seventeen tons, or 260 ft^3 (U.S. Department of Energy and U.S. Environmental Protection Agency 2005, 2).

Of course, normal commuting also means emitting other substances that affect the environment. For example, the release of nitrogen oxide causes acid rain while hydrocarbon emissions cause ozone smog. Gasoline, oil, radiator fluid, and other vehicle maintenance products that leak onto the roadways, washing into the waterways with every rainstorm.

Such business travel and commuting also create an ongoing demand for the infrastructure that makes such travel possible – the building and maintenance of road networks and, to a lesser extent, rail networks across vast landscapes, which changes the geomorphology and ecology of sites around the world. Plane travel requires the development and maintenance of an air travel infrastructure that consists of airports and the use of petroleum and other resources used in plane production, maintenance, and use.

Of course, the greenest means of business travel and employee commuting are no travel or commuting at all. Telecommuting (teleworking), teleconferencing, and other alternatives help to minimize the environmental effects of travel.

However, if travel is necessary, using public transportation is one way to reduce a company's environmental harm. Some firms have developed agreements with companies that offer public transit, thereby enabling employees to commute to and from work at reduced prices. Furthermore, as an incentive to their employees, some companies pay some of the costs associated with public transportation or provide incentives for biking, carpooling, or walking to work.

A thick brown haze of smoke, ozone, and other particles hangs over China. *Courtesy of NASA/ORBIMAGE.*

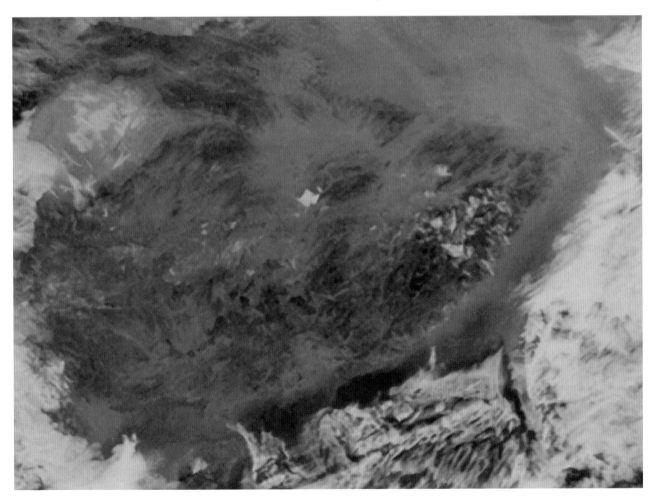

For example, Sun Microsystems Alternative Resources for Transportation (SMART) Commute Program has several options for employees, including:

* Subsidizes any employee who commutes by public transport or vanpool at least twice each week

* Provides regional shuttle services to move employees between campuses and public transportation

* Pays for a cab ride home whenever those who use alternative commutes have to stay overtime

* Provides public transport passes for employees who must travel between campuses at least twice each week

* Supports employees who bike to work by providing bike parking, showers, and lockers

* Provides ride-matching services for employees who wish to carpool

* Keeps alternative commuting program information on the company's internal web site

* Works to enhance employee awareness regarding alternative commute opportunities

* Holds a Bike to Work Week during which bike commuters are acknowledged (Sun Microsystems, 2005)

Sun Microsystems (2005) reports that it is one of the U.S. EPA's top five Best U.S. Workplaces for Commuters.

Some European cities are creating car-free urban areas. These have included Amsterdam, Bologna, and Zürich, all of which have developed systems that restrict vehicle traffic within cities (Mega 1999). This has created safer areas for people to walk and bike to work, both of which have health benefits as well.

Fortunately, some cities in United States, Europe, Asia, and other regions have created bicycle lanes, making it safer for cyclists to commute to work. However, this is not the case in many locales, so employees need to use their judgment regarding the safety of a bicycle commute.

In order to assist companies in reducing their environmental harm as it relates to travel, the U.S. Environmental Protection Agency developed a program called Transportation Partners. This program encourages telecommuting and greener transportation alternatives. The program encourages telecommuting from home or from "telecenters," which are places closer to home from which employees can work.

Telecommuting, also referred to as teleworking, is an important and often overlooked means of reducing vehicular traffic and associated pollution. With petroleum-based fuel prices on the rise, telecommuting is more appealing than ever. Telecommuting refers to working in a location other than the employer's office, and this location often is a home office. Electronic mail, the Internet, and other technologies have enabled workers in many industries to stay off the roads and work from home.

Telecommuting provides several advantages. First, because there typically are fewer interruptions during their workday, telecommuters tend to be more productive than when at the company office. Additionally, telecommuters often feel more empowered and in control of their lives. With extra time added to their days that once was spent preparing for and traveling to and from work, telecommuters can be calmer and better rested. Furthermore, telecommuters may work longer hours because there is no geographic separation between home and work. Because no commute is involved, telecommuters might begin work earlier and work later in the day than normal commuters.

Telecommuting has helped to change the definition of the workplace as employees with laptop computers might not need to report to a centralized location from Monday through Friday. Those people who work in industries that do not require their presence (e.g., IT) can work from virtually anywhere. This can reduce the number of hours spent commuting, help reduce wear and tear on the family car, decrease the amount of money spent on gasoline or other fuel, reduce the amount of maintenance needed on a personal vehicle, eliminate any stress felt from sitting in traffic, reduce pollution, and provide more time at the beginning and end of every day for family or other priorities. By reducing or eliminating commuting time, workers might have more time to pursue their interests and feel happier and more fulfilled.

Even if full-time telecommuting is not an option, part-time telecommuting might be. Employees might visit the office only a few days each week or might come in only in the mornings or in the afternoons, spending the rest of the time working from their home offices. Otherwise, they can work at home full-time and visit the office for meetings and other special events. Additionally, telecommuting can be done on a temporary basis.

Telecommuting has another financial benefit for the company. When employees are responsible for working from their home offices, companies require a smaller space and less equipment in order to operate. It is between the companies and their employees as to who is responsible for purchasing and maintaining home office equipment, software, and so forth.

Aside from walking, bicycling is one of the greenest forms of transport. *Courtesy of the US Agency for International Development.*

Telecommuting is not for everyone. Some people suggest that they could never telecommute because they do not believe that they are disciplined enough or because they believe that other things at home might distract them. However, it is difficult to know whether, if a telecommute is full-time, they might be able to develop their own routines. Those who might not be effective telecommuters include individuals who are uncomfortable being alone, need to supervise others, require frequent supervision, need to provide frequent reports, or are just starting a new project that requires working closely and in person with others.

Successful telecommuters are likely to be self-motivated, love their work, work hard, be creative and flexible, work best without close supervision, be comfortable with computers and other associated technologies, and be committed to helping their companies' telecommuting programs be successful.

If a company is considering starting a telecommuting program, it might first want to determine the best employees for telecommuting – mean-

ing those who are self-starters and do not need to be at the office to do their jobs – and try a pilot program. If the company's experience is successful, it might broaden its program to include other workers and allow them to work full-time from home.

Crowded, high-traffic cities like Washington, D.C., could benefit greatly from increased telecommuting. *Townsend.*

Food Services

Providing employees with *food services* – such as cafeterias and vending services – is another of the many aspects of a company's operations that need to be greened. Again, this is a large topic that cannot be covered in the scope of this book; however, it deserves at least cursory mention. Cafeterias can be a source of considerable environmental impacts with regard to the choice of food that is served; the plates, cups, napkins, and utensils that it uses; its use of industrial equipment (e.g., dishwashers, food processors); and food waste.

Recycline's Preserve Plateware and cutlery is made using recycled materials, is reusable, and is recyclable. *Courtesy of Planet Friendly PR.*

With regard to greener food, companies might want to buy locally grown foods that are fresher, require less energy to transport, and support local farmers, thereby contributing to the stability of the local economy. They might also want to purchase foods that are organically grown both to ensure the ongoing health of soils and local ecology and to prevent the use of petroleum-based fertilizers, toxic herbicides, and other unhealthy biocides that create ecological imbalances and can poison their manufacturers, users, local communities (e.g., via crop-dusting), groundwater, and streams.

Stella harvesting certified organic wild leeks on the Food for Thought farm. *Courtesy of Food for Thought.*

Pesticide-free foods are particularly important for children, whose small bodies take in disproportionately large amounts of pesticides on fruits and vegetables, and for women, whose bodies absorb pesticides and, then, feed them to their children via breast milk. Some of the chemicals found in human breast milk have included chlordane, DDT, dioxins, furans, heptachlor, hexachlorobenzene, mirex, nitro musks, toxaphene, PBDEs, PCBs, solvents, and heavy metals, such as cadmium, lead, and mercury.

The levels of these persistent organic pollutants tend to be highest in the first few months of breastfeeding and in first-time mothers (Natural Resources Defense Council, 2005). Commercially produced milk also is problematic because it often contains pesticide residues as a result of the non-organic feed that is given to cattle.

Although meat was once a popular source of proteins, it has come under scrutiny for health reasons over the past decade. Not only is mad cow disease of concern, but many of the animals raised in factory-like conditions are fed with chemical feed, treated regularly with antibiotics and other drugs, are kept in inhumane conditions, and are sold for meat even if they are diseased.

With regard to plates, cups, napkins, and utensils, companies can use reusable products. Otherwise, they might want to choose disposable paper products (e.g., cups, napkins, plates) that are not bleached using chlorine and utensils that can be composted after use, such as those made of cornstarch.

More energy- and water-efficient kitchen equipment can be used as well as non-toxic, biodegradable cleaning products that will not pollute the water. Finally, food services can work to eliminate food waste by making less food. Invariably, some food is wasted. In that case, waste fruits, vegetables, grains, and other items that do not consist of meat or fats can be composted. Excess food that is safe for serving can be donated to homeless shelters and soup kitchens.

Fleet

The procurement and maintenance of a company *fleet* is another aspect of some companies' operations. There are several ways to make existing company fleets greener. These include investing in vehicles that are powered by ecologically friendly means, such the new and cleaner diesel cars, electric vehicles (particularly those that run on solar-created electricity), and hybrids. For more information on vehicles' fuel economy, visit the U.S. Department of Energy's web site www.fueleconomy.gov. This site is compiled by the agency's Energy Efficiency and Renewable Energy group.

Another option is to use greener fuels, such as used vegetable oil or biodiesel. Biodiesel fuels can vary in the amount of vegetable oil that they contain but can be up to 100 percent vegetable-based with some additives. Maintaining company fleets is another way to be greener; regularly changing gaskets and hoses can help to prevent leaks and the associated loss of (and pollution by) fluids. Additionally, companies can recycle their used oil and purchase recycled oil.

Employees stand beside a vegetable oil-powered truck. *Courtesy of T.S. Designs.*

Organic wild blueberry Merlot preserves baked over brie cheese. *Courtesy of Food for Thought.*

Hiring

Of course, companies cannot be green without the existence of green employees throughout. Though this was discussed earlier, the necessity for *hiring* new employees and training both new and existing employees in greener approaches to their work cannot be overstated. If companies are to respond to environmental issues in an integrated manner, then employees at all levels need to develop rational and technical competence in a number of areas. As important as this is, most companies are neither knowledgeable nor skilled in ecological issues (Dobers and Wolff 1995). The development and maintenance of environmental competence occurs more easily in businesses that proactively and openly pursue learning and change (Dobers and Wolff 1995). Of course, greener hiring requires human resources departments to be ecologically literate so that interviewers know what to ask potential employees and how to ask them.

Investing

Green *investing*, also referred to as socially responsible investing (SRI), has received a considerable amount of attention over the past several years as both methodologies and mutual funds have been created to ensure that investors can invest with a conscience. Just as it is important for companies to behave in an ecologically friendly manner themselves, it is also important for them to ensure that their profits are invested in companies that share their environmental and social goals and values. Investing in environmentally degrading companies and industries enables them to continue operating in harmful ways. Conversely, investing in greener companies, industries, and technologies is an important way for companies to show their commitment to greening and to support greener business. It also helps to support the development of a growing number of greener firms from which companies can purchase greener supplies and services, which helps to ensure that companies can run in a greener manner.

In the mid- to late 1990s, about $600 billion were invested by people and companies using social criteria (Buss, Dale D. 1997, "Pure Profit" in *Bloomberg Personal*, 102-109, March/April 1997. Skillman, NJ: Bloomberg L.P.). In 2003, the Social Investment Forum reported that over one in nine dollars managed professionally in the U.S. are invested in more socially responsible companies, totaling $2.16 trillion in assets (2003, i). Clearly, green investing is becoming more mainstream. Parnassus, Calvert, Sierra Club, Pax

World, Domini, and others have created funds that use social, environmental, and/or other criteria to select those companies that will be in their portfolios. The Social Investment Forum, Coop America, *Green Money Journal*, and SocialFunds.com all provide information on SRI and specific companies and funds in which firms can invest.

Several companies, such as Social(k), offer greener investing solutions. *Courtesy of Social(k)*.

There are many criteria that companies can use to choose environmentally and socially preferable investments. For instance, a company might wish to invest in firms that are working to reduce their environmental harm, provide a fair and healthy workplace for their employees, and create worthy products/services. Also, it might choose to invest in companies that are active in their communities or trying to create a better world.

A company might want to avoid investing in firms that earn their money using practices or from products that are destructive and inhumane. These might include firms that are involved in defense and weapons, alcohol, tobacco, gambling, nuclear power, oil and gas drilling, animal testing, junk bonds, and other harmful industries. It might also choose to avoid companies that support repressive governments, have poor human rights records, have poor environmental records, or have a history of discrimination of any kind.

However, some investors specifically buy *small* amounts of stock in such companies in order to have shareholder voting rights with the idea that they might be able to exert some influence over company priorities and policies. If a firm believes that it will go to the effort of trying to sway the company as a shareholder, this might be a good option.

Keep in mind that, just as in any business venture, not all greener companies are well run. A firm will need to do its research and ensure that its investment choices are solid companies that meet its financial criteria.

One can learn something about a company's stated goals and policies by reviewing its environmental report, which often is located on the firm's web site. Issues to research before investing include the company's human rights record, employment practices, environmental policies, equal opportunity for minorities and women, labor relations, education, health care, child and eldercare, family benefits, and community relations.

Child laborers in twentieth century America portray the grueling conditions underage and underpaid workers might be forced to experience. *Courtesy of Department of Labor. Photos by Lewis Wikes Hine.*

Lobbying

Lobbying is another operations-related activity in which some companies are involved. As powerful as it is, businesses often use lobbying as a means of shaping or swaying public policy on any number of issues. Companies working toward sustainability should learn all they can about their own environmental impacts and develop effective ways to address those impacts. Then, they can work with regulators, politicians, and others to share their ideas so that they can move toward sustainability more quickly.

Marketing

Green *marketing* is important because it can help the company to establish a market for its products and services; share its environmental vision and performance with stakeholders; and be consistent with its mission and core values. A green company's ultimate success might depend, in part, on its ability to create a market for its greener products and services. Just as raising staff awareness is important, educating and raising the awareness and "caring capacity" of customers is equally essential. In part, this is because customers face many obstacles in choosing the greenest products and services because they might not have enough information to be able to differentiate between the products or services of different firms.

This gives the company a public way of sharing its environmental vision and performance and setting itself apart from its competition. More than a decade ago, a German company, Henkel, created a phosphate-free detergent in France. This detergent was touted as environmentally preferable to those containing phosphate, and the product represent 18 percent of France's detergent market. As positive a tool as green marketing can be, companies should be aware that green marketing can draw some unexpected responses from competitors. Henkel's main competitor, Rhone-Poulenc, claimed publicly that the German detergent was environmentally harmful and put up posters of dead fish, suggesting that they had been killed by Henkel's phosphate-free detergent. Henkel sued and won, forcing Rhone-Poulenc to take down the posters (Winsemius and Guntram 2002).

Of course, it is important that when companies are marketing their commitment to environmental performance, their actions back up their words. Winsemius and Guntram (2002) have stated that a firm's greening efforts should be consistent throughout the organization lest the company be accused of greenwashing – marketing itself as green(er) than it is.

Otherwise, the firm can lose the trust of multiple stakeholders, including customers, regulators, NGOs, and others, and might find that trust difficult to regain. In 2000, the company British Petroleum (BP) decided to change its image to embrace environmental values and long-term commitment to supply renewable energy. The company adopted the slogan "Beyond Petroleum." Shortly thereafter, Greenpeace criticized BP for spending more money – about $200 million – on its new greened campaign than it had on developing renewable energy (Winsemius and Guntram 2002). Furthermore, BP has been behind the development of a vast new oil pipeline between its Kovykta gas field in Siberia and China, which would result in continued environmental harm, although there is speculation that the Russian government might revoke BP's license to export the oil (Russian London Newspaper, 2005).

However, in other ways, the company appears to be committed to – or at least recognize the value of – sustainability. In October 1996, it withdrew its membership from the Global Climate Coalition, a fossil fuels lobbying group that was stonewalling the issue linking fossil fuels use with global climate change (Frankel 1998). The company believed the Coalition's position regarding fossil fuels and climate change to be unsound (Frankel 1998). The following year, the company's Group Chief Executive for BP America, John Browne, spoke out on the issue at Stanford University, announcing,

> "The time to consider the policy dimensions of climate change is not when the link between greenhouse gases and climate change is conclusively proven but when the possibility cannot be discounted and is taken seriously by the society of which we are part. We in BP have reached that point." (Frankel 1998, 192)

Such inconsistencies between corporate pronouncements, marketing, and actual investment in greener technologies can leave stakeholders uncertain regarding the depth of the firm's commitment to sustainability.

Printing & Graphics

In *printing and graphics*, it is important that all materials and technologies used in marketing support the company's commitment to the environment. Regarding print media, greener materials include things like papers (recycled, non-chlorine-bleached, tree-free) and inks (soy-based, no heavy metals) while technologies include energy-efficient equipment.

Procurement

Although operations involve many company activities, all of which affect environmental health, certain activities tend to be favored over others. For example, some companies might pay far more attention to recycling their waste (whether related to their operations, facilities and sites, or products and services) than they do in scrutinizing the products that they purchase; yet, *procurement* has enormous environmental implications, which can range from being ecologically devastating to being less harmful. This can occur for a number of reasons. For instance, a company might understand the concept and importance of recycling far better than it knows of some of the potential life cycle impacts of its procurement choices. Additionally, recycling might be free or provide some cost-savings opportunity for a company while greener procurement might be more expensive with regard to certain products. Yet, procurement is at least as important as recycling because it creates the demand for materials and resources in the first place. Greener procurement – such as purchasing tree-free and recycled paper products – has the potential to support greener companies, suppliers, manufacturing processes, and technologies. It also casts a company's vote for environmentally preferable products, and that sends a message to suppliers, companies, industries, and, ultimately, local and global markets.

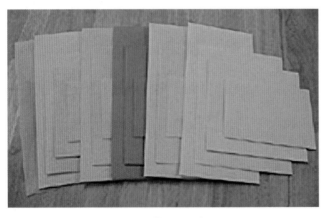

One hundred percent recycled fiber envelopes present a greener alternative to envelopes made of virgin resources. *Courtesy of Twisted Limb Paper.*

Office Supplies

With a growing interest in environmental issues, many companies are actively searching for greener office supplies. Office supplies include any non-electronic items that you use to keep the office running from paper and pens to whiteboards, calendars, and compost bins.

Paper is one of the most heavily purchased items in many offices and one that can have profound impacts on the environment. Paper made from trees results in deforestation, which removes habitat for numerous species, destroys soil communities, reduces the ability of the land to hold and cycle water, increases the amount of carbon dioxide (a greenhouse gas associated with climate change) in the atmosphere, and reduces the amount of oxygen produced in the atmosphere. Even trees that are engineered to grow quickly to provide fiber for paper and other products have ecological value that disappears when they are cut. In any instance, a tree has far more value when it is part of the living forest than it does when it is turned into paper.

The ecological value of these rich forests in Costa Rica and northeast India far outweighs their economic value. *Townsend.*

Moreover, most of the white, tree-based paper that is available has been bleached using chlorine. When chlorine mixes with the organic compounds in tree pulp, it can form of substance known as an organochlorine. Dioxin is one type of organochlorine. Highly toxic in minute doses, dioxin has been known to cause genetic mutations and other severe health effects. Because pulp and paper mills use water-intensive manufacturing processes, they often are located near large bodies of water into which they release contaminated water. As a result, frogs and other amphibians have been found with severe birth defects, a direct result of dioxin poisoning. Some paper companies have begun to bleach paper with oxygen rather than chlorine, thereby avoiding the production of dioxins and other organochlorines.

A field of hemp, which is a versatile fiber that holds great promise in the fiber industry. *Courtesy of Planet Friendly PR.*

Amphibians often serve as indicator species in highly polluted areas. *Townsend.*

Fortunately, there are several greener papers available. Some are made from a variety of paper that has been collected, de-inked, and manufactured into new paper while others are made from grasses (e.g., bamboo) or other plants that grow quickly and are truly a renewable resource. Many of these renewable species also result in papers with longer, stronger fibers that can be recycled into high-quality paper more times than paper that is made from trees. Finally, fibers like kenaf and hemp do not require any bleaching, resulting in a cleaner production process with fewer contaminants.

Energy-Efficient Equipment

Every year, U.S. companies and households spend $1.8 billion to operate office equipment, which is responsible for seven percent of all power use in the commercial sector (U.S. DOE, 2004). This translates to high energy bills and emissions of carbon dioxide and other pollutants related to non-renewable energy production.

Companies use a wide variety of office equipment, including computers, printers, copiers, scanners, fax machines, telephones, modems, servers, and so on. Staff kitchens also might have coffee makers, microwaves, refrigerators, stoves, and dishwashers. All of these items use energy, so how can a company find out which equipment is the most energy-efficient? Ensuring that products are maintained so that they run smoothly and that they are turned off when not in use are two ways to reduce energy use associated with any type of equipment that relies on electricity.

When purchasing new equipment, companies can look for greener versions of similar products. For instance, while a single computer/monitor together use about 150 watts of energy, laptops only use 15-25 watts when in use and less than a watt when powered-down (U.S. DOE, 2004). And if the laptop's AC adaptor is unplugged from the wall whenever the machine is not in use – or plugged into a power strip that can be turned off easily when not in use – it will prevent the transformer from drawing energy even while the laptop is turned off.

Companies can look for the U.S. government-backed Energy Star ® logo, which indicates that the equipment meets several energy-efficient criteria established by the Energy Star® program. For example, Energy Star ® computers have a power-saving mode. In power-down mode, they use 15 percent or less of the energy used in normal mode. Energy Star® monitors also have a power-down mode during which they use no more than 15 watts of energy following fifteen to thirty minutes of inactivity and no more than 8 watts following seventy minutes of inactivity. More than 3,300 office products carry the logo (U.S. DOE, 2004).

The Energy Star ® web site (www.energystar.gov) contains detailed information that can help companies looking for more energy-efficient equipment. Additionally, the American Council for an Energy-Efficient Economy produces online guides to energy-efficient office equipment, appliances, and commercial equipment (www.aceee.org).

Personal care products (restrooms, company fitness centers)

Personal care products are another area in which businesses can be greener. They include products like soaps, shampoos, conditioners, hand and body lotions, and feminine products that companies provide in employee restrooms, gyms, and other areas.

Suki Naturals' personal care products are made of natural ingredients. *Courtesy of Suki Naturals.*

Eve creating her Garden of Eve products. *Courtesy of Garden of Eve.*

Natural ingredients that go into Suki Naturals' personal care products. *Courtesy of Suki Naturals.*

Trillium Organics personal care products are all natural. *Courtesy of Trillium Organics.*

Greener products are those that are non-toxic, made of natural, renewable, organic ingredients, have minimal packaging made of recycled or renewable materials, have packaging that can be recycled or composted, and are not tested on animals.

Many companies (or their sub-contractors) engage in product testing on rabbits and other animals. *Townsend.*

Products to avoid include the following:

* Artificial colors: Might contain chemical dyes that irritate the skin, cause cancer, and contain dangerous heavy metals that are absorbed into the body, and are neither renewable nor biodegradable

* Fluoride: Might be carcinogenic and is banned by several countries in Europe

* Formaldehyde (also Quaternium-15): Toxic to humans and wildlife

* Mineral oil: Prevents the skin from breathing, dissolves the skin's germ-fighting sebum, is not biodegradable and is phototoxic, interferes with vitamin absorption, and is a suspected cause of cancer in humans

* Petrochemicals: Causes cancer and genetic mutation in humans and is neither renewable nor biodegradable

* Talcum powder: Might contain asbestos (a carcinogen), irritates eyes and lungs, and unhealthy for talc miners and babies, alike

Many products can be recycled, including aluminum, batteries, carpets, CD-ROMs, computer batteries, computers and other electronic equipment, construction waste, floppy disks, glass, hazardous waste, holiday cards, light ballasts, packing materials, paper, plastic, printer consumables, shoes, and software.

Recycling bins in the workplace provide a place for easy collection. *Courtesy of Interface Flooring Systems.*

Recycling Program

Recycling has taken hold as many companies realize the importance of minimizing the waste stream.

Recycling programs can help to eliminate the need for landfills as well as the act of illegal dumping. *Courtesy of Dr. James P. McVey, NOAA Sea Grant Program.*

Paper made by hand using recycled fibers and plant parts.
Courtesy of Twisted Limb Paper.

One company, Twisted Limb Paperworks, even uses the waste water from its studio's air conditioner and dehumidifier to produce its 100 percent post-consumer-content recycled papers.

Freecycle groups and waste exchanges also have become popular ways to give away unwanted items. Generally Internet-based, these groups allow companies and individuals to offer items that they no longer want. These items can include everything from excess packaging to surplus chemicals.

Whole Foods' recycling program helps to reduce the company's waste. *Courtesy of Whole Foods.*

Case Study: Patagonia

Patagonia has taken several steps to green its operations. Each department is directed to achieve a number of environmental goals, including educating customers regarding products' environmental benefits and impacts; educating suppliers about the firm's environmental criteria; being more resource efficient; using more green paper products; reducing paper use; decreasing energy use; increasing greener energy use; incorporating environmental costs into production and accounting systems; reducing waste produced at international facilities; and ending landfill-bound solid waste from domestic facilities (Rowledge, Barton, and Brady 1999). Some of these waste issues are relevant to the Products and Services element as well.

Additionally, every year, the company practices a Tithing Program. Through this program, Patagonia pays what it refers to as an "Earth tax" – a donation of either 10 percent of its pretax profits or 1 percent of its sales revenue (whichever is greater) to environmental organizations. Between 1985 and 1998, it gave over $13 million to environmental organizations (Patagonia, Inc. 1998, 25).

An unintended benefit of Patagonia's tithing, internships, and overall environmental and social commitment has been the $5-7 million/year's-worth of free media coverage that the company has gotten as a result. The company feels that this coverage has been more advantageous than if it had advertised itself.

One key aspect of a company's operations is the relationship that it develops with its customers. In one of its catalogues, Patagonia stated "everything we do pollutes" (Rowledge, Barton, and Brady 1999, 109). This type of transparency about its environmental impacts has helped to establish trust with a broad customer base. About 20 percent of Patagonia's customers buy its products because of the company's reputation and its commitment to environmental and social responsibility (Rowledge, Barton, and Brady 1999, 108). In its highly competitive industry, Patagonia believes that having differentiated itself through its commitment to environmental and social health has benefited the company.

Operations-related Activities

Below is a list of a few of the activities that a company wishing to green its operations might undertake:

* Integrate external costs into accounting and finance practices.

* Reduce employee commuting. Develop telecommuting programs and offer incentives to employees for telecommuting, bicycling, carpooling, or taking public transportation to work. Limit available parking to discourage individual employees from driving to work. Set up a carpool list on the company's internal web site to facilitate ride sharing.

* Reduce business travel; instead, set up teleconferences. When travel is necessary, use mass transit, hybrid rental cars, and greener forms of transport (e.g., subway, bicycle) whenever possible. For long trips, consider offsetting approximate carbon emissions by planting trees or donating to an environmental organization that does.

* In staff cafeterias, buy locally grown, organic foods. Compost coffee grounds and food scraps (except for meats and fats). Donate good leftovers to soup kitchens and homeless shelters. Keep lunchrooms and kitchens stocked with degradable utensils and non-chlorine-bleached, recycled paper napkins. Provide organic foods and beverages (e.g., shade-grown coffee) at meetings and workshops.

* Arrange to have unnecessary light bulbs within vending machines turned off.

* Purchase greener vehicles for the company's fleet and keep them well maintained for efficiency and durability. Use recycled oil, and recycle used oil.

* Articulate the company's environmental values up front. Hire employees whose values are aligned with the company's and who are environmentally aware.

* Invest in companies and funds with similar environmental and social values.

* Use marketing campaigns to share the company's vision, environmental progress, and information about greener products and services. Be honest and do not overstate how green the company is. If it still has a way to go, do not be afraid to explain the company's goals and what it must do in order to achieve them.

* Lobby for greener regulations that support both beneficial companies and the environment.

Help to shape business policies in proactive and creative ways. Support the end of ecologically harmful subsidies (e.g., the 1872 Mining Law) that enable non-green businesses to continue at an economic advantage.

* Use only greener (recycled, tree-free, non-chlorine-bleached) papers and inks in printing and graphics work.

* Purchase greener (environmentally and socially responsible) office products, equipment, and supplies.

* Use only as much as needed when using materials. Reuse products whenever possible as long as it will not provide a safety hazard. Reuse or recycle everything from paper, cans, and glass to toner cartridges, motor oil, and furniture.

* Dispose safely of hazardous materials.

* Exercise healthy trade policies for all involved, including ecological systems.

Summary

This chapter explored the many facets of greening a company's operations. "Operations" provide an umbrella for many activities, including accounting, company investing, purchasing, recycling, and so forth. As such, it is an important area for greening because so many activities are included within it.

Cruise vessel passing through the Panama Canal.
Courtesy of Holland America Lines.

Chapter 6
Greening Your Facilities & Sites

This chapter focuses on greening company facilities and its sites. First, it discusses the building life cycle. Then, it very briefly explores things to consider when trying to green various aspects of company facilities. Finally, it explores the need to green sites and suggests that businesses need to be accountable to three types of site.

Not only is it important for businesses to have green mission statements, informed and proactive employees, and green operations – it also is important that their facilities and relationships with their sites are environmentally benign. Facilities refer to the buildings and structures in and through which the company does its business. They include such varied structures as office buildings, hospitals, warehouses, schools, manufacturing facilities, airports, hotels, and home offices.

Sites typically refer to the geographic location that a company inhabits; however, my definition of a site is much broader. For the purposes of this book, I developed a typology of three site types, which reflect those locations that a company inhabits, uses, and affects.

As with greening any other human activity or artifact, the life cycle impacts of the firm's facilities and sites should be taken into account. This means that greening can be considered in every step of the facilities' and sites' existences – from the first stages of their design to their construction, habitation, operations and maintenance, renovation, and reuse or deconstruction. This will require that green thinking be a natural and continuous part of the facilities and sites throughout their entire lives.

Herman Miller's Design Yard – the Front Door space was awarded LEED Gold certification. *Courtesy of Herman Miller, Inc.*

Facilities and sites are important because most facility and site activities do not consider the ecosystems that they affect. As a result, they miss opportunities for working with the characteristics of the landscape, such as the wind and water flows, and with biological communities. Instead, they often damage soil communities, remove feeding and nesting areas, destroy routes for migratory species, wipe out or impair habitat for multiple species, and remove trees and other species that undergo photosynthesis, thereby reducing oxygen production while releasing carbon dioxide into the atmosphere and contributing to climate change.

For example, the designs and activities of facilities and sites affect Earth's hydrological cycle through such simple actions as paving roads, walkways, and parking lots and channelizing rivers and other waterways.

Filthy building systems can lead to unhealthy buildings. *Courtesy of Environmental Building Systems.*

Heavy machinery often has detrimental impacts on the landscape. *Townsend.*

When rainwater falls on unpaved ground, depending on the slope of the land, health of the soils, and the vegetation present, much of it is absorbed and filtered by soils and stone before ultimately draining into and recharging the underground aquifers that provide Earth's fresh groundwater. It also runs down the surface of land, feeding into streams, rivers, lakes, and oceans.

Building on the coastline without any buffer area often reduces a coastal ecosystem's ability to respond to changes in the environment. *Townsend.*

Channelized areas such as this one provide water access further inland; they do not account for the meandering flow of healthy waterways. *Townsend.*

When portions of Earth's surface are made impermeable by roads, buildings, and other impervious surfaces, rainwater cannot be absorbed to feed soils and recharge streams and aquifers. Instead, it picks up pollutants, such as road oil, cigarette butts, and other debris, and moves quickly along paved surfaces and down through sewers into large bodies of water, polluting them and causing hazards for aquatic and coastal life. Impervious surfaces also change the microclimate of an area, and they force water to move unnaturally, causing erosion. Other facility- and site-related activities, such as agriculture and deforestation, also interfere with hydrological processes.

This unimpeded Alaskan stream illustrates the natural, non-linear flow of water. *Townsend*.

Malta's garigue habitat benefits from unimpeded rainfall. *Townsend*.

Facilities

There are many different stages in the life of a building, and it is important to incorporate green considerations into each one. The first stage begins with conceptualization and design. This stage is extremely important because it helps to determine what the company's relationship to its sites will be by specifying its location, its placement, its systems, and the procurement of materials from which it will be made.

Green architects typically do what is called a design "charette" at the start of the design process. This is a working meeting in which the building's stakeholders (e.g., building owners, users, community) and designers (architects, landscape architects, engineers) find ways to meet the needs of the buildings' users while designing a building that functions as an integrated system. Green features can include solar orientation, thermal mass, pervious paving, counter tops made of soy flour, and other greener materials and products.

Children's Museum of Pittsburgh was designed to be one of the first LEED-certified children's museums in the United States. *Photo ©Albert Vecerko/Esto, Koning Eizenberg Architecture, Perkins Eastman Architects. Courtesy of Children's Museum of Pittsburgh*.

The Children's Museum of Pittsburgh made it a point to create a healthy museum filled with child-safe exhibits and activities. *Courtesy of Children's Museum of Pittsburgh.*

The Limb Bender, a climbing structure, is made using reclaimed wood. The nearby green-colored flooring is low-VOC carpet. *Photo ©Albert Vecerko/Esto. Courtesy of Children's Museum of Pittsburgh.*

One mistake that some businesses make is to hire an architect with little to no greening experience and, after the blueprint is drawn up, contact a green architect or consultant for greening tips. This step, alone, causes the company to miss out on the best greening opportunities (e.g., facility orientation) because they were not incorporated into the conceptualization and design of the building. If that company, then, decides to add green features to an existing, ecologically insensitive blueprint, those features are likely to increase the costs that are associated with both facilities construction and operations.

Construction of the facility is the next design stage. Construction is important because through it occurs the physical manifestation of the architect's blueprint. This is the first stage in which the company's impact on the building site is experienced by local ecosystems. Companies that wish to have green facilities need to be mindful of the impacts that their new facilities have on the land during construction. For example, heavy construction equipment tends to rely on non-renewable resources and is energy-intensive. Moreover, the use of heavy equipment tears ecological communities apart, compacts soils, and suffocates plant roots.

The Inn of the Anasazi in Santa Fe, New Mexico, was designed with several green features in mind. *Townsend.*

This is coupled with the degradation of more distant sites from which the building's materials are taken. Thus, building construction typically represents the degradation of multiple sites, the full ecological consequences of which will never be known in detail. Not only is the construction process often energy-intensive with the use of heavy equipment, but many of the materials used in the construction process often are energy- and resource-intensive as well. In fact, Van der Ryn and Cowan have reported that "building construction, materials, and maintenance" consume about 40 percent of the energy in the U.S. (1996, 13). Thus, it is important for companies to use greener materials (e.g., carpets and floor coverings, wallboard). Furthermore, carpets and other flooring products, paint and wallpaper, furniture, and construction materials (e.g., adhesives, solvents) can cause temporary or permanent harm to organisms throughout their life cycles.

Both sick building syndrome and chemical sensitivity are associated with exposure to toxic materials and might affect materials manufacturers, building users, and others, including later generations.

Habitation is the third stage in a building's life. This is the period in which the company inhabits and uses the building. The environmental impacts associated with habitation are numerous. They are due, in part, to the use of water, electricity, oil, and other resources needed to run the building's systems. Greener habitation does not depend solely on the facilities manager; it also relies on the building's users. For example, building inhabitants do environmental harm when they waste water by leaving faucets running and waste energy by leaving their lights and equipment on in their offices when they are not needed. Habitation also can affect the landscape. For example, the ways in which the building's users move through and use the site can affect the health of ecological communities.

Durapalm® coconut palm plywood is made of reclaimed coconut palms using no-formaldehyde adhesives. Quicksilver Design. *Photo by Brett Drury. Courtesy of Smith & Fong.*

Heavy equipment compacts soils, degrades habitat. *Townsend.*

Plyboo® bamboo-ply is made using 100 percent rapidly renewable bamboo and adhesives that are strong and free of emissions. Factory 1 Design. *Courtesy of Smith & Fong.*

Volunteers move planting material to Eastern Neck Island, Maryland. *Courtesy of the National Oceanic and Atmospheric Administration's Restoration Center.*

Like construction, renovation has the potential to harm the ecosystems on a building site through the use of heavy machinery as well as by the extraction, transport, and processing of materials used in the renovation process.

Demolition or deconstruction and reuse are the final stages of a facility's life. Demolition refers to the destruction the building, which is the most wasteful way to end a building's life. Building waste (e.g., construction and demolition) accounts for a large amount of landfill waste in the United States.

Deconstruction is a greener alternative. It refers to the intentional disassembly of a building. The site impacts associated with deconstruction generally are less harmful than those associated with the demolition of a building and hauling of demolished materials. Additionally, it allows companies the option of reusing materials (e.g., doors, windows, bricks, furnishings) so that they remain valued and used rather than discarded.

A Word about Leased Facilities

As important as it is to green its facilities, some companies lease, rather than own, their workplaces and other buildings. In that event, they may have little, if any, decision-making authority over renovations or maintenance done to the building and site. In some instances, lessees have been able to work with facility owners to make green improvements, such as replacing standard lighting with energy-efficient lighting. Alternatively, some building owners who have created greener buildings have experienced a competitive advantage in commercial real estate markets. Though a company might have little control over its leased facilities, it still can be greener by focusing on the other four elements – mission, employees, operations, and products and services.

Building Systems
Power Sources

There are several greener sources of energy. They include geothermal, passive solar, photovoltaics, and wind. *Geothermal* energy is created by harnessing the steam created by hot water within the earth. *Passive solar* energy comes from the sun and is used to heat building spaces without mechanical systems. Passive solar energy also can be used in solar hot water heaters, which can reduce your company's energy bills. *Photovoltaics*, or active solar power, uses solar panels to collect the sun's energy and store and distribute it using water or air as a medium. *Wind* energy, which is created when wind moves a turbine, is growing in popularity, particularly in Europe.

Mechanical Heating and Cooling

There are four primary types of mechanical heating sources. *Boilers* generally are used in large buildings, use fossil fuels, and heat and distribute steam or water through a series of pipes. *Electric resistance* heats either local air for circulation within a room or wall and ceiling surfaces for radiation into the room. It is used in larger buildings' air ducts in order to reheat air before it enters rooms, and it also is used in smaller buildings. *Furnaces* generally are used in larger buildings, use fossil fuels, and heat and distribute air through ducts. *Heat pumps* use refrigeration techniques to heat air and water. They remove heat from the outdoors and use it to heat indoor air and are considered more energy-efficient than the other sources. Heat pumps generally are used in small and medium-sized buildings.

There are two main methods of mechanical cooling. *Absorption* uses liquids, such as ammonia or lithium bromide, to absorb water. It can be used with solar collectors and inexpensive heat sources. *Vapor compression* is less expensive, in use more frequently than is absorption, and it can be used as a heat pump. This method requires moving refrigerant through metal pipes to remove heat.

Heating, ventilation, and air conditioning systems that are integrated are referred to as HVAC systems. There are four types of HVAC systems. *All-air systems* clean and heat/cool and humidify/dehumidify the air by moving it through ductwork. When the outdoor temperature drops below fifty to fifty-five degrees Fahrenheit, these systems can use that air and eliminate the need for mechanical cooling. *Air-water systems* provide forced ventilation and controlled humidity and can respond rapidly to fluctuating demands from various zones. Both air and water are sent to each space, and either one or both can be used to control the air temperature. These systems use only about one-sixth of the fan power that all-air systems require to circulate water. *All-water systems* both cool and dehumidify air by circulating water or chilled brine through coils. They are commonly used in smaller spaces, such as apartments or motels. *Unitary systems* use refrigerant and include window air conditioners and packaged terminal air conditioners (PTACs). Natural convection, radiant heating, and forced-air units also fall within the category of unitary systems and are powered by gas or electricity.

For additional information on determining which type of system to use, refer to Fuller Moore's *Environmental Control Systems* (McGraw-Hill). Refer to the Energy Star® web site (www.energystar.gov) for ways to increase the efficiency of your facilities' mechanical heating and cooling systems.

Natural Heating & Cooling

There are several things that your company can do to take advantage of natural heating and cooling opportunities. For example, in order to reduce heat loss, your company can design a compact building, with or without multiple stories; this building would have well-insulated ceilings, walls, and floors. Windows and doors would be caulked and weather-stripped, and closets and other uninhabited spaces can be placed on exterior walls.

To reduce heat infiltration, the company can plant a hedge of evergreens or create an earth berm along its building's windward side in order to move air around your building. Similarly, it can use an exterior overhang or wall to protect the entrance from wind.

To enhance solar gain, the company can design the building to face south with the most heavily used rooms on the south side. Additionally, a sunspace with thermal mass can be constructed on the south side to collect the sun's heat by day and release it at night. Furthermore, most of the building's windows can be on the south side in order to take advantage of the sun's radiant heating and daylight.

Solar panels. *Courtesy of the US Department of Energy's Energy Efficiency and Renewable Energy Division.*

Wind has long been used as a power source. *Townsend*.

To reduce the amount of solar heat that the building experiences, the company can use overhangs or exterior shades on south-facing windows. Outside shutters and indoor shades also can reduce the amount of sunlight that enters the building, thereby keeping it cooler. The roof and the building can be light-colored, which will reflect the sunlight rather than absorb it. Outdoor areas can be placed on the north side of the building and shaded in order to ensure that people feel comfortable during the heat of the summer.

To avoid fluctuations of indoor temperatures, the company can use thick walls for added insulation or put a living roof on the building, which provides both additional insulation and habitat for birds, insects, and other species. Furthermore, the construction of the building either fully or partially below ground level will take advantage of stable underground temperatures. Insure, however, that any underground ducts are sealed well in order to prevent radon gas from seeping into them.

This south-facing building enjoys plenty of sunlight and radiant heating due to its thermal mass. *Townsend*.

The natural buildings of Mesa Verde in southern Colorado provided radiant heating and natural protection from the elements. *Townsend.*

To enhance the building's ventilation, the company can use a narrow floor plan design to encourage circulation across the building. Raised floors, added vents, clerestory windows on the building's leeward side, roof belvederes, open interiors, and landscape features (e.g., hedges, outdoor walls) that direct breezes toward the building all help to enhance interior ventilation.

Green roofs such as this one serve as habitat for birds and insects, augment a roof's insulating abilities, slow the movement of rainwater, and add natural beauty to a building. *Courtesy of Emory Knoll Farms.*

Operable windows at the Chesapeake Bay Foundation's headquarters allow breezes to flow through the building. *Photo by Jennifer Wallace, Chesapeake Bay Foundation.*

To increase cooling, the company can use a desiccant cooling system, indoor greenhouses or pools, roof ponds, wetted curtains, fountains, outdoor overhead sprinklers, and water-sprayed walls and roofs.

Lighting

Artificial Lighting: Conventional lighting systems typically are the largest consumers of energy in commercial buildings. However, there are several things companies can do to improve their lighting efficiency. Replacing incandescent bulbs with compact fluorescent bulbs can reduce lighting energy use by more than half. Because compact fluorescent bulbs can last up to ten times longer than incandescent bulbs, they will need to be replaced much less frequently, which will save time and money. Although the bulb is important, the lighting fixture also can affect energy use. Fixtures that carry the Energy Star® logo are judged by several criteria, including their even distribution of light, longevity, and a two-year warranty. Energy Star® products also are available in exit signs, traffic signals, and ceiling fans.

Encouraging employees to turn off lights when they are not needed is another way of saving energy and money. Motion sensors can be used to turn lights off automatically when a room is empty.

Companies interested in greening their lighting systems can contact the Energy Star® program and the U.S. EPA's Green Light's Program, which is a voluntary program through which specialists work with companies to find ways to improve their energy efficiency in ways that benefit the firms' bottom lines.

Daylighting: Another means of providing light is through the use of daylighting. Daylighting refers to the use of sunlight and can be incorporated into the office setting in several ways – through windows, light shelves, skylights, sunpipes, and other means. Clearly, sunlight is a free source of light and warmth by which businesses can benefit, particularly in the early stages of building design/redesign. Well-designed daylighting systems can reduce drastically the need for artificial lighting. Additionally, daylighting is an important component of human health. People who spend time in daylit buildings tend to be happier, healthier, and more productive than those working in artificial lighting (Heschong 2002; Monroe 2004).

Rainwater Collection

With impervious road surfaces, sidewalks, and rooftops, much of the rain that falls runs down gutters and storm drains picks up cigarette butts, oil, radiator fluid, plastic bags, and other forms of pollution along the way. Not only does this contribute to the pollution of our waterways, but it also represents a wasted opportunity.

A free natural resource, rainwater can be collected and used for irrigation and industry. Every year, about 50 trillion gallons of rainwater runs off of American lawns, and this represents about half of the U.S. water budget, which includes industry and irrigation needs. Using low water landscaping and indoor water conservation measures discussed earlier, many companies can reduce their need to buy water from the local water authorities.

A day lit interior at the Chesapeake Bay Foundation. *Photos by Loretta Jergensen, Chesapeake Bay Foundation.*

Toilets & Waste Treatment

Many of us are accustomed to thinking of the toilet as a repository for human waste. Yet, by using an ordinary toilet that relies upon clean water as a flushing agent, we waste water and the opportunity to feed that human waste back in the local ecosystem. Although most areas in the U.S. have municipal water treatment facilities, the complex system of piping waste out to a distant location is costly and, often, somewhat ineffective. Additionally, the practice of using chemicals in toilets pollutes our water supply.

Composting toilets, such as those used at the Chesapeake Bay Foundation's headquarters in Annapolis, Maryland, are odor-free, resource-conserving alternatives to the traditional water toilet. Other companies have chosen to create on-site ecosystems, such as the Living System developed by John and Nancy Todd, to handle human waste. Other no-flush toilets use propane or electricity to incinerate waste, converting it into sterilized ash. Finally, low-flush toilets use less water than traditional toilets. Regardless of the toilet chosen, the most environmentally friendly toilet paper is that which is made out of non-rebleached, 100 percent recycled fibers.

Rainwater-fed restroom sinks at the Chesapeake Bay Foundation's headquarters. *Photo by Jennifer Wallace. Chesapeake Bay Foundation.*

Water Waste & Efficiency

U.S. manufacturing companies have been estimated to use over 9 trillion gallons of freshwater annually (U.S. EPA, 2003). Because the amount of freshwater on this planet is finite, is important to conserve water and prevent it from becoming polluted.

Conservation can be carried out by ensuring that manufacturing equipment, sinks, dishwashers, washing machines, and any other equipment that uses water are in proper working order. Pipes should be checked regularly for leaks, and showerheads can be fitted with flow restrictors, aerators, and sprayers, which can reduce water use by half.

Building Materials
Concrete

In the early 1900s, an innovative product named autoclaved cellular concrete (ACC) was created in Sweden. ACC, sometimes referred to as autoclaved aerated concrete, is a lightweight concrete block that contains tiny cells. This product is touted to be nontoxic and inert and has a far higher R-value than regular concrete.

Another promising concrete product is a concrete additive made by Hycrete® Technologies. Concrete is the most used material in the construction industry. Although it provides many useful functions, its porosity allows moisture to travel through its pores and corrode any rebar or structural components within a concrete structure. The Hycrete® additive is a water-based solution that contains a type of salt. When added to concrete, this solution makes it waterproof, thereby increasing the durability of concrete buildings and eliminating the need for plastic membranes used around building foundations, beneath living roofs, and so on. Company CEO David Rosenberg says of the firm, "It's taking the most used material in the construction industry and fixing its fundamental flaw" (personal communication 2005). This product has received Cradle to Cradle™ environmental certification as a biological nutrient from McDonough Braungart Design Chemistry.

Insulation

One important aspect of a greener building is its insulation. Insulation is important because it helps to keep indoor temperatures fairly steady, regardless of the weather outdoors. No matter what type of heating or cooling system a company has, insulation is key and can enhance the energy efficiency of its facilities significantly.

There are many kinds of greener insulation available, each with its own environmental benefits. For example, earthen buildings, such as those made using adobe or straw bales, are well insulated naturally due, in part, to the thickness of their walls and ceilings.

Hycrete® Concrete Additive makes concrete waterproof. *Courtesy of Hycrete® Technologies.*

Adding Hycrete® to concrete on the construction site. *Courtesy of Hycrete® Technologies.*

CEO David Rosenberg accepting an award on behalf of Hycrete® Technologies. *Courtesy of Hycrete® Technologies.*

123

Cellulose insulation is a loose-fill insulation that is made largely of recycled newspapers, is considered non-toxic, and contains fire retardant, which makes this product less flammable than standard fiberglass insulation. Because there is some concern over the effect that cellulose insulation containing ammonium sulfate might have in corroding metal, a company can check with installers about protecting pipes. Cotton insulation made from recycled, pre-consumer denim scraps also is available and is considered healthier than fiberglass. Icynene® and Bio-based® insulation are two types of non-toxic cellulose insulation that are sprayed into the wall's cavities, filling the nooks and crannies, prior to drywalling. Icynene is largely made of petroleum products, and Bio-based contains both petroleum and soy. Mineral fiber is odorless, non-corrosive, inflammable, and does not support bacterial or fungal growth. Mineral fiber, also called mineral wool, comes in two types – slag wool (from blast furnace slag) and rock wool (from natural rocks). Silicate foam, also referred to ask Air-krete®, is a wet insulation that is sprayed into frame, masonry, or concrete structures and is characterized by low-toxicity. Fiberglass is not particularly environmentally friendly, primarily because it requires more than 200 times the amount of electricity to produce per pound than does cellulose insulation (Smart Places, n.d.). However, if no other insulation is readily available, fiberglass is a good alternative to no insulation at all.

Finished earthen building. *Courtesy of David Eisenberg.*

Earthen building detail. *Courtesy of David Eisenberg.*

Earthen building interior with plenty of daylight and thermal mass. *Courtesy of David Eisenberg.*

Pavement

Impervious surfaces force rainwater to run off the land rather than soak into the ground and nourish soils and plants. Pervious paving materials allow rainwater to soak in and can be used in company parking lots, sidewalks, and roadways.

Plastic Wood

Plastic wood is made of recycled plastic; depending on the manufacturer, it also might contain wood waste. It is durable, skid-resistant, resists insects and rot, and can be stained. Plastic wood often is used to manufacture park benches and decks.

Roofing

There are several types of roofing options. These include organic asphalt shingles that contain recycled waste paper and/or mineral slag; however these shingles are not easily recycled. Slate is problematic because it is a finite natural resource, but the shingles

Icynene® insulation installed in a ceiling. *Courtesy of Home Energy Partners.*

Icynene® installed in a wall. *Courtesy of Home Energy Partners.*

are durable, and the quarrying associated with slate is less environmentally damaging than that associated with some synthetic roofing materials. Although clay tiles can be used in roofing, they are susceptible to the freeze-thaw cycle that occurs in some regions. Roofing tiles made of 100 percent recycled-content metal also are available. Though popular in some parts of the country, cedar shakes rely on cedar, which is a slow-growing, threatened species. Fiber-cement or plastic mock shingles can be used in place of cedar shakes.

Siding

Though a popular siding material, vinyl is not environmentally friendly. Fiber-cement siding is more durable and fire-resistant than is wood siding. Metal siding with high recycled content also is available. Of course, earthen buildings do not require siding – although they might do well sprayed with cement stucco.

Windows

Traditionally, windows have been a major source of heat loss in buildings. Old-fashioned, single-pane windows had an insulating capacity of approximately R-1, which meant that heat passed easily through the glass. Today's double- and triple-pane windows are rated at about R-2 and R-4, respectively. Some of today's improved windows are made using two layers of glass that are coated with a low-emissivity (low-e) finish and contain argon gas between the layers, reducing the amount of heat lost. Though these windows may cost more, the energy saving may have them pay for themselves within a year or two. Windows with higher R-values are available as well.

Another way to reduce heat loss through windows is by using insulating blinds. Not only do these blinds add to the insulating value of a window, but they also reduce air infiltration that can come in around the windows. Caulking to seal cracks and drafts around windows can help a company to be more energy-efficient and save money as a result.

Wood

Wood has long been a key component in building construction. Greener wood use is available and includes salvaged rather than virgin wood, certified-sustainable wood, plastic wood, and wood made from wheat straw or other quickly renewable resources.

Note: According to the journal *Science*, after three decades of remote sensing, scientists have discovered that selective logging – even in certified-sustainable forests – is causing immense harm to the rainforests of the Amazon basin (Asner et al., 2005).

Preparation for Icynene® insulation in a crawl space. *Courtesy of Home Energy Partners.*

Furnishings
Carpets

Carpets can facilitate indoor air quality problems because their fibers create dust when they flake off; they can harbor dust mites, molds, and mildews; and they are difficult to clean from the top of the fiber down to the backing. Additionally, most carpets contain a host of harmful chemicals and dyes, which can pose significant health threats. However, they provide sound insulation, a soft environment under foot, and help to keep floors warmer in the winter.

Plyboo® bamboo-ply, natural flat grain. Cheng Design. *Photo by Matthew Millman. Courtesy of Smith & Fong.*

Dust mite on carpet fibers. *Courtesy of Interface Flooring Systems.*

Greener carpets are those made using organic, non-toxic fibers and dyes or that are made of recycled products. Some of the most durable carpets are made of wool, which are available without added chemicals. Carpets made of recycled PET bottles and other synthetic products help to close the recycling loop and enhance the market for recycled products.

Non-toxic, recycled/organic carpet backing is available as well. In order to avoid the toxic adhesives used in carpet installation, some companies have elected to have their carpets tacked to the floor rather than glued to it.

Furthermore, rather than installing wall-to-wall carpeting, some firms are opting for carpet tiles, which can be replaced individually when some areas become worn or stained over time. This ensures the longevity of most of the carpet as high-traffic areas can be replaced while low-traffic areas can remain in situ.

Flooring

There are several choices of greener flooring. Many producers of ceramic tile incorporate recycled glass into their tiles and recycle their waste tiles into their new tiles. By using natural, unglazed ceramic tiles, your company also can avoid toxic dyes and glazes. Greener flooring choices also can include those made of natural, renewable resources, such as linoleum, cork, stone, paper, and bamboo. Linoleum is made using natural materials, including cork, linseed oil, rosin binders, and wood flour. Cork is the outer bark of the cork oak tree, or *Quercus suber*. This tree grows primarily in the Mediterranean basin, and most cork comes from Portugal, Algeria, Spain, and Morocco. The cork layer can be stripped off without harming the tree and can be harvested from the same tree every eight to fourteen years. Stone is a durable flooring material but is best purchased locally due to the high transportation costs associated with its weight. Most stone will need to be sealed against stains, and greener sealants are available. Paper also has been used experimentally on floors, including my dining room floor. It is lightweight, can be made from recycled or renewable resources, can be left natural or dyed with vegetable-based dyes, can be handmade, and requires less energy to transport than heavier flooring materials. Like wood, paper flooring requires a sealant, which can be low-toxic or non-toxic. Because of its rapid growth, bamboo is a readily renewable resource that can be grown easily without pesticides and makes a strong and beautiful floor.

Durapalm coconut palm flooring, manufactured from reclaimed coconut palms. *Photo by Matthew Millman. Courtesy of Smith & Fong.*

Plyboo® bamboo sport floor, natural edge grain at Singing Hills Recreation Center, Dallas. *Photo by John Benoist. Courtesy of Smith & Fong.*

Paints & Wallcoverings

Paints typically contain many toxins that can offgas for years, long after the "new paint" smell dissipates. Toxins come from the paints' ingredients, which can include solvents, fungicides, preservatives, polyvinyl chloride (PVC), mold inhibitors, and pigments made from heavy metals. Cadmium, a toxic substance, is used as a drying agent. Oil-based paints tend to be more toxic than do acrylic paints, though both can make building occupants sick. Similarly, paint thinners, other solvents, and primer can create indoor air quality problems. Now, however, there are many non-toxic and low-toxic paints, primers, and paint strippers available. Be sure to read the back of the paint can to ensure that the product contains no VOCs.

Natural fiber, non-toxic wallcoverings and non-toxic adhesives are available as well. Due to their toxicity, vinyl and other plastic wallpaper should be avoided.

Window Covering

Blinds made from bamboo, organic fabrics, and other renewable resources can be used to minimize heat and glare during daytime hours. Similarly, non-toxic, natural-fiber curtains are available as well.

Furniture

Much of the furniture available today is made of wood, pressed wood, plastics, and/or metals. Some of it contains VOCs, such as benzene, toluene, and xylene. Even if it contains no toxic solvents, stains, or sealants, there are other issues to consider.

For example, if your company is considering purchasing wood furniture, it might want to select recycled wood over virgin wood or certified-sustainable virgin wood over non-certified wood. Wood from local, sustainably harvested resources is preferred to wood imported from abroad due to the embodied energy and other environmental impacts associated with transportation. Recycled and recyclable metal and plastic framed furniture are available as well.

Lamps made from a variety of materials, including recycled scrap wood and greener fibers. *Courtesy of Scrapile.*

Upholstery

Many textiles produced today are highly toxic throughout their lifecycles – from fiber production to dyeing to fabric manufacture. If your company prefers natural fibers, it can purchase textiles made of organically grown plants and non-toxic dyes or choose to go with the natural colors of the fibers. Additionally, it probably will want to avoid the toxic finishes that make much of today's upholstery stain-resistant but also worsens indoor air quality.

There also are textiles made of recycled products, such as PET bottles. Buying such products is a good way to help close the loop on recycling – by creating a demand for recycled products and encouraging the collection of recyclable materials.

Housekeeping

Cleaning Supplies

Most cleaning supplies contain toxic chemicals and can endanger employees' health through inhalation, skin contact, or accidental consumption. They poison the air when used indoors and also can poison our water when flushed down toilets or washed down the drain. If a company, or its cleaning crew, must use such chemicals, it is important to ensure that users work in a well-ventilated area, that they wear gloves, a respirator, and goggles to reduce their exposure, and that they are well trained in using such products.

There are numerous non-toxic and low-toxic cleaning products on the market today, and these can be found in health food stores, online, and in some hardware stores.

Air Fresheners

Although air fresheners might smell pleasant, they do not really freshen the air at all. Instead, they coat the lining of the sinuses with an oil or use nerve-deadening agents that inhibit the nose's ability to smell. If you would like to use air fresheners in a company restroom or other area, try using a natural herb mix, such as a small bowl of rosemary that is changed every week or two, or an all-natural, non-toxic, scented spray. Be aware that some people are especially allergic to particular scents, so a company might want to ask its employees if they have any such allergies.

Pest control

One of the unpleasant tasks that many businesses face is dealing with unwanted insect or mammalian visitors. There are non-toxic and humane ways to deal with both. The first course of action is prevention. Companies can search for potential entry points and seek to close them off by caulking or sealing cracks and other spaces through which insects, mice, rats, birds, and other creatures could come inside. Outdoor insect infestations or visitations by hungry mammals can be handled through alternative means as well.

Toxic pesticides can harm not only their target organisms but also the health of humans and beneficial organisms. *Townsend*.

There are natural means of pest control. These can be found at natural food/product stores, online, and in several books, such as *The Natural Garden Book* and *Slug Bread and Beheaded Thistles*. Additionally, mice, rats, and other creatures that have made their way inside can be captured with live traps and released back into the wild or taken to a local nature center. Poisons and glue traps can be considered inhumane, and poisons also are an added source of indoor toxicity.

Natural elements have shaped this Land of Giants – majestic freestanding cliffs, or *tepuis*, tower over interlocking undulations of savannah and rainforest in the Gran Sabana National Park, southeast Venezuela. *Courtesy of Angus Gemmell.*

Hot Pepper Wax repels insects and animals without harming them. *Courtesy of Hot Pepper Wax.*

Sites

Primary, Secondary, and Tertiary Sites

Sites are affected – either for better or worse – throughout the company's entire life. A site generally refers to a specific geographic location. For a company, the site typically is where the company's facilities are located. My use of the term, however, is much broader.

A site contains not just spatial but also relational and temporal components. Thus, a site is not merely a spatial backdrop for business activities, but it is part of an ecosystem that, no matter how degraded it is, experiences and is affected by ecological processes, such as rainfall or wind. Of course, human activities also affect a site.

As indicated previously, I have divided the sites into three mutually exclusive types for ease of discussion. I refer to these as the primary, secondary, and tertiary sites, and none is necessarily more important or of higher priority than the others. I suggest that businesses wishing to be green would be accountable to all of them. In this book, a "site" refers not only to a geographic (spatial) location but also to a complex network of simultaneous, overlapping, multi-scaled relationships among biotic and abiotic ecological components. In any site, some of these relationships fall within and some extend beyond the site's conceptually constructed boundaries. Sites are dynamic and continuously change on multiple scales as the circumstances within and around them change. For this book, I developed a typology of sites – referred to as primary, secondary, and tertiary sites – and suggest that businesses need to be accountable to these three site types. *Primary* sites are those that a company inhabits through its facilities. They are the specific locations of corporate headquarters, storage facilities, and even non-terrestrial or temporary facilities, such as boats or spacecraft. *Secondary* sites refer to the places that businesses use for their resources. Examples might include a bauxite mine, a river used for hydropower, or a forest from which the firm takes some of the materials it uses in production or for facility construction or renovation. *Tertiary* sites are those locations that are affected by businesses and might include such diverse locales as the global climate, the ozone layer, or a frog's reproductive organs.

Even when a business has identified its particular sites, it might be difficult to track some of the effects that it has on those sites. That is because it requires a company to learn about the sites' ecological characteristics and processes and comprehend the company's effects on those processes, some of which may not be apparent. For example, a company may be able to quantify the siltation that it causes in a nearby river; however, until it really learns a site well, it might not know how that siltation affects a particular beaver family that lives in that river or a particular plant species upon which a certain population of migrating birds depends.

Migratory birds can be affected by changes in the areas upon which they rely during their long journeys. *Townsend.*

Additionally, it might be impossible to know the precise life cycle impacts that a company's products have on specific sites once its products are out of its control – for instance, once they are transported to warehouses and stores or purchased, used, and disposed of by customers. Tracking the life-cycle effects of their products may be a little less problematic for companies that lease their products and take them back for recycling or reuse at the end of their useful lives.

Greening Primary Sites

Most of today's businesses that are interested in greening focus only on greening their primary sites – those places where their facilities are located. Like facilities, primary sites (it might have multiple facilities) have a life cycle that begins at the conception and design phase. It is important that environmental health drive the company's relationship with its primary site(s) because of its potential to regenerate or enhance environmental health.

The construction phase of the site typically begins with deforestation, land-moving, paving, and other landscape-related activities that are associated with the development of facilities and subsequent landscaping. Because sites often are so affected by facilities construction, they could be said to go through two construction processes – that of facilities (a degradation process) and that of landscaping (a reconstruction and, often, a degrading process). While landscaping typically focuses on making a site look pleasing, it rarely focuses on making it healthy by rebuilding soils, strengthening existing ecological communities, reintroducing native species (which generally require less water and care), and so on.

By studying its local and regional ecosystems, a company can become more informed about the plants that are native to its primary site. *Townsend.*

131

The life cycle of a site from the company's perspective also includes the habitation phase, which comprises site use and maintenance. Common activities might include pruning, weeding, pesticide treatments, and mowing. Many companies have landscapers visit regularly to spray pesticides and use energy-intensive leaf blowers, trimmers, and mowers to keep a landscape looking manicured. However, today's greener landscape habitation practices include avoiding the use of chemical fertilizers and pesticides; maintaining landscapes by hand or with low-energy equipment; and working to restore the health of degraded ecosystems.

"Demolition" does not mean the same thing for a site as it does for a building since the site always will exist in some state or other. Some sites undergo seasonal demolition. For instance, landscaping companies might be called in seasonally to remove one species of flowering plant and replace it with another. Plants often are discarded rather than reused or sold to consumers. These practices are energy-intensive and wasteful. They also do not allow ecological communities to develop and mature; for instance, landscaping plants often are not native species, which means that firms lose the opportunity to renew ecosystems and habitats for local species of flora and fauna. Moreover, by removing the plants, root systems are unable to develop fully, and this inhibits or degrades nutrient cycling, hydrological cycling, the reestablishment of habitat, and soil health. Instead, the purpose of green site development can take on a deeper meaning by focusing more on renewing ecological health than on creating a pleasant display although both can be accomplished simultaneously.

Unfortunately, most businesses do not consider their far-reaching environmental impacts on their primary sites, let alone how they affect their secondary and tertiary sites. However, there are many ways in which sites can be greened if companies are committed and use specific ecological knowledge to inform their decisions. In this way, they can help to ensure that their facilities design, products, and activities nourish sites rather than deplete them.

Native plants

Native plants – particularly perennials – are a key component in sustainable sites. That is because they have been part of a co-evolving community of insect, mammalian, aquatic, and other plant species. By keeping native plants in place or by replacing non-native plants with native ones, a company can begin to enlarge habitat for local species, which often lose their needed habitat to human development. Additionally, native plants generally require less water than plants that have not evolved locally. This translates to a lower water bill, particularly during summer months.

The North Carolina National Wildlife Federation has created a voluntary program by which it helps companies to enhance habitat for local wildlife. This program is called Wildlife and Industry Together (WAIT). Like the National Wildlife Federation's Backyard Habitat program, WAIT's primary emphasis is on ensuring that sites provide food, water, shelter, and a place to raise young for multiple species.

Several states and nonprofit organizations also have compiled lists of native plants, and there is a growing number of companies that specialize in selling native plants or seeds. This is particularly important due to the loss of biodiversity around the world. By replanting sites with native species, companies can help to enhance biological diversity, ecological resilience, and evolutionary potential for the larger ecosystem.

Buckeye and fern are native to the Western North Carolina forest. *Townsend.*

Xeriscaping

Xeriscaping® is a word that was used first by Denver, Colorado's Water Department in 1981 following a period of severe drought. The origin of the word comes from the Greek "xeros," or "dry." It refers to a type of water-conserving landscaping, which has proven to be particularly beneficial in drier areas, such as the desert Southwest.

The plants that tend to need the least care and water are native species, which are particularly suited to a specific region. Therefore, the use of native plants is common in xeriscaping. For example, non-native species might have a difficult time in the Tucson, Arizona climate and soils while native scrub and cacti would thrive.

This method of landscaping can reduce water use by 25 to 75 percent (City of Albuquerque, 2005). It requires advance planning as the landscape is divided into three zones. The first is the oasis zone, which is located near the building. This is the area that will require the most care and watering and is the smallest in size. The second zone is a drought-tolerant one that is located further away, with native plants that require watering every week or so. The third and farthest zone is the natural zone. This final zone is made up of native plants that will only require rainwater after they are established.

Though grass might be used as an accent plant, it does not make up most of the xeriscaping lawn. Mulched beds or ground cover comprises much of the landscaped area, keeping the ground cooler in the summer and warmer in the winter, thereby helping to protect the roots. This mulch or ground cover also helps to prevent soil erosion as well as the evaporation of much-needed moisture.

Dust caused by erosion blows off of southern Africa's west coast. *Courtesy of NASA's Visible Earth team (http://visibleearth.nasa. gov/). the SeaWiFS Project, NASA/Goddard Space Flight Center, and ORBIMAGE.*

133

Xeriscaping has many benefits, including less water use, easier landscape maintenance, reduced run-off of irrigation and storm water, healthier soils, lower heating and cooling bills as a result of properly placed shrubs and trees, lower maintenance of topsoil, and more wildlife habitat. All of these benefits can result in reduced landscaping costs.

Watering

Because companies often landscape their sites, tremendous amounts of water are used and wasted. The use of aboveground hoses and sprinklers might result in too little water sinking deeply into the soil. As a result, the plants' roots tend to migrate upward toward the moist surface where they become more vulnerable to temperature swings; this also can destabilize a plant because its roots do not dig deeply into the soil.

Aboveground hoses and sprinklers also can cause runoff. When this occurs, a company can allow the water to soak into the soil before it continues watering. It might take time for the soil to drink in the water deeply. The use of underground watering systems and native plants can help to reduce the amount of water required and wasted. Also, a company can water only in the morning and allow the plants to dry out during the day. When it is watered in the afternoon and to dampen overnight, plants are more susceptible to disease.

Grasscycling

If a company does have a grassy area, it might wish to consider grasscycling. Grass recycling, or "grasscycling," is an activity by which grass clippings are left on a freshly mown lawn. As these clippings decompose, their embodied nutrients nourish the soil and help to ensure a healthy, beautiful lawn without the use of chemicals. Grasscycling offers other benefits as well. For example, it provides mulch for the lawn and helps to keep roots cooler and moister during the summer. It also helps to prevent soil compaction and run-off. Finally, it helps to inhibit the growth of weeds and the introduction of disease.

Although some people are concerned with thatch buildup, excessive thatch is a result of poor watering methods and too much fertilizing rather than grasscycling. If a company is concerned with appearance, it can keep the grass clippings short – one inch or less – so that they can fall down to the soil level and not be seen easily. For longer clippings, it can mow twice, perpendicular to the first cut, in order to shorten them. For the healthiest grass, it can avoid cutting more than one-third of the grasses' length at a time.

Companies that grasscycle also forgo the need to rake and bag grass clippings, both of which account for about half of the time spent "mowing" a lawn. As a result, it saves money. Additionally, money is saved when the grass itself is able to fertilize the lawn and no additional chemical fertilizers are used.

Typically, grass clippings are bagged and taken to a landfill, where they can make up to 10 percent of municipal solid waste (Montgomery County, Maryland, Department of Environmental Protection, *Grasscycle* video). During spring and summer, grass clippings can make up to 50 percent of all household solid waste. Although composting facilities do exist to accept grass clippings, from both financial and energy perspectives, the collection, transport, and processing of these clippings is costly and wasteful.

Grasscyclers need no special mower – just a lawnmower with sharp blades as dull blades can produce a poor cut and allow the introduction of disease. It is important to mow without the bag attached, allowing to the grass to stay on the lawn.

Composting

Each day, employees and companies in the food industry throw away precious minerals as food scraps head for the landfill. The next time company food service workers peel an onion, they can consider transforming that onionskin from trash into compost.

Compost is partially decayed organic material. Dark in color, it crumbles easily and has an earthy smell. When fully decomposed, it becomes dark and powdery and is called humus. Compost can be used to improve the health and fertility of soil in landscapes, gardens, or plant pots. It is particularly helpful for improving degraded soils that contain little organic matter and helps them retain both water and nutrients.

Composting is easy to do and precludes the expense and energy associated with having organic waste hauled away to a centralized facility. Finished compost can be used in indoor office plants, to improve soils, or for mulch in office landscaping gardens.

Chemical Fertilizers & Pesticides

Chemicals fertilizers and pesticides are relatively new additions to the landscape. Used heavily since the twentieth century, these products are known to disrupt ecological processes and cause harm to biota, including beneficial organisms. Such chemicals have gotten into our waterways, air, drinking water, and food supplies.

They also have decreased the vitality of soils and made plants more vulnerable to disease and infestation.

Algal blooms like this one off the coast of Portugal have many causes, including pollution from pesticides and fertilizers. *Courtesy of Jacques Descloitres, MODIS Land Rapid Response Team at NASA GSFC, and NASA's Visible Earth team (http://visibleearth.nasa.gov/).*

Some non-native species become invasive, replacing local species that once played key ecosystem roles. *Townsend.*

Most chemical fertilizers provide plants with only a few nutrients, such as phosphorus, nitrogen, and potassium. This "diet" does not provide the long-term nutrients that plants need in order to be healthy. Because many landscapes are created using annuals, long-term plant health often is not taken into consideration. However, this means that plants grown in depleted soils provide less nutritional value for the species that eat them. This can have long-term health effects on species, their offspring, and the evolutionary process as human activities reduce other species' abilities to survive.

Many pesticides and other biocides (e.g., fungicides, herbicides) are toxic to humans and other animals. Most commercial pesticides contain chemicals that can cause cancer, birth defects, neurological problems, reproductive problems, kidney damage, liver damage, and harm to babies.

If a company must fertilize with something more than grass and other plant clippings, it can use a slow-release, organic fertilizer. Fertilization should occur only in the fall before the first frost arrives.

Mowers

Most lawn mowers are environmentally damaging because mowers are run using gasoline or electricity. To avoid both the air pollution and the noise pollution associated with gas and electric mowers, a company can use a manual push mower. These have staged a comeback in recent years and come in a variety of sizes.

If the landscape is larger and the idea of a push mower is unappealing, the company can use a re-chargeable, battery-powered lawnmower. These are more energy-efficient than gas-powered lawn mowers. Additionally, they tend to be quieter, cause less pollution, and are easier to maintain.

For those businesses that want to try something different, there are self-directed solar powered lawn mowers. These mowers sense when there are changes in the landscape, such as flower gardens, and turn themselves accordingly.

Leaf Blowers

In spite of their popularity, leaf blowers are energy-hungry tools that cause air pollution, noise pollution, and may cause hearing loss in unprotected users. For every hour of operation, leaf blowers release five pounds of pollution (City of Portland's Office of Sustainable Development, 2002). The greener alternative to a leaf blower is the good, old-fashioned rake.

Case Study: Patagonia

Patagonia has been mindful of the environmental impacts of its facilities and has sought to be greener through better architectural design, improvements in energy use, and the reuse of materials. The company requires all of its divisions to decrease the environmental damage associated with building construction and operations. Toward this end, the company renovated its headquarters building using greener products, such as reclaimed materials and recycled concrete and steel.

In 1996, the company employed greener methods to build its new Patagonia Customer Service Center outside Reno, Nevada. Photovoltaic panels were incorporated into the building, and they provide some of its energy. Unlike most buildings, the company's facilities were designed to heat only workstations and not other areas of the building. It does this by using 205 radiant heat panels and a closed-loop heating system that loses very little heat. Smart mirrors on the roof follow the sun's movements and reflect daylight into the building while vents on the roof draw in fresh air and allow it to circulate through the building. With regard to construction materials, Patagonia used formaldehyde-free, compressed field straw in some of its interior walls and 100 percent recycled polyester carpeting. Countertops in the bathrooms are made of 100 percent recycled plastic. Additionally, Patagonia created an organic garden that is cared for by the staff. The plants in the landscape require little water. Runoff from the parking lot and roof are filtered and used to irrigate the landscape.

Patagonia was the first company in California to make a commitment to use 100 percent wind energy for all of its California facilities. The company has reduced its annual energy consumption by about 20 percent, which has offset the cost of the company's conversion to 100 percent renewable energy (Rowledge, Barton, and Brady 1999, 108).

Facilities & Site-related Activities

Companies that want to green their facilities and sites might carry out several activities, including:

* Avoid building unless there is no other choice – the greenest facilities are none at all. Instead, consider renovating an existing building.

* If you must build, consider using a brownfield or already degraded site.

* Use pervious paving to allow water to soak into the ground, thereby feeding the soils underneath and recharging the groundwater.

* Design and build facilities that work with the site, taking advantage of natural windbreaks, solar orientation, and other features.

* Use non-toxic, natural materials in constructing and renovating facilities.

* Consider environmental impacts throughout the life cycles of both facilities and sites.

* Support the ecological systems in which the company's facilities are embedded.

* Ensure the site's health by keeping harmful development to a minimum and regeneration to a maximum.

* Restore the site's health by planting native plants and providing healthy habitat for native species of insects, animals, and other organisms.

* Support the natural flows of water and remove unnecessary blockages that have been added.

* Ensure that no toxic pesticides or plant-related products are used inside or outside.

Summary

This chapter explored the importance of greening company facilities and sites. Facilities refer to any structures in which the company exists or that the company uses. They can be as varied as airports, office buildings, cruise ships, and underground bunkers. Sites are those places that a company inhabits, uses for resources, and affects. This definition of sites is far broader in scope than those generally used in greening company landscapes. As a result, it requires a greater degree of environmental awareness and accountability from companies.

Interface employees work to "redesign commerce" by taking inspiration and lessons from the natural world in their product designs. *Courtesy of Interface Flooring Systems.*

Chapter 7
Greening Your Products and Services

This chapter examines the need to green products and services. It asks if all products should exist and provides an example of industrial ecosystems. Then, it touches briefly on a few issues related to the greening of production and provides some examples of greener products and services.

The Importance of Greening Products and Services

Just as greening the other four elements is important for any company interested in sustainability, greening a company's products and services is essential. Though greening products and services requires businesses to undergo some fundamental changes in their manufacture and other areas, it can result in some fairly substantial benefits for companies. These include an enhanced reputation, a competitive edge over other businesses, the creation of new business opportunities for greener products and technologies, increased profits, positive publicity from the development of greener products, staying ahead of legislation, gaining stakeholder (e.g., employee, customer) loyalty, and raising customer awareness regarding the environmental impacts of their purchasing decisions.

Truly green products and services are those that benefit the environment throughout their entire lives. Their lives begin with conception and design and in- clude materials extraction and transport, product manufacture and use, and recycling or disposal. Green products and services do not harm their manufacturers, users, or the environment. The life cycle of company services also needs to be considered, which includes the entire development process of the service – from planning and organization to the offering and disuse of the service.

Truly green products and services of the future would have several important qualities throughout their entire life cycles, a few of which do not exist and might be difficult to imagine today. From their concept and design stages, the product or service would be imagined and designed to do more ecological and social good than harm, giving back more than it takes. Like the complex "products" of nature, it would be designed not for one purpose but for multiple functions for numerous species.

Nature's "products" have multiple functions and benefit numerous species. *Townsend*.

The energy that would be required to make and transport it would be 100 percent renewable, while the materials from which it is made come either from recycled products, thereby placing no burden on virgin resources, or from readily renewable resources.

Trees provide food, shelter, and a place to raise young for multiple species; are actively engaged in the hydrological and nutrient cycles; and are valued as a resource for human use. *Townsend.*

Its manufacture, use, and disposal would be healthy for producers, users, or others, including other species. This vision can be a guiding one as firms move toward redefining the business and manufacturing paradigm.

Even though today's greener products and services are several steps away from giving back at least as much as they take from an ecological perspective, they still have many important qualities. These include increased resource-efficiency (e.g., materials, energy, water, labor), the use of at least some renewable energy sources for manufacturing, transport, use, and all other energy-intensive aspects of the product life cycle, and no toxicity to the environment, manufacturers, and users.

Wind turbine operating in Baja, Mexico. *Townsend.*

Photovoltaic array at Interface Flooring Systems facility in LaGrange, Georgia. *Courtesy of Interface Flooring Systems.*

Some qualities that are associated with enhanced environmental performance, such as creating zero waste, remains a dream in most producers' minds. However, U.S. carpet manufacturers Collins & Aikman and Interface, Inc., have begun to extend their product responsibilities by retrieving their customers' old carpets and using them as materials for new products. In 1998, Collins & Aikman realized a 300 percent increase in production and achieved zero landfill waste (Motavalli 2001).

Durability has become another issue related to greener products. Some (DeSimone and Popoff 1997) have suggested that products should be durable and of high quality so that they last longer and need not be replaced unnecessarily. Although durability is an important feature for many products, I would qualify this by stating that products should have *durability appropriate to their functions*. This means that products with short life spans should not be designed for longevity (e.g., disposable chopsticks made of wood, non-recyclable plastic carry-out containers).

On the farm. *Courtesy of Food for Thought.*

Instead, the product's use should be matched with its materials and construction. If not intended for re-use, products with short life spans should be constructed to break down or be taken apart easily and their parts recycled easily at the end of their useful lives. For example, packaging that is made from corn-based plastics rather than petroleum-based products indicates a recognition that products that are intended to be short-lived need to be made of materials that can cycle back into the environment easily. However, such packaging would need to be made of corn that is grown free of pesticides and artificial fertilizers. Wal-Mart's recent switch to corn-based plastic packaging (made of polylactic acid) is an example of a mainstream giant moving in a greener direction. The company's vice president for product development and private brands, Matt Kistler, stated, "With this change to packaging made from corn, we will save the equivalent of 800,000 gallons of gasoline and reduce more than 11 million pounds of greenhouse gas emissions," (Brubaker, 2005, C1). The company anticipates that there will be more stability surrounding the price of corn-based plastic than there is for petroleum-based plastics, which have been increasing due to the rise in oil prices. This switch to corn-based packaging strengthens the market for Cargill subsidiary NatureWorks L.L.C., a producer of corn-based plastics.

Should This Product Exist?

A company's greenness depends not only on the usual list of green attributes (e.g., green materials, renewable energy, compostable/biodegradable), but it also depends on the inherent value of the products that it makes (North 1992). For example, some products might be inherently incompatible with sustainability (Winsemius and Guntram 2002). Regardless of how little energy it takes and how green the materials are that are used to make a product, companies and societies need to begin identifying those products that have true value and determine what types of products and services they want in the future. Each product and service that a firm provides will alter ecosystems, and firms will need to be wise in determining which (human and non-human) resources to use to ensure that only products of value to humans and the rest of nature are created. It takes more than recycled materials and solar energy to make a green product. It takes a worthy purpose and ecological benefits – not just the minimization of ecological harm.

Perhaps there will be a time in the future when this is not true, but, today, the greenest products are

Many items are so durable they outlive their usefulness and are not cycled back into production – biological or technical – at the end of their useful lives. *Townsend.*

no products. In other words, if a manufacturer is torn between the notion of developing a new product and not developing one, the best answer from an ecological perspective would be to decide against developing that product. However, some companies develop greener products to replace less green ones, and this might prove a useful strategy as we transition to sustainability. The corollary for existing products is to take harmful goods off the market. The same can be said of many companies as well – that the greenest companies are the ones that do not exist but that, in the transition toward sustainability, perhaps it is best to replace non-green companies with greener ones.

An important note: Companies should never contract out their dirtier jobs and, then, sell themselves as green (North 1992). It is dishonest and, if discovered, is likely to result in the loss of trust among multiple stakeholders and call into question the company's overall integrity.

Industrial Ecosystems

One of the ways in which some companies have sought to develop greener products and services has been through the creation of industrial ecosystems.

Industrial ecosystems are created when companies form relationship networks in order to use one another's wastes and byproducts, thereby reducing their inputs of natural resources and their outputs of waste. In this way, industrial ecosystems are meant to mimic the interdependent processes of ecosystems.

Richards, Allenby, and Frosch[1] (cited in Stead and Stead 1996) have written that there are three increasingly difficult stages of industrial development. The first stage is the Type I industrial ecosystem, which represents the classical industrial model. It is represented by linear processes of inputs and outputs and significant material and energy waste. Though the Type II industrial ecosystem is characterized by some recycling of both materials and energy, it still relies on linear input-output processes using virgin materials and funneling waste into ecosystems. The Type III industrial ecosystem is represented by "ecologically symbiotic" business relationships that rely strictly on renewable energy inputs and closed-loop operations as nearly all materials that are used are recycled. The only type of waste produced in this third stage of industrial evolution is heat. This stage is meant to mimic mature ecosystems with minimal entropy.

Businesses are looking to nature for ideas on environmentally friendly processes and products. *Townsend.*

These shells are beneficial throughout their life cycles, providing housing for organisms that live inside them and breaking down into minerals that can be reabsorbed and used in their ecosystem. *Townsend.*

Kalundborg, an eco-industrial park in Denmark, provides an example of a system that is somewhere between a Type II and Type III industrial ecosystem. Several companies at Kalundborg exchange wastes. For example, a coal-fired power plant produces waste heat, waste steam, and gypsum. An aquaculture facility uses the power plant's waste heat while a Novo Nordisk pharmaceutical plant uses waste steam from the power plant. Meanwhile, the pharmaceutical plant processes its sludge and turns it into fertilizer for local farmers. A Statoil oil refinery also uses waste steam from the power plant while the power plant uses some of the wastewater that Statoil produces. A plasterboard manufacturer uses the power plant's waste gypsum rather than virgin gypsum. Together, these companies reduce their yearly resource use by 600,000 cubic meters of water, 30,000 tons of coal, and 19,000 tons of oil, thereby saving between $12 and $15 million annually (Winsemius and Guntram 2002).

Natural ecosystems can serve as models for businesses that wish to move beyond mimicry and toward intentional ecological integration. *Townsend.*

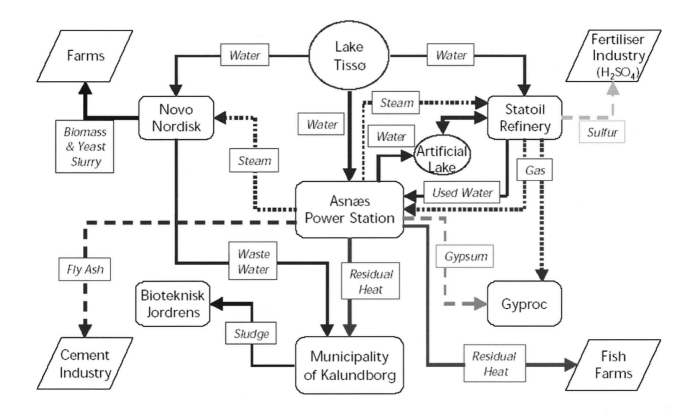

The Industrial Symbiosis in Kalundborg, Denmark. *Courtesy of UNEP (Environmental Management for Industrial Estates: Information and Training Resources, Case Study/Kalundborg – p. 2, http://www.unepie.org/pc/ind-estates/ pdf_documents/Resource Kit/05 percent20Case percent20Studies/01 percent20Kalundborg-Case-Study.pdf).*

The industrial ecosystem typology put forward by Richards, Allenby, and Frosch is an excellent one because it helps to define industrial *evolution* while providing a direction and vision for businesses that are working toward sustainability. Though it is a vast improvement over most of today's business practices, I propose that this Type III industrial ecosystem ultimately will not result in sustainable industry. Nonetheless, it will provide a vitally important transitional step to what I would imagine is a Type IV industrial ecosystem.

This Type IV industrial ecosystem would be a business-ecological system. This system would move beyond the concept of businesses closing the resource and waste loop with one another and would focus, instead, on *closing the loop with nature itself*. In other words, Type III industrial ecosystems are a brilliant solution to today's glut of technical resources – those human-made materials and products with which Earth's ecosystems have not evolved and that either accumulate as waste or cause harm as pollutants. Type III industrial ecosystems will work as long as there are

technical (and biological) resources and wastes for companies to share. Eventually, however, today's technical resources are likely to degrade in quality as they are reused repeatedly and will need to be replaced by new resources – hopefully, biological ones. When this occurs, and as the demand for biological resources continues over time, businesses will need to know how to relate to nature in a way that meets the needs and desires of humans and all other life on the planet. Though many of today's greener businesses are seeking ways to mimic nature by closing their waste loops with other businesses, they are missing one key element: nature's cycles of production, waste, and other activities *include* humans and human enterprise. However, many businesses still operate within the old humans-as-separate-from-nature paradigm and seek to develop cycles that *exclude* nature or, at least, keep it somewhat peripheral. This approach is inherently nonsustainable because it is based on practices that, while greatly improved, will hasten entropy. Yet, businesses that wish to be sustainable will need to move on to a regenerative, relational approach with nature.

Therefore, in this fourth stage, rather than developing networks of business that use one another's resources and exchange one another's wastes, industries will need to open up their relationships to nature, itself, so that nature is an active partner in industrial ecosystems. Rather than simply modeling industrial relationships after natural systems, but excluding those systems from an explicit relationship, firms will need to include ecosystems in those relationships for mutual benefit. Thus, business enterprises will need to develop proactive, adaptive, ecologically informed *partnerships with ecosystems* in ways that benefit both.

Working with Suppliers

A company's products are not green as long as its supplies are not green. After all, as far as products are concerned, sourcing materials is one important step in the product's life cycle. Nearly all companies are involved with suppliers of some sort – whether it is to purchase office supplies for their daily operational activities or buying supplies for manufacturing processes or services. Regardless, companies should focus on identifying suppliers that offer greener products and that are green in the other elements of their businesses as well.

Firms with existing supplier relationships might want to educate suppliers about why greening is important and help them transition to greener practices. If suppliers are not responsive to green requests, companies can look for greener suppliers. Some companies, such as Ben & Jerry's and Apple Computer, have boycotted certain suppliers when their suppliers did not follow the companies' social and environmental codes of conduct (Winsemius and Guntram 2002).

Commercial Equipment

Most companies use a significant amount of energy to power their commercial equipment. Such equipment can include motors, lighting, transformers, elevators, refrigeration equipment (e.g., vending machines, walk-in freezers), heat pump water heaters, and so on. Other equipment used at various stages of product/service life cycles varies by industry, such as equipment used in farming, forestry, fisheries, agriculture, mining, and metal casting, etc. Because this equipment can use a tremendous amount of energy, policies have been developed to discuss energy savings associated with their use. For information on reducing energy use in commercial equipment, visit the web sites of the American Association for Energy Efficient Economy (www.aceee.org) or the Energy Star® program (www.energystar.gov).

Eliminating Waste

The concept of eliminating all waste associated with business activities has been mentioned previously. *Zero waste* is a concept that has been embraced by government, industry, and individuals alike. That is because waste is a symptom of an inefficient activity or set of processes. In nature, there is no waste; instead, every "waste" product cycles back into ecosystems. Companies that embrace the concept of zero waste are interested in mimicking nature by creating a closed-loop system by which waste is either prevented or can be cycled back into production.

Case Study: Patagonia

Over a decade ago, Patagonia began to look into the environmental effects of its own activities. It studied the lifecycle impact of the four fibers that it used for most of its clothing – cotton, wool, polyester, and nylon. Though the company expected that synthetic fibers would cause harm, it was surprised to learn of the severe environmental effects associated with conventional cotton. Cotton is the world's most pesticide-intensive crop grown, far from being a truly natural fiber by the time it is harvested (Bennett, 2002).

By studying the environmental and human histories of their local and regional landscapes, companies can find opportunities to feed back into their ecosystems through their products and services. *Townsend*.

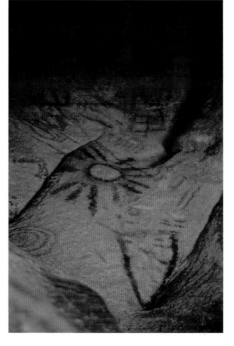

In 1992, Patagonia took some of its suppliers on a tour of cotton farms in the San Joaquin Valley in order to show them the great differences between organic and environmentally damaging, conventionally grown cotton farming. It also has taken over one-third of its employees on such tours. The company believed that by making the environmental impacts of its work personal, it could make a positive difference. In 1994, Patagonia committed to use only 100 percent organic cotton in all of its product lines by 1996.

The company held a three-day conference for its suppliers in 1996. Incorporated into its video presentation of cotton fields was the message that Patagonia and its suppliers can and should leave a better legacy. The message was, "It is not Exxon – it is us. The problem is ours. It is not OK to assign blame for environmental degradation elsewhere – the production, distribution, and use of Patagonia products is causing damage" (Rowledge, Barton, and Brady 1999, 102).

Cotton fields. *Courtesy of Patagonia.*

Organic cotton display. *Courtesy of Patagonia.*

Moreover, Patagonia developed marketing materials to communicate to its customers and others about the environmental harm created by conventionally grown cotton. However, the company had to determine what to do about the increased costs of purchasing only 100 percent organic cotton since organic cotton can cost between 15 and 40 percent more than conventionally grown cotton. Patagonia decided to absorb some of the costs itself and asked its customers to absorb some as well by accepting no more than a 20 percent price increase in the company's cotton products.

Patagonia also asked that others help to create a market for organic cotton. It persuaded Nike, Adidas, and Levi's to commit to ordering three bales of organic cotton for every 100 bales of conventional cotton that they purchased. In order to help create a stable market for organic cotton, in 1997, Patagonia created a new business called "Beneficial Ts." This has become a successful company that sells plain organic cotton T-shirts.

As far as its other fabrics are concerned, in 1993, Patagonia created a synthetic fleece fabric, "Synchilla," from recycled soda bottles. This decision alone prevented more than 100 million bottles from being disposed of in landfills over a six-year period. It also saved a great deal of oil, which would have been used to make synthetic fleece. Moreover, the company moved away from the use of PVCs in some of its products and is looking into using less environmentally harmful dyes as well.

Organic cotton extension cord pants. *Courtesy of Patagonia.*

Men's polo shirt made of organic cotton. *Courtesy of Patagonia.*

Recognizing that its clothing manufacture resulted in waste fabric on the cutting room floor (about 18 percent), Patagonia started an infant clothing line called "Seedling." The company's infant clothes are made of scraps left over from the manufacture of the outdoor clothing for which the company became known.

Ultimately, the company is interested in closing the product loop and eliminating waste by using materials that can be composted or that can be reused in manufacture. All in all, Patagonia's efforts to minimize production and facilities waste have resulted in a cleaner company. In the 1990s, the company opened a customer service and distribution center in Reno, Nevada. In the first two and a half years after it opened, that center created only three 36-40-yard dumpsters of waste (Rowledge, Barton, and Brady 1999, 110).

Synchilla vest. *Courtesy of Patagonia.*

Products & Services-related Activities

There are several steps that a company can take in order to green its products and services. These include:

* Consider the environment in every stage of the product or service, from the product's/service's conception, design, and extraction of raw materials to its transport, production, use, and disposal/recycling.

* Develop products that require little energy and other resources (e.g., water) to use and maintain.

* Manufacture products that are non-toxic. For existing products, replace toxic materials with non-toxic ones.

* Educate consumers about the impacts of non-green products and why greener products are important. This might be one of the only ways that consumers have to learn about the environmental impacts of particular products.

* Transition to renewable energy sources to power production processes.

* Work with suppliers to ensure that they and their products are environmentally friendly.

* Create products that are appropriately durable.

* Ensure that products benefit the environment throughout their lives, including their disposal, by feeding resources back into ecosystems.

Summary

This chapter discussed the need for a company to green its products and services. It explored the importance of greening a product/service through its entire life cycle. It also addressed the need to green the supply chain and identify greener suppliers in order to ensure that a product/service is green through its life cycle.

The chapter suggested that a company interested in sustainability might choose to not develop or to discontinue offering one of its products/services if it learns that it causes environmental harm. Finally, it stated that companies will need to enter into mutually beneficial relationships with nature in order to be ecologically sustainable.

Companies will need to take the road less traveled to achieve
ecological sustainability. *Townsend.*

Chapter 8
The Future of Green Business

This chapter provides a brief overview of this book. Then, it suggests what I believe to be the future direction of green business.

The move toward greening has occurred against a backdrop of changing social, economic, and environmental forces. Though some have suggested that firms' increased attention to the environment is just a fad, green business research seems to indicate otherwise. Few companies were considering the environment seriously in the early 1990s; however, the majority of large companies today are reported to incorporate environmental considerations into their strategic decision-making processes. Companies have begun to use green business best practices, voluntarily sign onto corporate codes of conduct, and adopt goals, such as sustainable development and the triple bottom line (see Glossary). With a growing number of companies committing to ecological sustainability and/or other green business principles, green business is likely to continue to gain momentum and become increasingly sophisticated.

Despite the environmental progress made by greener companies, some (Rowledge, Barton, and Brady 1999) have expressed uncertainty regarding the exact approach needed to achieve ecological sustainability. Moreover, Winsemius and Guntram have stated that a proactive response to greening "can be scary since the very nature of the business might be challenged" (2002, 17). For example, "the service or product – say, cars or detergents (as we know them today) – is inherently incompatible with sustainability if the global atmosphere or waters are not able to carry the burden" (Winsemius and Guntram 2002, 17).

Large-scale salt mining and transport on the Baja peninsula in Mexico. *Townsend.*

Others have indicated that today's best companies are not sustainable. Rowledge, Barton, and Brady have stated, "Our corporations and society are a long way from the end-point of an environmentally and socially sustainable industrial system" (1999, 16). They have added, "We deeply understand the shortcomings of industry, even those companies described here [*Volvo, Suncor, AssiDoman, Patagonia, Interface Flooring Systems, Sony, ASG, SC Johnson, DaimlerChrysler, Center for Technology Assessment, Henkel, SJ Rail, TransAlta*] as being exemplary.... We see the fatal flaws in our current system of commerce, the cultural *zeitgeist*, and the societal metabolism in which today's organisations are embedded" (Rowledge, Barton, and Brady 1999, 16). Similarly, Elkington has stated, "Although many of the companies profiled in this [*Rowledge, Barton, and Brady's*] book of case studies have already been recognised for their environmental and/or social achievements, they are not – and most would not claim to be – anywhere near their final destination" (Foreword to Rowledge, Barton, and Brady 1999, 14).

This is partially a result of current green business best practices. Though these best practices have decreased the environmental harm caused by many companies, they do not and cannot result in green businesses for one or more of several reasons. First, their reliance on *reduction and replacement (not renewal) strategies* means that they depend on resource efficiency and replacing toxic substances with less toxic ones. Though these practices are important, they are not enough to result in ecological sustainability. Second, today's green business best practices use almost exclusively *quantitative tools*, which neglect the qualitative aspects of ecosystems. Third, they often fail to incorporate all *elements* of a business in their greening. These elements are defined here as the company's mission, employees, operations, facilities and sites, and products and services. Fourth, many green business best practices address only *single scales* in space and time rather than the multiple scales within and across ecosystems and the relationships among those scales. Fifth, though standardization can make greening easier, many best practices are *generic* in their approaches, meaning that they are not informed or driven by the specific constraints and opportunities of particular sites. Sixth, most best practices are not *multi-disciplinary* and *transdisciplinary*, thereby offering a somewhat limited perspective and approach to the greening of business. Seventh, by using best practices, many companies wish to *reduce their environmental harm* in order to achieve ecological sustainability. As important as these practices have been in helping firms to improve their environmental performances, such approaches will make

sustainability impossible, as anything less than renewing ecological systems will result in a rapid increase toward entropy. (These issues will be discussed in more depth in an upcoming book.)

If green business best practices are to result in ecologically sustainable companies, they will need to overcome these limitations. This is not to say that green business best practices should not be employed. Together, these best practices have made an enormous difference in reducing the environmental harm done by firms and should be embraced wholeheartedly until improved best practices become available. However, many practitioners in the field of greening recognize that most of today's best practices ultimately cannot deliver us to economic-ecological sustainability regardless of the progress made thus far.

If businesses are to become ecologically sustainable, they will need to use an ecologically based approach to greening. In essence, they will need to understand how ecosystems function in general and develop local ecological knowledge with regard to the sites that they inhabit through their facilities, use for resources, and otherwise affect. Then, they will need to focus on ecological renewal in order to rebuild natural capital. Ultimately, green business will be characterized by renewing ecosystem health through the creation of mutually beneficial business-to-nature (B2N), integrated relationships. I refer to this as *business ecology*.

This book suggested that only by greening in their entirety will a firm have a hope of becoming ecologically sustainable. However, incorporating the entire firm into greening activities is only half the picture. Companies that wish to move beyond reducing their environmental harm will need to develop ecologically based, site-specific approaches.

Firms that wish to be green will need to integrate with ecosystems in mutually beneficial ways. *Townsend.*

Therefore, firms will need to green in their entirety, which, in this book, is characterized as the five elements of greening. Each of these elements needs to be integrated into any firm's greening efforts. Though the green business literature has recognized the need to green firms in their entirety, that "entirety" often is left undefined and varies across the bodies of literature.

Furthermore, companies will need to embrace business ecology or something akin to it if they wish to achieve or move significantly toward ecological sustainability. Ecology is the study of the relationship between organisms and their environments. Thus, *business ecology is the study of the reciprocal relationship between business and organisms and their environments. The goal of business ecology is ecological sustainability through the complete ecological synchronization and integration of a business with the sites that the business inhabits, uses, and affects.* Business ecology represents a complete shift in the business paradigm to a business-ecological partnership that takes its lead from the opportunities and constraints of specific sites and ecosystems rather than solely those of economic markets. I believe that this is the only way in which businesses can be ecologically sustainable.

This has repercussions across a variety of disciplines, and this book suggested that greening businesses fully will require expertise from numerous fields. For example, information on green missions is scant but present in the green business literature while suggestions for greening employees and others can be found in the green business and environmental education literatures. Meanwhile, greening operations falls across several literatures, from socially responsible investing and ecological economics to greener transportation. Facilities and sites information is found in the green architecture and landscape design literatures, respectively, while information on greening products is located in the realm of industrial ecology. The multidisciplinary/trans-disciplinary nature of green business might leave companies feeling overwhelmed at having to weave together the patchwork of best practices that emerge from each discipline. Indeed, few green business consulting firms span more than a few disciplines. Nonetheless, companies committed to ecological sustainability will need to include their entire firms in the effort and rely on a broad variety of expertise to do so.

Though the future of green business is uncertain, if current trends are any indication, a growing number of companies will continue to recognize the importance of greening. As this book reported, such recognition might result from increased government regulations, enhanced awareness of the economic benefits of conservation or of being a business pioneer, growing environmental awareness and accountability on the part of business leaders, new environmental catastrophes, and increasing public pressure for businesses to act responsibly with regard to the environment. Despite the cause, it will result in fundamental changes in the relationships between businesses and the environment.

Glossary

These are business, business ecology, design for environment, eco-efficiency, ecology, ecological systems/ecosystems, ecosystem goods and services, landscape, limiting factors, living systems, natural capital, the Natural Step, non-production sustainability strategy, oecology, reduce/reuse/recycle, reduction and replacement strategies, stakeholder, sustainable, sustainable development, and systems thinking/systems theory, triple bottom line, and volatile organic compound. Each is discussed below.

Business: In this book, business refers not only to corporations (one kind of business entity) but to any type of organization, regardless of its legal status (e.g., S corporation, limited liability company, sole proprietorship, non-profit organization). It is used interchangeably with "firm" and "company."

Business Ecology: I define business ecology as the complete ecological synchronization and integration of a business with the sites that it inhabits, uses, and affects.

Design for Environment: Design for Environment (DfE) was developed as a set of practices that promote more ecologically friendly design by incorporating all known environmental factors into the design process. Led primarily by the electronics industry (Allenby, 1999), the goal of DfE is to use eco-friendly production processes that result in eco-friendly products while ensuring competitiveness in both price and performance (Allenby as cited in Stead and Stead, 1996). According to Allenby, DfE is the means by which companies can apply industrial ecology.

Eco-efficiency: The term *eco-efficiency*, coined by Stephen Schmidheiny in his book *Changing Course*, refers to both economic and ecological efficiency. It indicates the efficient use of both economic and ecological resources, thereby creating value for both the environment and the customer (DeSimone and Popoff, 1997).

Ecology: Originating from the word *oecology*, *ecology* is "the study of relationships between organisms and the environment" (Molles 1999, 2). Developed primarily by biologists and zoologists, ecology "signified a dynamic, experimental approach to the study of adaptation, community succession, and population interactions" (Molles 1999, 2). Ecology is important to the discussion of sustainability, which is concerned with maintain-

ing the integrity of natural systems to allow the healthy continuation of life on Earth. For more information on the importance of natural systems and the supportive services that they provide, see Daily 1997.

Ecological Systems/Ecosystems: An ecological system, or ecosystem, as been defined as "[A] community and its physical and chemical environment. Its biotic (living) component includes producers, consumers, decomposers, and detritivores (organisms that feed on non-living organic materials). Its abiotic (nonliving) component includes soils, temperature, and rainfall" (Starr and Taggart, 1989, Glossary). Similarly, it has been defined as "a community of different species interacting with one another and with their nonliving environment of matter and energy" (Miller 2002, 72). Thus, ecological systems refer to networks of relationships among abiotic and biotic elements. Such relationships can occur on multiple scales, from a microscopic soil community to an entire alpine meadow. Brussard et al. (1998) have explained, "Ecosystems are not bounded, balanced, cybernetic systems, although there are some self-reinforcing interactions among some of their components. Furthermore, ecosystems rarely have discrete boundaries because all 'leak' individuals, species, nutrients, and energy to one degree or another" (11). Though some are more bounded than others (a lake versus a field), they are always affected by their contexts on multiple scales. Brussard et al. (1998) have suggested that ecosystems can be divided into three types – high integrity (showing little sign of human influence), impacted (modified by human activity and without much original ecological integrity), and cultural (modified by humans in "structure, composition, and functional organization") (12-13).

Ecosystem Goods and Services: Nature provides many services when its ecosystems are healthy and functioning, including soil building, oxygen production, water purification, climate maintenance, flood control, plant pollination, ecosystem functioning, wetlands development and maintenance, seed dispersal, prairie development and maintenance, nutrient cycling, waste decomposition, protection from harmful solar ultraviolet radiation, and the multitude of other processes and products that Earth provides. Both biotic and abiotic processes work together to produce benefits for all species on many temporal and spatial scales. For instance, hydrological cycling – the uptake and transpiration of water by plants, accumulation and movement in the atmosphere, and release through rain, snow, mist, and other hydrological activities – occurs on multiple scales. This cycling of water occurs globally, regionally, locally, and even microscopically, enlivening ecosystems on numerous spatial scales. In comparison, today's recycling of products appears overly simplistic, typically occurring only on one scale – the scale of the product. Though ecosystem services are important because they are needed for the survival of humans and other species, they also do something else. They provide something that Daily (1997) refers to as *ecosystem goods*. These are the "seafood, forage, timber, biomass fuels, natural fiber, and many pharmaceuticals, industrial products, and their precursors" upon which businesses and others depend (3). To deplete ecosystem services and the goods that they provide and, then, try to recreate them would be impossible because we know so little about how they function. According to the National Research Council, "there are still too many scientific uncertainties to understand relatively 'simple' modifications to ecosystems and to ascribe causality to the observed patterns (as cited in Castilla 2000, 9). Additionally, attempting to recreate ecosystem functions would be extraordinarily expensive to try (Daily 1997, xviii).

Landscape: In ecology, particularly the sub-discipline of landscape ecology, the term "landscape" has been defined as, "an area that is spatially heterogeneous in at least one factor of interest," such as a watershed (Turner, Gardner, O'Neill 2001, 7). It differs from an ecosystem in that, while an ecosystem is defined by its set of relationships and often is viewed as an "irreducible whole," a landscape is defined by its spatial configuration *and* its ecological processes. However, they are similar in that both can refer to an area of any size. For instance, a landscape can be so large as to include several ecosystems or so small that it is visible only with a microscope. Generally, however, landscapes refer to large-scale areas.

Limiting Factors: Limiting factors determine the carrying capacity of an entity in an ecosystem. They include territory, food, water, predators, competitors, and other factors that limit a population's size and ability to survive.

Living Systems: Capra (1996) defined living systems as "integrated wholes whose properties cannot be reduced to those of smaller parts" (36). For Capra (1996), living systems meet the following three criteria: 1) organization ("the configuration of relationships that determines the system's essential characteristics"), 2) structure ("the physical embodiment of the system's pattern of organization"), and 3) life process ("the activity involved in the continual embodiment of the system's pattern of organization") (161).

Natural Capital: The concept of natural capital has been discussed by several authors, including Daily (1997) and Hawken, Lovins, and Lovins (1999). Natural capital refers to the economic value, in human terms, that ecosystem "services" provide. Gretchen C. Daily (1997), a research scientist at Stanford University's Department of Biological Sciences, defines ecosystem services as "…the conditions and processes through which natural ecosystems, and the species that make them up, sustain and fulfill human life" (3).

Natural Step, The: Developed in 1989 by Swedish oncologist Karl-Henrik Robert, The Natural Step (TNS) is a set of four non-prescriptive principles that was developed to identify the basic ecosystem requirements for life. These principles provide a very general, scientifically based framework upon which companies can ground their decisions and operations. Robert used these four principles to identify system boundaries, which he refers to as "system conditions." Violating any of these four system conditions will result in ecological damage.

Non-production sustainability strategy: This indicates a company's decision to stop producing a product due to the environmental harm that the product causes.

Oecology: Coined by German zoologist Ernst Haeckel in the 1860s, oecology was developed in order to study "the multifaceted struggle for existence" discussed in Darwin's *On the Origin of Species* (Real and Brown, 1).

Reduce, Reuse, Recycle: This trio often is said in one breath, but each of the three concepts is different and is listed in order of importance. Reducing is the most important of these three concepts because it is tied to the concept of prevention at the source. One might reduce pollution by turning lights off when they are not in use, by driving less, by buying an item with less packaging. Each of these choices helps to reduce resource use and pollution at the time of initial consumption. Once purchased, many products can be reused until their useful lives are done. If a product cannot be used any longer, it can be recycled and turned into another product. Though recycling is an important activity in minimizing waste, it often is a resource-intensive process. Nonetheless, producing a can made of recycled aluminum rather than virgin aluminum saves a tremendous amount in resources. Once a product exists, it is important to reuse it until it cannot be used anymore.

Reduction and replacement strategies: This refers to the reduced use of resources through efficiency and the replacement of harmful substances with less harmful ones. Most greening efforts employ reduction and replacement strategies rather than regenerative or restorative ones.

Stakeholder: Ulhoi, Madsen, and Hildebrandt (1996) have explained that a stakeholder is a person who both has interest in the firm *and* can affect its direction, viability, or existence (247). These persons can include individuals (human and non-human), communities, local populations, shareholders, boards of directors, environmental organizations, the media, and others who have a "stake" in the impacts of business. Others, however, have suggested that stakeholders are not limited to persons but include other species and the environment. In fact, because all other stakeholders are entirely dependent upon Earth's functioning, the environment is *the* key stakeholder (Stead and Stead 1996; Callenbach et al. 1992; Bansal and Roth 2000).

Sustainable: *Sustainable* comes from the Latin term *sustinere*, which means to uphold or support. In an ecological context, something that is ecologically sustainable supports ecosystem health. Starik and Rands (1995) have suggested that a sustainable company is one that "can continue indefinitely without negatively affecting the *limiting factors* that permit the existence and flourishing of other groups of entities, including other organizations" (909). This means that ecologically sustainable companies will not use natural resources more quickly than they can be renewed naturally, than ecosystems' regenerative rates are exceeded before new technologies or sustainable resources can replace, or than recycling rates (917). In essence, sustainable firms will be those that are locally self-sufficient. I use sustainable and green interchangeably.

Sustainable Development: The concept of "sustainable development" (SD) has gained widespread use since the early 1990s. "Development," derived from the French *developp*(er), means "to bring out the capabilities or possibilities of; bring to a more advanced or effective state" (Dilithium Press, 1989,

394). Based on the definition of its two root words, sustainable development implies drawing out or realizing the potential of something in a supportive manner. The concepts underlying sustainable development are not new. Garrett Hardin's well-known *Tragedy of the Commons* discussed the related idea of carrying capacity (see Glossary of Terms). Moreover, a 1972 article in *The Ecologist*, "Blueprint for Survival," emphasized the need "to create a society which is sustainable and which will give the fullest possible satisfaction to its members" (Hutchinson 1995, 84). The concept of a sustainable society also was mentioned in a 1973 policy statement published by The Conservation Trust. One of the most common interpretations of sustainable development was issued by the Brundtland Commission, which defined it as "development that meets the needs of the present without comprising the ability of future generations to meet their own needs" (Starik and Rands 1995, 908). This definition, while one of the most commonly used, has been criticized for reasons, including what some believe to be its anthropocentric bias as well as a general disagreement on how to achieve it (Brockhoff, Chakrabarti, and Kirchgeorg 1999; Starik and Rands 1995). The definition also does not specify what is sustained (e.g., ecological health, cultural integrity) and what is developed, or brought to a higher level. Additionally, it remains general enough to be unwieldy and open to multiple interpretations depending on individual and organizational values, assumptions, knowledge, and desires. Furthermore, Lee has suggested that it is unlikely that sustainable development will be attained but that, like the concepts of justice and freedom, it is a goal toward which we should strive (as cited in Holling, Berkes, and Folke 1998, 349).

Yet, the basic idea behind sustainable development is that human development should support, rather than degrade, the functioning of Earth's ecological systems. Rowledge, Barton, and Brady (1999) have suggested that "Sustainable development requires the 'dematerialization' of our economy by decoupling economic growth from growth and material resource inputs and waste 'outputs', designing more equitable and socially beneficial industrial practices, and replacing quantitative growth with qualitative development" (34). Costanza (1991) has differentiated between economic growth and economic development. While economic growth indicates a quantitative increase and cannot be sustainable in a context of planetary finiteness, economic development indicates improvement in the quality of life without necessarily increasing resource use (Costanza 1991). However, Pasqual and Souto (2003) have expressed that "most specialist [sic] are beginning to lose faith in the idea that economic development in itself can bring about better environmental quality" (57).

Systems Thinking/Systems Theory: The idea of systems has become important in the greening of business. Capra (1996) has stated that life is not composed of individual parts; rather, it is made of living systems that are defined by "connectedness, relationships, and context" (36). The fact that we see "things" (e.g., trees, people) merely indicates that most of us are unable or have not been trained to perceive systems and their complex interconnections (Capra 1996). As Werner Heisenberg explained, "What we observe is not nature itself, but nature exposed to our method of questioning" (Capra 1996, 40).

Systems theory, supported by discoveries in quantum mechanics, has provided the green business field with insights into how ecological and human systems work thereby giving companies a fresh understanding of their impacts on those systems and potential models for new organizational and product designs. In their efforts to become more ecologically sustainable, a growing number of companies have begun to apply systems thinking (Capra 1996; Laszlo 1996b) to their businesses in order to optimize resources, reduce or eliminate waste, or find a template for sustainability (de Geus 1997; Senge 1990; Wheatley 1999).

Triple Bottom Line: One popular notion of sustainability is that it comprises three factors — environment, society, and equity. Together, these factors sometimes are referred to as the "triple bottom line."

Volatile organic compound (VOC): Harmful substances found in many common products, such as adhesives, paints (including most nail polish), furniture, fabrics, and carpet.

Endnotes

Introduction

1. Ford, for example, is interested in cutting greenhouse gas emissions in its production processes and in its products (Michael J. Radcliffe, "The Auto Industry Responds," *green@work*, 10, November/December 2001).

2. Most companies might be unaware that the diesel engine was invented to run on vegetable oils, and the use of a petroleum-based diesel fuel occurred later.

3. The life cycle impacts of waste oil and virgin oil will differ. I believe that waste oil is environmentally preferable because it is has been used already and is being recycled for use. Meanwhile, growing the market for virgin oil, which generally is produced using petroleum-intensive, non-sustainable agricultural methods, might provide little, if any, environmental benefit.

4. The ISO 14000 family of standards, developed by the International Organization for Standardization in 1996, is used increasingly by companies that want to become greener. ISO 14000 was created to provide a consistent way to monitor and carry out environmental management and to reflect current environmental and design practices and technologies. Through ISO certification, companies and organizations that use ISO standards gain public, government, and industry recognition for their efforts to reduce their harmful effects on the environment. This family of standards includes 23 different standards, each of which covers a broad range of environmental concerns and has its own guidelines and technical reports.

5. What began as the Coalition for Environmentally Responsible Economies, Ceres is an organization that developed a set of principles, known as the CERES Principles, to improve business relationships with the environment.

6. Hemp often is grown without pesticides or synthetic fertilizers and produces a strong yarn that does not require a great deal of processing. Conversely, cotton is the United States' most pesticide-intensive agricultural product. The fact that hemp is grown without the petroleum-based inputs of fertilizers and pesticides, which often contain other components that are environmentally harmful, makes it an environmentally preferable fiber.

7. LEED is the acronym for "Leadership in Energy and Environmental Design." The LEED Green Building Rating System was designed by the U.S. Green Building Council. LEED is a voluntary rating system for buildings. Buildings must meet a variety of criteria related to greener, "high performance" building in order to attain LEED certification.

8. Such a strategy also would include those products that were never created because of their potential environmental harm; however, it is likely that few people would ever be aware of these products simply because they were never developed.

9. The Business Charter for Sustainable Development consists of sixteen environmental management principles for businesses. These principles were designed by the Business Council for Sustainable Development (BCSD), which was created by Maurice Strong, then-Secretary General of the U.N. Conference on Environment and Development, and headed by industrialist Dr. Stephan Schmidheiny. At the time of its creation in 1990, Strong understood the need to bring business and industry into the sustainability dialogue and appointed Schmidheiny, Chairman of the Swiss company UNOTEC, as his principal advisor for business and industry. Schmidheiny assembled the heads of fifty multinational corporations as members of the new BCSD, and, together, they designed a set of principles that are intended to guide the environmental management activities of companies around the world. In 1995, the BCSD merged with the World Industry Council for the Environment to become the World Business Council for Sustainable Development (WBCSD). Today, the WBCSD is a coalition of 170 international companies from twenty industries and forty countries. The Council's primary directive is to promote corporate social responsibility, eco-efficiency, and innovation in order to move toward sustainable development. The BCSD's principles stand out in their focus on issues that are specific to business, such as the need for employee education, advice to customers, and preparing for emergencies.

10. Ecobag, or sandbag, construction was developed largely by California architect Nader Khalili based on sandbag bunkers used in wartime. Buildings are constructed using bags, generally made of burlap, and filled with sand or soil. To learn about Khalili's work, you can visit http://www.calearth.org/

naderkha.htm. He is at the Southern California Institute of Architecture (CalEarth) - http://www.calearth.org/.

11. Developed in France, isochanvre is a building material comprising the pithy interior of hemp stalks and lime.

12. Living "off the grid" refers to a somewhat self-reliant lifestyle in which a household provides for its own energy needs through using one or more methods (e.g., geothermal, passive solar, photovoltaics, hydropower, wind). It also might collect rainwater and process all sewage wastes on site. Therefore, it is not connected to any utilities or human-created water/sewage infrastructures.

13. The use and reliance upon technical nutrients ultimately is not environmentally friendly because it still locks what Earth uses as nutrients into forms that cannot be accessed easily by nature, thereby contributing further to ecological entropy.

CHAPTER 1

1. Ray Anderson is Interface's Chairman of the Board and Chairman of the Board's Executive Committee.

2. An environmental impact assessment is a study that identifies the impacts that a product, service, or activity will have or is likely to have on the environment. Developed to ensure compliance with environmental regulations, it takes into account both qualitative and quantitative measures, such as a product's effects on threatened species and its pollution outputs, respectively.

3. Energy Star is a voluntary program of the Environmental Protection Agency by which equipment manufacturers commit to specific energy-efficiency standards. In exchange, manufacturers are allowed to use the EPA's Energy Star logo on their equipment.

4. The best things that a manager can do to increase the comfort and productivity of a building's users are to provide a) the best lighting possible (daylight) for all employees, b) individual control over their light, temperature, and air flow, and c) better air quality, cooling, and heating.

5. Air-krete is made from magnesium salts and whipped seawater. It is pumped into the wall cavities as a liquid. Then, it foams and fills the wall crevices, hardening into a non-toxic and nonflammable insulation.

6. Because the research into the health effects of PFCs is ongoing, it is difficult to anticipate the long-term impact of 3M's PFC production will have on the company. Although it appeared to have averted a crisis with its initial phase-out announcement, it is too early to know what the penultimate view of 3M's role in PFC production will be. In February 2006, a report on PFC contamination was delivered to the Senate Environment Committee (see http://www.peer.org/docs/mn/06_27_2_pfc_ report.pdf). Additional information is being made public.

CHAPTER 8

1. Deanna Richards is with the Center for Sustainability in Engineering at California Polytechnic State University. Braden Allenby is an Arizona State University's Lincoln Professor of Engineering and Ethics. Dr. Allenby is a former Vice President for Environment, Heath and Safety at AT&T and serves as Chair of the AAAS Committee on Science, Engineering, and Public Policy. Robert Frosch is a senior research fellow at the Center for Science and International Affairs at Harvard University's John F. Kennedy School of Government and at the National Academy of Engineering. He is a former vice president of research at General Motors and former NASA administrator.

M. "Perfluorooctane Sulfonate: Current Summary of Human Sera, Health and Toxicology Data." 1999.
_____. *3M Phasing out Some of Its Speciality Materials Press Release* 2000 [cited October 30 2003]. Available from http://www.chemicalindustry archives.org/dirtysecrets/scotchgard/pdfs/226-0641.pdf#page=1.
_____. *3M's Environmental Tradition* 2003 [cited October 23 2003]. Available from http://www.3m.com/about3m/sustainability/policies_ehs_tradition.jhtml.
_____. *Environmental Highlights* 2003 [cited October 23 2003]. Available from http://www.3m.com/about3m/sustainability/78-6920-0070-2.pdf.
Aarkrog, Asker. "Input of Anthropogenic Radionuclides into the World Ocean." *Deep Sea Research Part II: Tropical Studies in Oceanography* 50, no. 17-21 (2003): 2597-606.
Abe, Joseph M., Patricia E. Dempsey, and David A. Bassett. *Business Ecology: Giving Your Organization the Natural Edge.* Boston, MA: Butterworth-Heinemann, 1998.
Abram, David. *Spell of the Sensuous.* New York, NY: Vintage Books, 1996.
Abram, Stephen. "What's Ahead for 2000? Prognostications from 13 Information Industry Leaders." *Information Today*, January 2000 [cited August 6, 2002]. Available from http://www.infotoday.com/it/jan00/ahead.htm.
Acheson, James M., James A. Wilson, and Robert S. Steneck. "Managing Chaotic Fisheries." In *Linking Social and Ecological Systems: Managment Practices and Social Mechanisms for Building Resilience*, edited by Fikret Berkes and Carl Folke. New York, NY: Cambridge University Press, 1998.
Adam, Barbara. *Timescapes of Modernity: The Environment and Invisible Hazards.* New York, NY: Routledge, 1998.
Adam, Barbara, and Stuart Allan, eds. *Theorizing Culture: An Interdisciplinary Critique after Postmodernism.* New York, NY: New York University Press, 1995.
Adamo, M. Arienzo, M. Pugliese, V. Roca, and P. Violante. "Accumulation History of Radionuclides in the Lichen *Stereocaulon Vesuvianum* from Mt. Vesuvius (South Italy)." *Environmental Pollution.* In press (2003).

Adizes, Ichak. *Corporate Life Cycles: How and Why Corporations Grow and Die and What to Do About It.* Paramus, NJ: Prentice-Hall, 1988.
Alexander, Christopher. *The Timeless Way of Building.* New York, NY: Oxford University Press, 1979.
Allenby, Braden R. *Industrial Ecology: Policy Framework and Implementation.* Englewood Cliffs, NJ: Prentice Hall, 1999.
Amato, Ivan. *Stuff: The Materials the World Is Made Of.* New York, NY: Avon Books, 1997.
American Council for an Energy-Efficient Economy. *Guide to Energy-Efficient Office Equipment.* Washington, D.C.: ACEEE, 1996.
Anderson, Dan. "Expanding Environmental Risk Management." *Risk Management* 46, no. 7 (1999): 21.
Anderson, Ray C. *Mid-Course Correction.* Atlanta, GA: Peregrinzilla Press, 1998.
Andrews, Clinton J. "Putting Industrial Ecology into Place: Evolving Roles for Planners." *Journal of the American Planning Association* 65, no. 4 (1999): 364-75.
Anema, Taco, and Michel Szulc-Krzyzanowski. *World of Energy.* Amsterdam: De Verbeelding Publishers, 2000.
Anheuser-Busch Companies. "Environmental, Health & Safety Report 2000." St. Louis, IL: Anheuser-Busch Companies, Inc., 2000.
_____. *Our Vision.* Anheuser-Busch Companies, Inc., 2002 [cited August 6, 2002]. Available from http://www.anheuser-busch.com/misc/vision.html.
Anonymous. "'Enviropreneurial' Strategy Is a Free-Market Approach." *Marketing News* 31, no. 3 (1997): 22.
_____. "Purchasing Increases Role in Environmental Metrics." *Purchasing* 124, no. 2 (1998): 27.
_____. "In the Green." *CMA Management* 74, no. 6 (2000): 58.
_____. "Accounting for Renewable and Environmental Resources." *Survey of Current Business* 80, no. 3 (2000): 26-51.
Anton-Luca, Alexandru. *Gregory Bateson.* n.d. [cited April 9, 2004]. Available from http://www.indiana.edu/~wanthro/bateson.htm.
Anzovin, Steven. *The Green Pc: Making Choices That Make a Difference.* New York, NY: Windcrest/McGraw-Hill, 1993.

Arrow, Kenneth, Bert Bolin, Robert Costanza, Partha Dasgupta, Carl Folke, C.S. Holling, Bengt-Owe Jansson, Simon Levin, Karl-Goran Maler, Charles Perrings, and David Pimentel. "Economic Growth, Carrying Capacity, and the Environment." *Ecological Economics* 15 (1995): 91-95.

Asmus, Peter. "A Template for Transition: How Mitsubishi and the Rainforest Action Network Found the Natural Step." *Corporate Environmental Strategy* 5, no. 4 (1998): 50-59.

Asner, Gregory P., David E. Knapp, Eben N. Broadbent, Paulo J.C. Oliveira, Michael Keller, Jose N. Silva. "Selective Logging in the Brazilian Amazon." *Science* 310 (2005).

Atkins, W. *The Periodic Kingdom*. New York, NY: BasicBooks, 1995.

Audesirk, Teresa, and Gerald Audesirk. *Life on Earth*. Upper Saddle River, NJ: Prentice-Hall, Inc., 1997.

Auer, Charles. *Phaseout of Pfos*. Internal EPA memo, 2000 [cited October 31, 2003]. Available from http://www.chemicalindustryarchives.org/dirtysecrets/scotchgard/pdfs/226-0629.pdf#page=2.

Aveda Corporation. *Press Releases - Aveda Celebrates Earth Month with the Launch of Indigenous Products....* Aveda, November 2001 [cited August 6, 2002]. Available from http://www.aveda.com/about/press/indigenous_earthmonth02.asp.

———. *Employment*. Aveda, 2002 [cited August 6, 2002]. Available from http://www.aveda.com/about/employment/default.asp.

———. *Press Releases - Profit for the Planet: A Business Model for Sustainability*. Aveda, 2002 [cited August 6, 2002]. Available from http://www.aveda.com/about/press/dcrelease.asp.

———. *What We Do*. Aveda, 2003 [cited October 30, 2003]. Available from http://www.aveda.com/protect/we/default.asp.

———. *What We Do: The Aveda Babassu Community Project*. Aveda, 2003 [cited October 30, 2003]. Available from http://www.aveda.com/protect/we/babassu.asp.

———. *What We Do: Environmental Sustainability Policy*. Aveda, 2003 [cited October 30, 2003]. Available from http://www.aveda.com/protect/we/esp.asp.

———. *Horst Rechelbacher, Aveda Founder*. Aveda, 2003 [cited October 30, 2003]. Available from http://www.aveda.com/about/bio/default.asp.

———. *Facilities*. Aveda, 2003 [cited October 30, 2003]. Available from http://www.aveda.com/about/facilities/default.asp.

———. *The Aveda Mission*. Aveda Corporation, 2003 [cited October 30, 2003]. Available from http://www.aveda.com/home.asp#.

Babakri, Khalid A., Robert A. Bennett, and Matthew Franchetti. "Critical Factors for Implementing Iso 14001 Standard in United States Industrial Companies." *Journal of Cleaner Production* 11 (2003): 749-52.

Badgley, Catherine. "Can Agriculture and Biodiversity Coexist?" In *The Fatal Harvest Reader: The Tragedy of Industrial Agriculture*, edited by Andrew Kimbrell, 199-207. Washington, D.C.: Island Press, 2002.

Ball, Philip. *The Self-Made Tapestry: Pattern Formation in Nature*. New York, NY: Oxford University Press, 1999.

Banerjee, Subhabrata Bobby. "Corporate Environmentalism." *Management Learning* 29, no. 2 (1998): 147.

Bansal, Pratima and Kendall Roth. "Why Companies Go Green: A Model of Ecological Responsiveness." *Academy of Management Journal* 43, no. 4 (2000): 717-36.

Barta, Suzette D. and Mike D. Woods. *Gap Analysis as a Tool for Community Economic Development*. Oklahoma Cooperative Extension Service, n.d. [cited April 13, 2004]. Available from http://osuextra.com/pdfs/F-917web.pdf.

Baskin, Ken. *Corporate DNA: Learning from Life*. Woburn, MA: Butterworth-Heinemann, 1998.

Battelle. "Quality Assurance Project Plan for Empirical Human Exposure Assessment Multi-City Study Sampling Task." Duxbury, MA: Battelle, 1999.

Beets, S. Douglas and Christopher C. Souther. "Corporate Environmental Reports: The Need for Standards and an Environmental Assurance Service." *Accounting Horizons* 13, no. 2 (1999): 129-45.

Bell, Christopher. "The Iso 14001 Environmental Management System Standard: One American's View." *ISO 14000 and Beyond* (1997): 61-89.

Bell, Simon. *Landscape: Pattern, Perception and Process*. New York, NY: E & FN Spon, 1999.

Bellamy, Jennifer A., Daniel H. Walker, Geoffrey T. McDonald, and Geoffrey J. Syme. "A Systems Approach to the Evaluation of National Resource Management Initiatives." *Journal of Environmental Management* 63 (2001): 407-23.

Bennett, David J. *Chinese Farmers Choked – on Pesticide*. The Scientific Alliance, March 4, 2002 [cited November 12, 2005]. Available from http://www.scientific-alliance.org/news_archives/biotechnology/chinesefarmerschoked.htm.

Benyus, Janine M. *Biomimicry*. New York, NY: Quill

Books, 1997.

Berkes, Fikret and Carl Folke. *Linking Social and Ecological Systems: Management Practices and Social Mechanisms for Building Resilience.* New York, NY: Cambridge University Press, 1998.

_____. "Back to the Future: Ecosystem Dynamics and Local Knowledge." In *Panarchy: Understanding Transformations in Human and Natural Systems,* edited by Lance H. Gunderson and C.S. Holling, 121-46. Washington, D.C.: Island Press, 2002.

Berry, Michael A. and Dennis A. Rondinelli. "Proactive Corporate Environment Management: A New Industrial Revolution." *The Academy of Management Executive* 12, no. 2 (1998): 38-50.

Berry, Thomas. *The Dream of the Earth.* San Francisco, CA: Sierra Club Books, 1988.

Berry, Wendell. *Life Is a Miracle.* Washington, D.C.: Counterpoint, 2000.

Bespalchuk, Pavel I., Sergey Kabak, Eugenij Cherstvoy, Yurij Demidchik, Boris V. Dubovik, Dmitry J. Romanovsky, and Alexander Stogarov. "Overview of Research and Future Prospects in Radiation Medicine Based on the Current Health Status in Belarus." *International Congress Series* 1258 (2003): 85-89.

Birkner, Lawrence R. and Ruth McIntyre Birkner. "Tools for Envisioning the Future of Occupational Hygiene." *Occupational Hazards* 64, no. 5 (2002): 79-82.

Bloom, Jeffrey W. "Patterns That Connect: Rethinking Our Approach to Learning and Teaching." Flagstaff, AZ: Center for Excellence in Education, 1999.

Blumberg, Jerald, Georges Blum, and Age Korsvold. "Environmental Performance and Shareholder Value." The World Business Council for Sustainable Development, 1997.

Boodro, Michael. "Armani Leads the Way." *Organic Style,* March/April 2002, 72-81.

Boons, Frank, Leo Baas, Jan Jaap Bouma, Anja De Groene, and Kees Le Blansch. "Trajectories of Greening." *International Studies of Management & Organization* 30, no. 3 (2000): 18-40.

Boons, Frank and Lars Strannegard. "Organizations Coping with Their Environment." *International Studies of Management & Organization* 30, no. 3 (2000): 7-17.

Booth, Wayne C., Gregory G. Colomb, and Joseph M. Williams. *The Craft of Research.* Chicago, IL: The University of Chicago Press, 1995.

Botkin, Daniel B. *Discordant Harmonies: A New Ecology for the Twenty-First Century.* New York, NY: Oxford University Press, 1990.

Boyatzis, Richard E. *Transforming Qualitative Information: Thematic Analysis and Code Development.* Thousand Oaks, CA: Sage Publications, Inc., 1998.

Boyce, Mark S. and Alan Haney, eds. *Ecosystem Management: Applications for Sustainable Forest and Wildlife Resources.* New Haven, CT: Yale University Press, 1997.

Boyd, James. "The Benefits of Environmental Accounting: An Economic Framework to Identify Priorities." Washington, D.C.: Resources for the Future, 1998.

BP. "(Advertisement)." *green@work,* September/October 2001, Inside cover.

Braden, Greg. *Awakening to Zero Point: The Collective Initiation.* Bellevue, WA: Radio Bookstore Press, 1997.

Brockhoff, Klaus, Alok K. Chakrabarti, and Manfred Kirchgeorg. "Corporate Strategies in Environmental Management." *Research Technology Management* 42, no. 4 (1999): 26-30.

Brown, Lester R. "Rising Sea Level Forcing Evacuation of Island Country." *Eco-Economy Update 2001-2, Earth Policy Institute 2001* (2001).

Brubaker, Harold. "Wal-Mart Goes More Eco-Friendly." *The Philadelphia Inquirer,* October 20, 2005, C1.

Brussard, Peter F., J. Michael Reed, and C. Richard Tracy. "Ecosystem Management: What Is It Really?" *Landscape in Urban Planning* 40 (1998): 9-20.

Buchholz, Rogene A. *Principles of Environmental Management: The Greening of Business.* Second Edition. Upper Saddle River, NJ: Prentice Hall, 1998.

Bunch, Richard. "Grey Pinstripes with Green Ties: Preparing Environmental Leaders." *Selections* 15, no. 2 (1999): 1-8.

Thayer, Burke Miller. "Way Station." In *Buildings for a Sustainable America Case Studies,* 23-26. Boulder, CO: American Solar Energy Society, 1994.

Callenbach, Ernest, Fritjof Capra, Lenore Goldman, Rudiger Lutz, Sandra Marburg. *Ecomanagement: The Elmwood Guide to Ecological Auditing and Sustainable Business.* San Francisco, CA: Berrett-Koehler Publishers, Inc., 1993.

Capra, Fritjof. *The Web of Life.* New York, NY: Anchor Books, 1996.

_____. *The Tao of Physics: An Exploration of the Parallels between Modern Physics and Eastern Mysticism.* Boston, MA: Shambhala, 2000.

Cardskadden, H., and D.J. Lober. "Environmental Stakeholder Management as Business Strategy:

The Case of the Corporate Wildlife Habitat Enhancement Programme." *Journal of Environmental Management* 52 (1998): 183-202.

Carson, Rachel. *Silent Spring*. New York, NY: Houghton Mifflin Company, 1962.

Castilla, Juan Carlos. "Rules of Experimental Marine Ecology and Coastal Management and Conservation." *Journal of Experimental Marine Biology and Ecology* 250 (2000): 3-21.

Catron, Bayard L. "Sustainability and Intergenerational Equity: An Expanded Stewardship Role for Public Administration." *Administrative Theory & Praxis* 18, no. 1 (1996): 2-12.

Center for Disease Control (CDC). *Baq Action Plan*. 1998 [cited October 30, 2003]. Available from http://www.cdc.gov/niosh/baqact.html.

Central Intelligence Agency. *The World Factbook*. November 1, 2005 [cited November 11, 2005]. Available from http://www.cia.gov/cia/publications/factbook/rankorder/2001rank.html.

Cespedes-Lorente, Jose, Jeronimo de Burgos-Jimenez, and Maria Jose Alvarez-Gil. "Stakeholders' Environmental Influence. An Empirical Analysis of the Spanish Hotel Industry." *Scandinavian Journal of Management* 19 (2003): 333-58.

Champion, David. "Environmental Management: Spreading the Green." *Harvard Business Review* 76, no. 6 (1998): 20.

Cheremisinoff, Nicholas P. "Conduct a Pollution Prevention Audit - Part 2." *Pollution Engineering* 34, no. 4 (2002): 16-19.

Children's Museum of Pittsburgh (2005). *The Green Museum*. Children's Museum of Pittsburgh, 2005.

Childs, Craig. *The Secret Knowledge of Water: Discovering the Essence of the American Desert*. Seattle, WA: Sasquatch Books, 2000.

Chinander, Karen R. "Aligning Accountability and Awareness for Environmental Performance in Operations." *Production and Operations Management* 10, no. 3 (2001): 276-91.

Christmann, Petra. "Effects of 'Best Practices' of Environmental Management on Cost Advantage: The Role of Complementary Assets." *Academy of Management Journal* 43, no. 4 (2000): 663-80.

City of Albuquerque. *What Is Xeriscape?* [cited November 12, 2005]. Available from http://www.cabq.gov/waterconservation/xeric.html.

City of Portland's Office of Sustainable Development. *Green Pages Household Worksheet* 2002 [cited November 12, 2005]. Available from http://www.sustainableportland.org/greenpages/Work sheet.htm.

Clark, David D. *Affinity between Living Systems Theory Subsystems* 1997 [cited October 23, 2003]. Available from http://www.srl.gatech.edu/education/ME3110/catalog/affinity.html.

Clif Bar. *Moving Towards Sustainability*. 2005 [cited November 13, 2005]. Available from http://www.clifbar.com/ourstory/document.cfm?location=environment&webSubsection=hammond.

Clift, Roland. *Environment '97 Web Page* 1997 [cited 2001]. Available from http://www.environment97.org/framed/reception/r/all_papers/t3.htm.

Coalition for Environmentally Responsible Economies. *The Ceres Principles* 1989 [cited August 8, 2002]. Available from http://www.ceres.org/our_work/principles.htm.

_____. *About Us: Coalition Members* CERES, April 2001 [cited August 6, 2002]. Available from http://www.ceres.org/about/coalition_members.htm.

_____. *About Us: Endorsing Companies* CERES, n.d. [cited August 6, 2002]. Available from http://www.ceres.org/about/endorsing_companies.htm.

Cohen, Stephen, J. Bradford DeLong, and John Zysman. *Tools for Thought: What Is New and Different About the E-Conomy*. Brad DeLong, July 3, 2000 [cited October 30, 2003]. Available from http://econ161.berkeley.edu/OpEd/virtual/technet/TfT.html.

Collins & Aikman. *C&A Floorcoverings*. Melia Design Group, 2001 [cited August 6, 2002]. Available from www.powerbond.com.

Conservation International Foundation. *Conservation Programs – Ecotourism*. CI, 2002 [cited August 6, 2002]. Available from http://www.conservation.org/xp/CIWEB/programs/ecotourism/ecotourism.xml.

Cordano, Mark and Irene Hanson Frieze. "Pollution Reduction Preferences of U.S. Environmental Managers: Applying Ajzen's Theory of Planned Behavior." *Academy of Management Journal* 43, no. 4 (2000): 627-41.

Corraliza, Jose A. and Jaime Berenguer. "Environmental Values, Beliefs, and Actions: A Situational Approach." *Environment and Behavior* 32, no. 6 (2000): 832-48.

Costanza, Robert, ed. *Ecological Economics*. New York, NY: Columbia University Press, 1991.

Costanza, Robert and Carl Folke. "Efficiency, Fairness, and Sustainability as Goals." In *Nature's Services: Societal Dependence on Natural Ecosystems*, edited by Gretchen C. Daily. Washington, D.C.: Island Press, 1997.

Cotlier, Moira. "Gaiam Launches Magalog." *Catalog Age*, September 2001, 6.

Creswell, John W. *Research Design: Qualitative & Quantitative Appro*. Thousand Oaks, CA: Sage Publications, 1994.

Curtis, Fred. "Eco-Localism and Sustainability." *Ecological Economics* 46 (2003): 83-102.

Daily, Gretchen C. *Nature's Services: Societal Dependence on Natural Ecosystems*. Washington, D.C.: Island Press, 1997.

Daily, Gretchen C., Pamela A. Matson, and Peter M. Vitousek. "Ecosystem Services Supplied by Soil." In *Nature's Services: Societal Dependence on Natural Ecosystems*, edited by Gretchen C. Daily. Washington, D.C.: Island Press, 1997.

Daly, Herman E. and John B. Cobb, Jr. *For the Common Good*. Boston, MA: Beacon Press, 1994.

Danish Environmental Protection Agency. *Green Accounting in Denmark* (March 27, 2000) 2000 [cited October 23, 2003]. Available from http://www.mst.dk/indu/05030100.doc.

Dar & Company. *Dar & Company: Inventing Business Models*. Dar and Company, 2001 [cited August 6, 2002]. Available from www.darandcompany.com.

Dar, Vinod. *The Web as Business Ecology*. As cited in Power Executive, September 22, 1999, 1999 [cited August 6, 2002]. Available from http://www.energyecomm.com/bsneco.html.

de Armond, Paul. *Big Body Features: Are Corporate Bodies Really Alive?* Online conference, Posted March 9, 2000 [cited 2001]. Available from http://www.nancho.net/bigmed2000/bbonline.html.

de Geus, Arie. *The Living Company*. Boston, MA: Harvard Business School Press, 1997.

DeLong, Bradford. *Why the Valley Way Is Here to Stay*. May 2000 [cited August 6, 2002]. Available from http://www.business2.com/articles/mag/0,1640,7823,FF.html.

Dermody, Janine and Stuart Hanmer-Lloyd. "Greening New Product Development: The Pathway to Corporate Environmental Excellence?" *Greener Management International*, no. 11 (1995): 73-88.

DeSimone, Livio D. and Frank Popoff. *Eco-Efficiency: The Business Link to Sustainable Development*. Cambridge, MA: The MIT Press, 2000.

Deutsch, Lisa, Carl Folke, and Kristian Skanberg. "The Critical Natural Capital of Ecosystem Performance as Insurance for Human Well-Being." *Ecological Economics* 44 (2003): 205-17.

Dilithium Press, Ltd. *Webster's Encyclopedic Unabridged Dictionary of the English Language*. New York, NY: Gramercy Books, 1989.

Dobers, Peter, and Rolf Wolff. "Managing Ecological Competence: Empirical Evidence and Theoretical Challenges." *Greener Management International*, no. 11 (1995): 32-48.

Dobson, Andrew P. *Conservation and Biodiversity*. New York, NY: Scientific American Library, 1998.

Doppelt, Bob. *Leading Change toward Sustainability*. Sheffield, UK: Greeleaf Publishing Limited, 2003.

Dregne, H., M. Kassas, and B. Rozanov. "A New Assessment of the World Status of Desertification." *Desertification Control Bulletin* 20 (1991): 6-18.

Drew, Christopher and Richard A. Oppel Jr. "Lawyers at E.P.A. Say It Will Drop Pollution Cases." *The New York Times*, November 6, 2003.

Durning, Alan. *How Much Is Enough? The Consumer Society and the Future of the Earth*. Washington, D.C.: Worldwatch Institute, 1992.

EarthLink. *Eleven Nations Agree to Moratorium on Offshore Oil Rig Disposal* [EPA News Service]. August/September 1995 [cited August 6, 2002]. Available from http://www.ee/lists/infoterra/1995/09/0033.html.

Eco Management Consulting Co. *International Standard 14001, Environmental Systems Management – Specification with Guidance for Use*. 1996 [cited August 8, 2002]. Available from http://ecoland.hihome.com/ImportedFiles/ems-eng.htm.

Egan, Dave and Evelyn A. Howell, eds. *The Historical Ecology Handbook: A Restorationist's Guide to Reference Ecosystems*. Washington, D.C.: Island Press, 2001.

Egri, Carolyn P. and Susan Herman. "Leadership in the North American Environmental Sector: Values, Leadership Styles, and Contexts of Environmental Leaders and Their Organizations." *Academy of Management Journal* 43, no. 4 (2000): 571-604.

Ekins, Paul, Carl Folke, and Rudolf De Groot. "Identifying Critical Natural Capital." *Ecological Economics* 44 (2003): 159-63.

Elkington, John. "Foreword." In *Mapping the Journey: Case Studies in Strategy and Action toward Sustainable Development*, edited by Lorinda R. Rowledge, Russell S. Barton, and Kevin S. Brady. Sheffield, UK: Greenleaf Publishing, 1999.

Engebretson, G. "A mission's a must." *Credit Union Management* 20(3) (1997): 16.

Environmental Defense Fund. *Environmental Release Report: Entire United States*. Environmental Defense Fund, 2003 [cited October 22, 2003]. Available from http://www.scorecard.org/env-releases/us.tcl.

_____. *Environmental Defense Fund Scorecard.* Environmental Defense Fund, 2003 [cited October 22, 2003]. Available from http://www.scorecard.org/env-releases/us.tcl.

_____. *About Scorecard: What's New.* Environmental Defense Fund, 2003 [cited October 22, 2003]. Available from http://www.scorecard.org/about/txt/new.html.

_____. *About the Chemicals: By Industrial Sector (Mercury Compounds).* Environmental Defense Fund, 2003 [cited October 22, 2003]. Available from http://www.scorecard.org/chemical-profiles/rank-industrial-sectors.tlc?edf_substance_id=EDF%2d033 &edf_chem_name=MERCURY%20 COMPOUNDS&type=mass&category=total_env& modifier=na&fips_state_code=Entire%20United% 20States&how_many=100.

_____. *Pollution Locator: Facility Response to Information Presented on Scorecard (Shell Chemical Co. Deer Park).* Environmental Defense Fund, 2003 [cited October 22, 2003]. Available from http://www.scorecard.org/env-releases/facility-response. tcl?tri_id=77536SHLLLHIGHW.

_____. *Pollution Locator: Environmental Release Report (Du Pont Delisle Plant).* Environmental Defense Fund, 2003 [cited October 22, 2003]. Available from http://www.scorecard.org/env-releases/facility.tcl?tri_id=39571DPNTD7685K.

Environmental Defense Fund. *Pollution Locator: Animal Waste (National Report).* Environmental Defense Fund, 2003 [cited October 22, 2003]. Available from http://www.scorecard.org/env-releases/aw/us.tcl#trends.

_____. *Pollution Locator: Environmental Release Report (Tropicana Prods. Inc.).* Environmental Defense Fund, 2003 [cited October 22, 2003]. Available from http://www.scorecard.org/env-releases/facility.tcl?tri_id=33482TRPCN6500G.

_____. *Pollution Locator: Environmental Release Report (Georgia-Pacific Corp. Paper Mill).* Environmental Defense Fund, 2003 [cited October 22, 2003]. Available from http://www.scorecard.org/env-releases/facility.tcl?tri_id= 32078GRGPCSTATE.

_____. *Pollution Locator: Environmental Release Report (U.S. Sugar Corp. Clewiston Mill).* Environmental Defense Fund, 2003 [cited October 22, 2003]. Available from http://www.scorecard.org/env-releases/facility.tcl?tri_id= 33440SSGRC1731A.

_____. *Pollution Locator: Toxic Chemical Releases from Industrial Facilities.* Environmental Defense Fund, 2003 [cited October 22, 2003]. Available from http://www.scorecard.org/env-releases/us-map.tcl.

_____. *Pollution Locator: Land (Superfund Site Report: Love Canal).* 2003 [cited October 23, 2003]. Available from http://www.scorecard.org/env-releases/land/site.tcl?epa_id=NYD000606947.

_____. *Pollution Locator: Land (Superfund Site Report: Rocky Flats Plant (Usdoe)).* 2003 [cited October 23, 2003]. Available from http://www.scorecard.org/env-releases/land/site.tcl?epa_id=CO7890010526.

Environmental Working Group. *3M and Scotchgard: "Heroes of Chemistry" or a 20-Year Coverup?* 2001 [cited October 30, 2003]. Available from http://www.chemicalindustryarchives.org/dirtysecrets/scotchgard/1.asp.

Epstein, Marc. "Managing Corporate Environmental Performance: A Multinational Perspective." *European Management Journal* 16, no. 3 (1998): 284.

Ericsson. "Ericsson Sustainability Report 2001." Stockholm, Sweden: Ericsson, 2001.

Ericsson. *Financial Highlights.* Ericsson, 2001 [cited August 7, 2002]. Available from http://www.ericsson.com/annual_report/2001/eng/fs/fin_highlights.shtml.

_____. *Company Facts.* Ericsson, July 24, 2002 [cited August 6, 2002]. Available from http://www.ericsson.com/about/compfacts/.

_____. *Mission and Vision.* Ericsson, July 24, 2002 [cited August 6, 2002]. Available from http://www.ericsson.com/about/mission.shtml.

_____. *Sustainability & Environment.* Ericsson, n.d. [cited August 6, 2002]. Available from http://www.ericsson.com/sustainability/supplier_guides.shtml.

_____. *Environmental Self-Assessment Form.* Ericsson, n.d. [cited August 6, 2002]. Available from http://www.ericsson.com/sustainability/download/excel/SAform.xls.

Estee Lauder Inc. *Estee Lauder.* Estee Lauder, 2002 [cited August 19, 2002]. Available from http://www.esteelauder.com/home.tmpl.

European Chemical Industry Council. *About Us.* Karakas Graphic Communications, 2002 [cited August 6, 2002]. Available from http://www.cefic.be/Templates/shwStory.asp?NID=11&HID=108.

Feld, Steven and Keith Basso. *Senses of Place.* Santa Fe, NM: School of American Research Press, 1996.

Finnegan, Lisa. "Sustainable Development: Business without Footprints." *Occupational Hazards* 61, no. 5 (1999): 54-56.

Flannery, Brenda L. and Douglas R. May. "Environmental Ethical Decision-Making in the U.S. Metal-Finishing Industry." *Academy of Management Journal* 43, no. 4 (2000): 642-62.

Food and Agriculture Organization. *The State of World Fisheries and Aquaculture*. Rome, Italy: FAO, 2002.

Food and Drug Administration. *New Animal Drug for Increasing Milk Production*. Food & Drug Administration, November 1993 [cited August 6, 2002]. Available from http://www.fda.gov/opacom/backgrounders/bst.html.

Forero, Juan. "A Swirl of Foreboding in Mahogany's Grain." *The New York Times*, September 28, 2003, 8.

Forum, The Sustainable Office. *Paper Buyers' Checklist*. The Sustainable Office Forum, n.d. [cited August 7, 2002]. Available from http://www.tsof.org.uk/chcklst.html.

Frankel, Carl. *In Earth's Company: Business, Environment and the Challenge of Sustainability*. Stony Creek, CT: New Society Publishers, 1998.

Franz, Neil. "Bill Pushes for Audit Protection." *Chemical Week* 163, no. 7 (2001): 38.

Freedman, Julian. "Far's Environmental Study Is Honored." *Management Accounting* 78, no. 10 (1997): 66.

Fuad-Luke, Alastair. *Eco Design: The Sourcebook*. London, England: Thames & Hudson, Ltd., 2002.

Gentile, J.H., M.A. Harwell, Jr., W. Cropper, C.C. Harwell, D. DeAngelis, S. Davis, J.C. Ogden, and D. Lirman. "Ecological Conceptual Models: A Framework and Case Study on Ecosystem Management for South Florida Sustainability." *The Science of the Total Environment* 274, no. 1-3 (2001): 231-53.

Gladwin, Thomas N., James J. Kennelly, and Tara-Shelomith Krause. "Shifting Paradigms for Sustainable Development: Implications for Management Theory and Research." *The Academy of Management Review* 20, no. 4 (1995): 874-907.

Global Ecolabeling Network. *What Is Ecolabelling?* GEN General Affairs Office, 1999 [cited March 24, 2004]. Available from http://www.gen.gr.jp/eco.html.

Global Reporting Initiative. "Sustainability Reporting Guidelines on Economic, Environmental, and Social Performance." Boston, MA: Global Reporting Initiative, 2000.

_____. *Global Reporting Initiative Vision and Mission Statements*. GRI, 2002 [cited August 6, 2002]. Available from http://globalreporting.org/AboutGRI/MissionVision.htm.

_____. *Companies Using the Gri Sustainability Reporting Guidelines*. GRI, 5 August 2002 [cited August 6, 2002]. Available from http://www.global reporting.org/GRIGuidelines/Reporters.htm.

Goldberg, Rob. *The Big Picture: Life Cycle Analysis*. Academy of Natural Sciences, 1992 [cited May 1992]. Available from http://www.acnatsci.org/research/kye/big_picture.html.

Goldin, Owen and Patricia Kilroe, eds. *Human Life and the Natural World: Readings in the History of Western Philosophy*. Orchard Park, NY: Broadview Press, 1997.

Golley, Frank Benjamin. *The History of the Ecosystem Concept in Ecology: More Than the Sum of the Parts*. New Haven, CT: Yale University Press, 1993.

Golley, Frank B. *The Primer for Environmental Literacy*. New Haven, CT: Yale University Press, 1998.

Gorman, Michael E., Matthew M. Mehalik, and Patricia H. Werhane. *Ethical and Environmental Challenges to Engineering*. Upper Saddle River, NJ: Prentiss-Hall, Inc., 2000.

Goudie, Andrew. *The Human Impact on the Natural Environment*. Cambridge, MA: The MIT Press, 2000.

Green Mountain Energy Company. "Green Mountain Energy Company 2000 Environmental Report." Burlington, VT: Green Mountain Energy Company, 2001.

Groenewegen, Peter, Kurt Fischer, Edith G. Jenkins, and Johan Schot. *The Greening of Industry Resource Guide and Bibliography*. Washington, D.C.: The Island Press, 1996.

Gruber, Tom. *2021: Mass Collaboration and the Really New Economy* (Electronic version) April 4, 2002 [cited November 1, 2003]. Available from http://www.next20 years.com/newsletter/futures/archive/v01-05 business.html.

Gunderson, Lance H. and C.S. Holling. *Panarchy: Understanding Transformations in Human and Natural Systems*. Washington, D.C.: Island Press, 2002.

Gussow, Joan Dye. "Ecology and Vegetarian Considerations: Does Environmental Responsibility Demand the Elimination of Livestock?" *American Journal of Clinical Nutrition* 59, no. (Supplement 5) (1994): 1110S-16S.

Haan, Cees de, Henning Steinfeld, and Harvey Blackburn. *Livestock & the Environment: Finding a Balance – Introduction*. Suffolk, England: Food and Agriculture Organization, n.d.

Habermas, Jurgen. *Legitimation Crisis*. Boston, MA: Beacon Press, 1975.

Haggard, Ben. *Green to the Power of Three.* March 1, 2002 [cited August 11, 2002]. Available from http://www.edcmag.com/CDA/ArticleInformation/coverstory/BNPCoverStoryItem/0,4118,75525,00.html.

Hagmann, Jurgen and Edward Chuma. "Enhancing the Adaptive Capacity of the Resource Users in Natural Resource Management." *Agricultural Systems* 73 (2002): 23-29.

Haldane, J.B.S. "Essay on Science and Ethics." *The Inequality of Man* (1932): 113.

Halfpenny, Elizabeth and Nicole R. Otte. *Not Just Nature.* 1999, February [cited August 8, 2002]. Available from http://www.ourplanet.com/imgversn/101/otte.html.

Halfpenny, James C. *Winter: An Ecological Handbook.* Boulder, CO: Johnson Books, 1989.

Hamilton, Martha M. "Irresistibly Drawn toward a More Hopeful Future." *The Washington Post Business* (2000): 16-18.

Handy, Charles. *The Hungry Spirit: Beyond Capitalism: A Quest for Purpose in the Modern World.* New York, NY: Broadway Books, 1998.

Harrison, Paul and Fred Pearce. *Aaas Atlas of Population & Environment.* Berkeley, CA: University of California Press, 2000.

Hart, Stuart. "Beyond Greening: Strategies for a Sustainable World." *Harvard Business Review* 75, no. 1 (1997).

Hart, Stuart L. "A Natural-Resource-Based View of the Firm." *Academy of Management Review* 20, no. 4 (1995): 986-1014.

Hart, Stuart L. and Mark B. Milstein. "Global Sustainability and the Creative Destruction of Industries." *Sloan Managemenet Review* 41, no. 1 (1999): 23-33.

Hartman, Cathy L. "Green Alliances: Building New Business with Environmental Groups." *Long Range Planning* 30, no. 2 (1997): 184.

Hawken, Paul. *Growing a Business.* New York, NY: Fireside, 1987.

_____. "Natural Capitalism." *Mother Jones* (1997): 40-62.

Hawken, Paul, Amory Lovins, and Hunter Lovins. *Natural Capitalism: Creating the Next Industrial Revolution.* New York, NY: Little, Brown and Company, 1999.

Herman Miller. *Aeron Chairs.* 2003 [cited October 30, 2003]. Available from http://www.herman miller.com/CDA/SSA/Product/0,1592,a10-c440-p8,00.

html.

_____. *Mirra Chairs.* 2003 [cited October 30, 2003]. Available from http://www.hermanmiller.com/CDA/SSA/Product/0,1592,a10-c440-p205,00.html.

Heschong, Lisa. "Daylighting and Human Performance." *ASHRAE Journal* (2002).

Hessburg, Paul F. and James K. Agee. "An Environmental Narrative of Inland Northwest United States Forests, 1800-2000." *Forest Ecology and Management* 178, no. 1-2 (2003): 23-59.

Hibbit, C. and N. Kamp-Roelands. "Europe's (Mild) Greening of Corporate Environmental Management." *Corporate Environmental Strategy* 9, no. 2 (2002): 172-82.

Higgins, Margot. *Global Warming Ruffles Wildlife, Study Says.* (February 15, 2000) Environmental News Network, 2000 [cited 2001]. Available from http://www.enn.com/enn-news-archive/2000/02/02152000/cchange_10004.asp.

Hill, J. "Thinking About a More Sustainable Business – an Indicators Approach." *Corporate Environmental Strategy* 8, no. 1 (2001): 30-38.

Hoffman, Andrew. "Institutional Evolution and Change: Environmentalism and the US Chemical Industry." *Academy of Management Journal* 42, no. 4 (1999): 351-71.

Holling, C.S. "From Complex Regions to Complex Worlds." Gainesville, FL: University of Florida, 2003.

Holling, C.S. and Lance H. Gunderson. "Resilience and Adaptive Cycles." In *Panarchy: Understanding Transformations in Human and Nature Systems,* edited by Lance H. Gunderson and C.S. Holling, 25-62. Washington, D.C.: Island Press, 2002.

Holling, C.S., Lance H. Gunderson, and Donald Ludwig. *In Quest of a Theory of Adaptive Change, Panarchy.* Washington, D.C.: Island Press, 2002.

Holusha, John. "For Office Towers, Being Green Can Be Beneficial." *The New York Times,* June 30, 1996, 9.

Hukkinen, Janne. *Institutions of Environmental Management: Constructing Mental Models and Sustainability.* New York, NY: Routledge, 1999.

Hutchinson, Colin. *Vitality and Renewal: A Manager's Guide for the 21st Century.* London, England: Adamantine Press, 1995.

ICF Consulting. "Statement of Qualifications: Sustainable Development." ICF Consulting, n.d.

IKEA. *Environment.* Inter IKEA Systems B.V., 2002 [cited August 8, 2002]. Available from http://www.ikea.com/about_ikea/code_of_conduct/

store.asp.

Industrial Designers of America. *We Are All Involved.* n.d. [cited October 30, 2003]. Available from http://www.idsa.org/whatsnew/sections/ecosection/index.htm.

Interface, Inc. *Sustainability Report.* Atlanta, GA: Interface, Inc., 1997.

_____. *Our Company.* Interface, Inc., 2002 [cited August 6, 2002]. Available from http://www.interfacesustainability.com/comp.html.

_____. *Recognitions and Awards.* 2003 [cited October 30, 2003]. Available from http://www.interfacesustainability.com/awards.html.

_____. *Interface Celebrates Ten Years of Sustainability in Action.* Press release. Atlanta, GA: Interface, Inc., 2004.

_____. *Interface, Inc. 2004 Annual Report.* Atlanta, GA: Interface, Inc., 2004.

Interface, Inc. *Sensitivity Hookup.* 2005 [cited November 18, 2005]. Available from http://oam.darwill.com/index.cfm?image=45798 &saveopendoc=768&.

International Chamber of Commerce. *The Business Charter for Sustainable Development - 16 Principles.* ICC, 2001 [cited August 7, 2002]. Available from http://www.iccwbo.org/sdcharter/charter/principles/principles.asp.

Investor Responsibility Research Center. *About IRRC.* IRRC, 2002 [cited August 6, 2002]. Available from http://www.irrc.org/subnav/about.html.

ISO World. *The Number of Iso14001/Emas Registration of the World.* ISO World, 2002 [cited August 6, 2002]. Available from http://www.ecology.or.jp/isoworld/english/analy14k.htm.

Iyer, Gopalkrishnan R. "Business, Consumers and Sustainable Living in an Interconnected World: A Multilateral Ecocentric Approach." *Journal of Business Ethics* 20, no. 4, Part 2 (1999): 273-88.

Jackson, Suzan L. "Avoid Environmental Embarrassments." *Power Engineering* 102, no. 1 (1998): 28.

Jackson, Wes. *Becoming Native to This Place.* Washington, D.C.: Counterpoint, 1996.

Jenkins, M. "What's Our Business?" *Black Enterprise* 36(3) (2005): 71.

Jennings, Michael D. *A Handbook for Conducting Gap Analysis.* National Biological Service, Idaho Cooperative Fish and Wildlife Research Unit, 2000 [cited April 13, 2004]. Available from www.gap.uidaho.edu/handbook/Imagery/default.htm.

Jennings, Devereaux and Paul A. Zandenbergen. "Ecologically Sustainable Organizations: An Institutional Approach." *Academy of Management Journal* 20, no. 4 (1995): 1015-52.

Jensen, Poul Buch. *Introduction to the Iso 14000 Family of Environmental Management Standards.* International Network for Environmental Management, 2000 [cited October 23, 2003]. Available from http://www.inem.org/htdocs/iso/iso14000_intro.html.

Kaminsky, Ilene. *Asps – Creating a New Business Ecology.* HTE8, Inc., May 2000 [cited August 6, 2002]. Available from http://www.hte8.com/artEcol.html.

Kaufman, Lois. "Selling Green: What Managers and Marketers Need to Know About Consumer Environmental Attitudes." *Environmental Quality Management* 8, no. 4 (1999): 11.

Kaufman, Les and Paul Dayton. "Impacts of Marine Resource Extraction on Ecosystem Services and Sustainability." In *Nature's Services: Societal Dependence on Natural Ecosystems,* edited by Gretchen C. Daily. Washington, D.C.: Island Press, 1997.

Kay, James J., Henry A. Regier, Michelle Boyle, and George Francis. "An Ecosystem Approach for Sustainability: Addressing the Challenge of Complexity." *Futures* 31 (1999): 721-42.

Keitsch, Martina Maria. *Sustainable Development: A Framework for Industrial Ecology.* Norwegian University of Science and Technology, 2001 [cited April 14, 2004]. Available from http://www.hausarbeiten.de/download/19843.pdf.

Kern, Stephen. *The Culture of Time and Space: 1880-1918.* Cambridge, MA: Harvard University Press, 1983.

Khanna, Madhu and Wilma Rose Q. Anton. "What Is Driving Corporate Environmentalism: Opportunity or Threat?" *Corporate Environmental Strategy* 9, no. 4 (2002): 409-17.

Kinetix. *Kinetix Business Ecology.* Kinetix LLC, 2002 [cited August 6, 2002]. Available from http://www.kinetixllc.com/Kinetix_[business_ecology].pdf.

King, Andrew. "Avoiding Ecological Surprise: Lessons from Long-Standing Communities." *Academy of Management Review* 20, no. 4 (1995): 961-85.

Kiuchi, Tachi. "What I Learned in the Rainforest." *Technology Review* 100, no. 8 (1997): 63-64.

Kling, Daniel and Stellan Flodstrom. *Metapatterns: An Overview.* 2002 [cited April 13, 2004]. Available from www.idt.mdh.se/kurser/cd5130/msg/2002lp3/download/CD5130%20VT02%20Metapatterns.pdf.

Knevitt, Charles. *Shelter: Human Habitats from around the World.* San Francisco, CA: Pomegranate Artbooks, 1996.

Knight, James R. and Eugene W. Myers. "Super-Pattern Matching." 1-26. Tucson, AZ: University of Arizona, 1996.

Kranz, Dorie and Susan Burns. "Combining the Natural Step and Iso 14001." *Perspectives on Business and Global Change* 11, no. 4 (1997).

Kuchli, Christian. *Forests of Hope: Stories of Regeneration.* Stony Creek, CT: New Society Publishers, 1997.

Kustin, Ira. "Limiting Architects' Liability for Indoor Air Pollution and Sick Building Syndrome." *N.Y.U. Environmental Law Journal* 7 (1999): 119-51.

LaBar, Gregg. "Substituting Safer Materials." *Occupational Hazards* 59, no. 11 (1997): 49.

Lambin, Eric F., B.L. Turner, Helmut J. Giest, Samuel B. Agbola, Arild Angelson, John W. Bruce, Oliver T. Coomes, Rodolfo Dirzo, Gunther Fischer, Carl Folke, S. George, Katherine Homewood, Jacques Imbernon, Rik Leemans, Xiubin Li, Emilio F. Moran, Michael Mortimore, S. Ramakrishnan, John F. Richards, Helle Skanes, Will Steffen, Glenn D. Stone, Uno Svedin, Tom A. Veldkamp, Coleen Vogel, and Jianchu Xu. "The Causes of Land-Use and Land-Cover Change: Moving Beyond the Myths." *Global Environmental Change* 11 (2001): 261-69.

Laszlo, Ervin. "Moral Behavior on a Small Planet: Groundwork for a Biospheric Systems Ethics." Paper presented at the International Society for Systems Sciences Meeting, Budapest, Hungary, September 18, 1996.

Laszlo, Ervin. *The Systems View of the World.* Cresskill, NJ: Hampton Press, Inc., 1996.

Lawrence Berkeley Labs. *Improved Indoor Environments Could Save Billions of Dollars.* Lawrence Berkeley Labs, n.d. [cited October 30, 2003]. Available from http://eetd.lbl.gov/New/Fisk-new.html.

Lazaroff, Leon. "Activists Hold Retailers Responsible for Logging." *Journal of Commerce* (1998): 9.A.

Leader to Leader Institute. *How to Develop a Mission Statement.* Leader to Leader Institute. 2005.

Ledgerwood, Grant. "The Global 500, Big Oil and Corporate Environmental Governance." *Greening the Boardroom* (1997): 189-205.

Lexus. *Environment/Technology* [Web site]. 2005 [cited November 12, 2005]. Available from http://www.lexus.com/about/corporate/environment_tech.html.

Lewis, Stephen. "An Opinion on the Global Impact of Meat Consumption." *American Journal of Clinical Nutrition* 59 (supplement) (1994): 1099S-102S.

Livesey, Sharon M. "Eco-Identity as Discursive Struggle: Royal Dutch/Shell, Brent Spar, and Nigeria." *The Journal of Business Communication* 38, no. 1 (2001): 58-91.

Locke, Lawrence F., Waneen Wyrick Spirduso, and Stephen J. Silverman. *Proposals That Work: A Guide for Planning Dissertations and Grant Proposals.* Thousand Oaks, CA: Sage Publications, 2000.

Logan, William Bryant. *Dirt: The Ecstatic Skin of the Earth.* New York, NY: Riverhead Books, 1995.

Lovins, Amory B., et al. "A Road Map for Natural Capitalism." *Harvard Business Review* (1999): 145-58.

Lyle, John Tillman. *Regenerative Design for Sustainable Development.* New York, NY: John Wiley & Sons, Inc., 1994.

Lyle, John Tillman. *Design for Human Ecosystems: Landscape, Land Use, and Natural Resources.* Washington, D.C.: Island Press, 1999.

Lynch, Kevin. *What Time Is This Place?* Cambridge, MA: The MIT Press, 1998.

Madsen, Henry and John P. Ulhoi. "Greening of Human Resources: Environmental Awareness and Training Interests within the Workforce." *Industrial Management + Data Systems* 101, no. 2 (2001): 57-65.

Magretta, Joan. "Growth through Global Sustainability: An Interview with Monsanto's CEO, Robert B. Shapiro." *Harvard Business Review* 75, no. 1 (1997): 78.

Mangrove Software, Inc. *Our Vision – Understanding the Ecology of Business.* Mangrove Software, Inc., 2001 [cited August 6, 2002]. Available from http://www.click4systems.com/corpvision.htm.

Molles, Manuel C. Jr. *Ecology: Concepts and Applications.* New York, NY: WCB McGraw-Hill, 1999.

Margulis, Lynn and Dorion Sagan. *What Is Life?* New York, NY: Simon & Schuster, 1995.

Matthews, Bonnye L. *Chemical Sensitivity: A Guide to Coping with Hypersensitivy Syndrome, Sick Building Syndrome and Other Environmental Illnesses.* Jefferson, NC: McFarland & Company, Inc., Publishers, 1992.

Maxwell, James, Sandra Rothenberg, Forrest Briscoe, and Alfred Marcus. "Green Schemes: Corporate Environmental Strategies and Their Implementation." *California Management Review* 39, no. 3 (1997): 118.

McCoy, Charles. "Two U.S. Members of Mitsubishi Group and Environmental Activists Reach Pact." *The Wall Street Journal,* February 11, 1998, 1.

McDonagh, Pierre and Alison Clark. "Corporate Communications About Sustainability: Turning Clever Companies into Enlightened Companies." *Greener Management International*, no. 11 (1995): 49-62.

McDonald, Mary. "Integrating Green into an Existing Management System: Performing a 'Green' Gap Analysis." Paper presented at the Quality Congress 2002.

McDonough, William. "Foreword." In *Leading Change toward Sustainability*, edited by Bob Doppelt. Sheffield, UK: Greeleaf Publishing Limited, 2003.

McDonough, William and Michael Braungart. "The Next Industrial Revolution." *The Atlantic Monthly* (1998): 82-92.

_____. *Cradle to Cradle: Remaking the Way We Make Things*. New York, NY: North Point Press, 2002.

McGarigal, Kevin. *Ecosystem and Landscape Dynamics* [PDF file]. n.d. [cited March 10, 2003]. Available from http://www.umass.edu/landeco/teaching/landscape_ecology/schedule/dynamics.pdf.

McGee, John. "Commentary on 'Corporate Strategies and Environmental Regulations: An Organizing Framework'." *Strategic Management Journal* 19, no. 4 (1998): 377.

McGinley, Kathleen and Bryan Finegan. "The Ecological Sustainability of Tropical Forest Management: Evaluation of the National Forest Management Standards of Costa Rica and Nicaragua, with Emphasis on the Need for Adaptive Management." *Forest Policy and Economics*, In Press (2003).

McNeill, J.R. *Something New under the Sun: An Environmental History of the Twentieth-Century World*. New York, NY: W.W. Norton & Company, 2000.

McSpirit, Kelly. "Sustainable Consumption: Patagonia's Buy Less, but Buy Better." *Corporate Environmental Strategy* 5, no. 2 (1998): 32-40.

Meadows, Donella H., Dennis L. Meadows, and Jorgen Randers. *Beyond the Limits: Confronting Global Collapse Envisioning a Sustainable Future*. Post Mills, VT: Chelsea Green Publishing Company, 1992.

Mega, Voula. "The Participatory City: Innovations in the European Union." *The Scout Report for Social Sciences Selection* 2, no. 11 (1999).

Melanie. *Environmental Education in Malta – Ecosystems*. n.d. [cited August 6, 2002]. Available from http://www.geocities.com/RainForest/Vines/6460/ecosys.html.

Mello, Tara Baukus. *Diesel Developments*. Edmunds.com, March 25, 2003 [cited November 11, 2005]. Available from http://www.edmunds.com/advice/specialreports/articles/93338/article.html.

Menon, Anil and Ajay Menon. "Enviropreneurial Marketing Strategy: The Emergence of Corporate Environmentalism as Market Strategy." *Journal of Marketing* 61, no. 1 (1997): 51-67.

Menzel, Peter. *Material World: A Global Family Portrait*. San Francisco, CA: Sierra Club Books, 1994.

Miller, G. Tyler, Jr. *Living in the Environment*. Belmont, CA: Wadsworth Group, 2002.

Miller, John. *Egotopia: Narcissism and the New American Landscape*. Tuscaloosa, AL: The University of Alabama Press, 1997.

Milliken & Company. *Welcome to Milliken & Company*. Dogwood Productions, 2002 [cited August 6, 2002]. Available from www.milliken.com.

Mitchell, John Hanson. *Ceremonial Time: Fifteen Thousand Years on One Square Mile*. New York, NY: Addison-Wesley Publishing Company, Inc., 1984.

Mollison, Bill. *Permaculture: A Designers' Manual*. Tyalgum, Australia: Tagari Publications, 1988.

Monroe, Linda K. "Light and Human Health." *Buildings* 98, no. 3 (2004): 20.

Montague Institute. *Ecology of Competition*. (May/June) 1993 [cited November 1, 2003]. Available from http://montague.montague.com/abstracts/ecology.html.

Montuori, Alfonso and Ronald E. Purser. "Complexity, Epistemology, and Ecology." *The Academy of Management Review* 21, no. 4 (1996): 918-20.

Moore, James F. *The Death of Competition: Leadership & Strategy in the Age of Business Ecosystems*. New York, NY: HarperBusiness, 1996.

Morgan, Gareth. *Images of Organization*. Newbury Park, CA: Sage Publications, 1986.

Motavalli, Jim. "Zero Waste." *E Magazine*, March/April 2001, 26-33.

Mullin, Rick. "Building Structure Behind the Scenes." *Chemical Week* 161, no. 14 (1999): 36.

Mumford, Lewis. *From the Ground Up: Observations on Contemporary Architecture, Housing, Highway Design, and Civic Design*. New York, NY: Harcourt Brace Jovanovich, Publishers, 1956.

Myers, Norman. "The World's Forests and Their Ecosystem Services." In *Nature's Services: Societal Dependence on Natural Ecosystems*, edited by Gretchen C. Daily. Washington, D.C.: Island Press, 1997.

Nabhan, Gary Paul and Stephen Trimble. *The Geography of Childhood*. Boston, MA: Beacon Press, 1994.

National Academy of Engineering. *The Industrial Green Game: Implications for Environmental Design and Management*. Washington, D.C.: National Academy Press, 1997.

National Audubon Society. *Audubon House: Building for an Environmental Future.* National Audubon Society, 2003 [cited October 30, 2003]. Available from http://www.audubon.org/nas/ah/.

National Institute of Standards and Technology – Office of Applied Economics. *Bees 2.0.* NIST, July 24, 2002 [cited August 6, 2002]. Available from http://www.bfrl.nist.gov/oae/software/bees.html.

National Occupational Health & Safety Commission – Commonwealth of Australia. *Cis Newsletter* (N° 99 DECEMBER-DECEMBRE 1997) National Occupational Health & Safety Commission, Commonwealth of Australia, 1997 [cited August 7, 2002]. Available from http://www.oshvn.net/OSH/ www.worksafe.gov.au/worksafe/11/cisd.html.

Nattrass, Brian and Mary Altomare. *The Natural Step for Business: Wealth, Ecology and the Evolutionary Corporation.* Gabriola Island, British Columbia, Canada: New Society Publishers, 1999.

Natural Resources Defense Council. *Healthy Milk, Healthy Baby: Chemical Pollution and Mother's Milk.* March 25, 2005 [cited November 12, 2005]. Available from http://www.nrdc.org/breastmilk/ chems.asp.

Nazarea, Virginia, ed. *Ethnoecology: Situated Knowledge/ Located Lives.* Tucson, AZ: The University of Arizona Press, 1999.

Ndubisi, Forster. *Ecological Planning: A Historical and Comparative Synthesis.* Baltimore, MD: The Johns Hopkins University Press, 2002.

Nelton, S. (1994). "Put Your Purpose in Writing." *Nation's Business* 82(2): 61-64.

Neuvelt, Carol Singer. "Eh&S Preparation – Meeting the Needs of Hiring Managers." *Corporate Environmental Strategy* 6, no. 4 (1999): 407-14.

New Zealand Ministry of the Environment. *The New Zealand Waste Strategy: Towards Zero Waste and a Sustainable New Zealand.* Ministry for the Environment, 2002 [cited August 6, 2002]. Available from http://www.mfe.govt.nz/about/publications/ waste/waste.htm#wastestrategy.

Newton, Tim. "Green Business: Technicist Kitsch?" *The Journal of Management Studies* 34, no. 1 (1997): 75.

North, Klaus. *Environmental Business Management.* Geneva, Switzerland: International Labour Office, 1992.

Orr, David. *The Nature of Design.* Santa Clarita, CA: Professional Programs, Inc., 2001. CD-ROM.

Orr, David W. *Earth in Mind: On Education, Environment, and the Human Prospect.* Washington, D.C.:

Island Press, 1994.

Osbahr, Henny and Christie Allan. "Indigenous Knowledge of Soil Fertility Management in Southwest Niger." *Geoderma* 111 (2003): 457-79.

Ottman, Jacquelyn A. "Back up Green Programs with Corporate Credibility." *Marketing News* 32, no. 22 (1998): 9-10.

_____. "Environmental Branding Blocks Competitors." *Marketing News* 32, no. 17 (1998): 8.

_____. "Proven Environmental Commitment Helps Create Committed Customers." *Marketing News* 32, no. 3 (1998): 5.

_____. "How to Develop Really New, New Products." *Marketing News* 33, no. 3 (1999): 5.

Papanek, Victor. *The Green Imperative: Natural Design for the Real World.* New York, NY: Thames and Hudson, 1995.

Parent, Elaine. "The Living Systems Theory of James Grier Miller." Paper presented at the International Society for Systems Sciences Meeting, Budapest, Hungary, September 18, 1996.

Park, Chris. *The Environment: Principles and Applications.* New York, NY: Routledge, 1997.

Parker-Pope, Tara. "Estee Lauder Sets Deal to Buy Aveda for $300 Million." *Wall Street Journal*, November 20, 1997, 1.

Parry, Pam. *The Bottom Line: How to Build a Business Case for Iso 14001.* Washington, D.C.: St. Lucie Press, 2000.

Pasqual, Joan and Guadalupe Souto. "Sustainability in Natural Resource Management." *Ecological Economics* 46 (2003): 47-59.

Patagonia. *Let My People Go Surfing.* 2005 [cited November 11, 2005]. Available from http://www. patagonia.com/culture/yc_book.shtml?seepromo =home.

_____. "Defining Quality: A Brief Description of How We Got Here." 2003.

_____. *Enviro Internship.* 2003 [cited October 23, 2003]. Available from http://www.patagonia.com/enviro/ internship.shtml.

Pauli, Gunter. *Upsizing: The Road to Zero Emission, More Jobs, More Income and No Pollution.* Sheffield, UK: Greenleaf Publishing, 1998.

Pearson, Christine M. "Crisis Management in Central European Firms." *Business Horizons* 41, no. 3 (1998): 50.

Percy, S.W. "Environmental Sustainability and Corporate Strategy: Why a Firm's 'Chief Environmental Officer' Should Be Its CEO." *Corporate Environmental Strategy* 7, no. 2 (2000): 194-202.

Pianin, Eric. "Warming Trend Shifting Bird Migration

Patterns." *The Washington Post* as shown on *The Holland Sentinel* web site, March 7, 2002 [cited August 6, 2002]. Available from http://www.holland sentinel.com/stories/030702/out_030702040.shtml.

_____. "Study Finds Net Gain from Pollution Rules." *The Washington Post*, September 27, 2003, A01.

Piper, Lennart. *Environmental Performance Assessment/Environmental Performance Reporting and Iso 14031.* Lennart Piper, June 18, 2000 [cited August 6, 2002]. Available from http://iso14031.net/epa/epa.htm.

Piper, Lennart. *Two Packages of Criteria.* Lennart Piper, June 18, 2000 [cited August 6, 2002]. Available from http://iso14031.net/epa/bild3kl.htm.

_____. *From Environmental Aspects to Significant Environmental Aspects.* Lennart Piper, June 18, 2000 [cited August 6, 2002]. Available from http://iso14031.net/epa/bild4kl.htm.

_____. *From Significant Environmental Aspects to Environmental Targets.* Lennart Piper, June 18, 2000 [cited August 6, 2002]. Available from http://iso14031.net/epa/bild5kl.htm.

_____. *Who Is Using the Criteria and Who Sets the Points?* Lennart Piper, June 18, 2000 [cited August 6, 2002]. Available from http://iso14031.net/epa/bild6kl.htm.

Pooley, Julie Ann and Moira O'Connor. "Environmental Education and Attitudes: Emotions and Beliefs Are What Is Needed." *Environment and Behavior* 32, no. 5 (2000): 711-23.

Post, James E., ed. "Research on Organizations and the Natural Environment: Some Paths We Have Traveled, the Field Ahead." *Research in Corporate Social Performance and Policy* (1995).

Postel, Sandra. *Growing More Food with Less Water.* February 2001. Available from http://www.sciam.com/article.cfm?articleID =0006AB09-13AC-1C71-84A9809EC588EF21&pageNumber =2&catID=2.

Pree, Wolfgang. *Meta Patterns – a Means for Capturing the Essentials of Reusable Object-Oriented Design.* n.d. [cited April 13, 2004]. Available from www.exciton.cs.rice.edu/comp410/frameworks/Pree/C010.pdf.

Radcliffe, Michael J. "The Auto Industry Responds." *green@work*, November/December 2001.

Ramus, Catherine A. and Ulrich Steger. "The Roles of Supervisory Support Behaviors and Environmental Policy in Employee 'Ecoinitiatives' at Leading-Edge European Companies." *Academy of Manage-*

ment Journal 43, no. 4 (2000): 605-26.

Ray, Paul H., Ph.D. and Sherry Ruth Anderson, Ph.D. *The Cultural Creatives: How 50 Million People Are Changing the World.* New York, NY: Harmony Books, 2000.

Rees, Robin, Executive Editor. *The Way Nature Works.* New York, NY: Macmillan Publishing Company, 1992.

Regenesis. "Damned If You Do – Damned If You Don't." *Regeneration*, Summer 2000, 1-3.

_____. *Sundance Resort Case Study.* Regenesis, 2002 [cited August 11, 2002]. Available from http://www.regenesisgroup.com/cssundance.html.

_____. *Regenesis Group Staff Contacts.* Regenesis, n.d. [cited August 6, 2002]. Available from http://www.regenesisgroup.com/contacts.html.

Reinhardt, Andy. *The New Intel.* The McGraw-Hill Companies Inc., March 13, 2000 [cited August 7, 2002]. Available from http://www.businessweek.com/2000/00_11/b3672001.htm.

Renesch, John E. *Getting to the Better Future: How Business Can Lead the Way to New Possibilities.* San Francisco, CA: New Business Books, 2000.

Richards, Deanna J., ed. *The Industrial Green Game: Implications for Enviromental Design and Management.* Washington, D.C.: National Academy Press, 1997.

Robinson, S. "Key Survival Issues: Practical Steps toward Corporate Environmental Sustainability." *Corporate Environmental Strategy* 7, no. 1 (2000): 92-105.

Rocky Mountain Institute, Alex Wilson, Jennifer L. Uncapher, Lisa McManigal, L. Hunter Lovins, Maureen Cureton, and William D. Browning. *Green Development: Integrating Ecology and Real Estate.* New York, NY: John Wiley & Sons, Inc., 1998.

Roddick, Anita. *Business as Unusual: The Triumph of Anita Roddick.* London, England: Thorsons, 2000.

_____. *Take It Personally: How to Make Conscious Choices to Change the World.* Berkeley, CA: Conari Press, 2001.

Romanyshyn, Robert D. *Technology as Symptom and Dream.* New York, NY: Routledge, 1989.

Romm, Joseph J. *Lean and Clean Management.* New York, NY: Kodansha International, 1994.

Ronnback, Patrik and Jurgenne H. Primavera. "Illuminating the Need for Ecological Knowledge in Economic Valuation of Mangroves under Different Management Regimes – a Critique." *Ecological Economics* 35 (2000): 135-41.

Roseland, Mark. *Toward Sustainable Communities: Resources for Citizens and Their Governments*. Stony Creek, CT: New Society Publishers, 1998.

Rosen, Robert H., Ph.D. and Lisa Berger. *The Healthy Company: Eight Strategies to Develop People, Productivity, and Profits*. New York, NY: Jeremy P. Tarcher/Putnam, 1991.

Rosenzweig, Michael L. *Win-Win Ecology: How the Earth's Species Can Survive in the Midst of Human Enterprise*. New York, NY: Oxford University Press, 2003.

Rothwell, William J., Roland Sullivan, and Gary N. McLean. *Practicing Organization Development*. San Francisco, CA: Jossey-Bass/Pfeiffer, 1995.

Rowledge, Lorinda R., Russell S. Barton, and Kevin S. Brady. *Mapping the Journey: Case Studies in Strategy and Action toward Sustainable Development*. Sheffield, UK: Greenleaf Publishing, 1999.

Ruben, Debra K., Mary B. Powers, William J. Angelo, and David B. Rosenbaum. "Revenue Grows in Green Markets." *Engineering News Record*, July 3, 2000.

Rudestam, Kjell Erik and Rae R. Newton. *Surviving Your Dissertation: A Comprehensive Guide to Content and Process*. Newbury Park, CA: Sage Publications, 1992.

Rugman, Alan M. "Corporate Strategies and Environmental Regulations: An Organizing Framework." *Strategic Management Journal* 19, no. 4 (1998): 363.

_____. "Corporate Strategy and International Environmental Policy." *Journal of International Business Studies* 29, no. 4 (1998): 819.

Russian London Newspaper. *Russia May Revoke Bp Gas License* 2005 [cited November 12, 2005]. Available from http://www.russianlondon.com/uknews/business/22176.

Sapp, Amy and Shannon McDonald. "Production and Consumption of Meat: Implications for the Global Environment and Human Health." Harvard University, 2001.

Sarkis, Joseph. "Evaluating Environmentally Conscious Business Practices." *European Journal of Operational Research* 107, no. 1 (1998): 159.

Schaltegger, Stefan and Terje Synnestvedt. "The Link between 'Green' and Economic Success: Environmental Management as the Crucial Trigger between Environmental and Economic Performance." *Journal of Environmental Management* 65 (2002): 339-46.

Schendler, A. "Trouble in Paradise: The Rough Road to Sustainability in Aspen." *Corporate Environmental Strategy* 8, no. 4 (2001): 293-99.

Schmidheiny, Stephan. *Changing Course: A Global Business Perspective on Development and the Environment*. Cambridge, MA: The MIT Press, 1992.

Senge, Peter M. *The Fifth Discipline: The Art & Practice of the Learning Organization*. New York, NY: Currency/Doubleday, 1990.

_____. *The Fifth Discipline Fieldbook*. New York, NY: Doubleday, 1994.

Sharfman, Mark P., Mark Meo, and Rex T. Ellington. "Regulation, Business, and Sustainable Development: The Antecedents of Environmentally Conscious Technological Innovation." *The American Behavioral Scientist* 44, no. 2 (2000): 277-302.

Sharma, Sanjay. "Proactive Corporate Environmental Strategy and the Development of Competitively Valuable Organizational Capabilities." *Strategic Management Journal* 19, no. 8 (1998): 729.

_____. "Corporate Environmental Responsiveness Strategies: The Importance of Issue Interpretation and Organizational Context." *The Journal of Applied Behavioral Science* 35, no. 1 (1999): 87.

_____. "Managerial Interpretations and Organizational Context as Predictors of Corporate Choice of Environmental Strategy." *Academy of Management Journal* 43, no. 4 (2000): 681-97.

Shaw Industries. *Shaw International*. Shaw International, n.d. [cited August 6, 2002]. Available from http://www.shawinc.com/International/Default.htm.

Shepard, Paul. *Coming Home to the Pleistocene*. Washington, D.C.: Island Press, 1998.

Shrivastava, Paul. "Ecocentric Management for a Risk Society." *Academy of Management Review* 20, no. 1 (1995): 118-37.

Sitarz, Daniel. *Sustainable America: America's Environment, Economy and Society in the 21st Century*. Carbondale, IL: EarthPress, 1998.

Slattery, Dennis Patrick. *The Wounded Body: Remembering the Markings of Flesh*. Albany, NY: State University of New York Press, 2000.

Smart Places, Inc. *Section 07210 – Building Insulation*. n.d. [cited November 13, 2005]. Available from http://www.smartplaces.com/sp/discuss/07200.htm.

Smith, Ronald S., Jr. *Profit Centers in Industrial Ecology: The Business Executive's Approach to the Environment*. Westport, CT: Quorum Books, 1998.

Society of Building Science Educators. "Bepac Explained." *SBSE News* (1995): 6.

Sosnowchik, Katie. "In the Driver's Seat." *green@work*, November/December 2001, 10-11.

175

_____. "Citizen Kraemer." *green@work*, January/February 2001-2002, 18-25.

Stafford, Edwin R. and Cathy L. Hartman. "Toward an Understanding of the Antecedents of Environmentalist-Business Cooperative Relations." *American Marketing Association* (1998): 58-63.

Starik, Mark and Archie B. Carroll. "Strategic Environmental Management: Business as If the Earth Really Mattered." Paper presented at the 1991 International Association for Business and Society Meetings, Sundance, UT, March 22-24, 1991.

Starik, Mark and Chandra Gribbon. "European Strategic Environmental Management: Toward a Global Model of Business Environmentalism." *Corporate Social Performance and Policy* 14 (1993): 167-97.

Starik, Mark and Mark Heuer. "Strategic Inter-Organizational Environmentalism: A Research and Teaching Framework." *Unpublished* (n.d.).

Starik, Mark and Alfred Marcus. "Introduction to the Special Research Forum on the Management of Organizations in the Natural Environment: A Field Emerging from Multiple Paths, with Many Challenges Ahead." *Academy of Management Review* 43, no. 4 (2000): 539-47.

Starik, Mark and Gordon Rands. "Weaving an Integrated Web: Multilevel and Multisystem Perspectives of Ecologically Sustainable Organizations." *Academy of Management Review* 20, no. 4 (1995): 908-35.

_____. "Interpretations of Sustainability." *Unpublished* (n.d.).

Starik, Mark, et al. "Toward Eco-Humanism." *Unpublished* (n.d.).

Starke, Linda, ed. *State of the World 2001*. Washington, D.C.: The Worldwatch Institute, 2001.

Stead, Jean Garner and W. Edward Stead. "Eco-Enterprise Strategy: Standing for Sustainability." *Journal of Business Ethics* 4, no. 2 (2000): 313-29.

Stead, W. Edward and Jean Garner Stead. *Management for a Small Planet*. Thousand Oaks, CA: Sage Publications, Inc., 1996.

Steger, Ulrich. "Organization and Human Resource Management for Environmental Management." In *The Greening of Industry Resource Guide and Bibliography*, edited by Peter Groenewegen, Kurt Fischer, Edith G. Jenkins, and Johan Schot. Washington, D.C.: Island Press, 1996.

Strang, Veronica. *Uncommon Ground: Cultural Landscapes and Environmental Values*. New York, NY: Berg, 1997.

Stuart, John. "World Review." *Greener Management International*, no. 11 (1995): 6-31.

Sun Microsystems. *Sun's Smart (Sun Microsystems Alternative Resources for Transportation) Commute Program*. 2005 [cited November 11, 2005]. Available from http://www.sun.com/aboutsun/ehs/ehs-commute.html.

Suncor Energy. *2001 Report on Sustainability: Our Journey toward Sustainable Development*. Calgary, Alberta, Canada: Suncor Energy, Inc., 2001.

_____. *Social Responsibility*. 2003 [cited October 23, 2003]. Available from http://www.suncor.com/bins/content_page.asp?cid=3.

_____. *About Suncor*. 2003 [cited October 23, 2003]. Available from http://www.suncor.com/bins/content_page.asp?cid=1.

Suncor Energy. *Renewable Energy Sources*. 2003 [cited October 30, 2003]. Available from http://www.suncor.com/bins/content_page.asp?cid=2-1464-1466-1470.

Sykes, Richard E. *American Studies and the Concept of Culture: A Theory and Method*. n.d. [cited April 13, 2004]. Available from http://xroads.virginia.edu/~DRBR/sykes.txt.

T.S. Designs (2005). *Sustainability*. 2005.

Tellus Institute. *About Tellus*. Tellus Institute, n.d. [cited August 6, 2002]. Available from http://www.tellus.org/general/about.html.

TerraChoice Environmental Services, Inc. *Terrachoice Environmental Services Inc*. TerraChoice, n.d. [cited August 6, 2002]. Available from www.terrachoice.com.

Thayer, B.M. "Way Station." *Solar Today* 8, no. 4 (1994): 17-20.

The American Heritage Dictionary. *The American Heritage Dictionary*. Second College Edition. Boston, MA: Houghton Mifflin Company, 1991.

The Associated Press. "Bush Administration Relaxes Air Pollution Rules." 2003.

_____. *Death Toll from Indonesia Floods Hits 101*. November 5, 2003 [cited November 7, 2003]. Available from http://www.nytimes.com/aponline/international/AP-Indonesia-Flood.html.

The Body Shop. *Values Report*. The Body Shop, 1997 [cited August 6, 2002]. Available from http://www.bodyshop.com/global/values/reporting/values97.pdf.

_____. *Who We Are*. The Body Shop, 2001 [cited August 6, 2002]. Available from http://www.bodyshop.com/global/who_we_are/index.asp.

The Chemical Industry Archives. *3M and Scotchgard: "Heroes of Chemistry" or a 20-Year Cover Up?* 2001 [cited October 30, 2003]. Available from http://www.chemicalindustryarchives.org/dirtysecrets/scotchgard/1.asp.

The Cooperative Bank. *About the Bank – Highlights from Our History.* The Cooperative Bank, 2000 [cited August 6, 2002]. Available from http://www.co-operativebank.co.uk/about/about_history. html.

_____. *Ecological Mission Statement.* 2000 [cited August 7, 2002]. Available from http://www.co-operativebank.co.uk/.

The Earth Council. *Biological Productivity Available on This Planet.* n.d. [cited October 30, 2003]. Available from http://www.ecouncil.ac.cr/rio/focus/report/english/footprint/biological.htm.

The H. John Heinz III Center for Science, Economics and the Environment. *The State of the Nation's Ecosystems: Measuring the Lands, Waters, and Living Resources of United States.* New York, NY: Cambridge University Press, 2002.

The Johnson Foundation, Inc. "The Natural Step to Sustainability." *Wingspread Journal* (1997).

The Sustainable Office Forum. *Paper Buyers' Checklist.* n.d. [cited October 2003]. Available from http://www.tsof.org.uk/chcklst.html.

The Way Station. *Way Station: A New Era of Mental Health Care Facilities.* Frederick, MD: The Way Station, n.d.

Third Millennium Systems, Inc. *Business Ecosystems Model Web Page.* Third Millennium Systems, Inc., 2000 [cited August 6, 2002]. Available from http://www.tmsinow.com/Living/ECommerce/business_ ecosystem.html.

Thomson, Alan J. "Elicitation and Representation of Traditional Ecological Knowledge, for Use in Forest Management." *Computers and Electronics and Agriculture* 27, no. 1-3 (2000): 155-65.

Thoreau, Henry D. *Faith in a Seed.* Washington, D.C.: Island Press, 1993.

Tickner, J.A. and C. Raffensperger. "The Precautionary Principle: A Framework for Sustainable Business Decision-Making." *Corporate Environmental Strategy* 5, no. 4 (1998): 75-82.

Toledano, Moises Daniel Diaz. *Meta-Patterns: A New Approach to Design Patterns.* 2002 [cited April 13, 2004]. Available from http://www.moisesdaniel.com /wri/metapatterns.html.

Townend, Ian. "Marine Science for Strategic Planning and Management: The Requirement for Estuaries." *Marine Policy.* In Press (2002).

Townsend, Amy. *The Smart Office: Turning Your Company on Its Head.* Olney, MD: Gila Press, 1997.

_____. "Business Ecology: The Future of Green Business?" In *New Horizons in Research on Sustainable Organizations: Emerging Ideas, Approaches, and Tools for Practitioners and Researchers*, edited by Sanjay Sharma and Mark Starik. Sheffield, UK: Greenleaf Publishing, 2004.

Treasury Board of Canada Secretariat. *Impediments to Partnering and the Role of the Treasury Board. (1998)* 2002 [cited October 31, 2003]. Available from http://www.tbs-sct.gc.ca/asd-dmps/imp/ais_e.asp.

Tronkoa, Mykola D., Olga O. Bobylyovab, Tetyana I. Bogdanovaa, Ovsiy V. Epshteina, Illya A. Likhtaryovc, Valentyn V. Markova, Valery A. Oliynyka, Valery P. Tereshchenkoa, Viktor M. Shpaka, Gilbert Beebed, André Bouvilled, Aaron Brille, David Burch, Daniel Finkf, Ellen Greenebaumf, Geoffrey Howef, Nicholas Luckyanovd, Ihor Masnykd, Robert McConnelld, Jacob Robbinsg, Terry Thomasd, and Paul Voilléquéh. "Thyroid Gland and Radiation (Ukrainian-American Thyroid Project)." *International Congress Series* 1258 (2003): 91-104.

Tsujii, Koichi. *Iso World.* 2003 [cited October 23, 2003]. Available from http://www.ecology.or.jp/isoworld/english/analy14k.htm.

_____. *Iso World.* December 2003-2004 [cited March 22, 2004]. Available from http://www.ecology.or.jp/isoworld/english/analy14k.htm.

Tucker, Kelley R. "Wildlife Health." In *The Fatal Harvest Reader: The Tragedy of Industrial Agriculture*, edited by Andrew Kimbrell. Washington, D.C.: Island Press, 2002.

Turner, B.L. II, W.C. Clark, R.W. Kates, J.F. Richards, J.T. Mathews, W.B. Meyer. *The Earth as Transformed by Human Action: Global and Regional Changes in the Biosphere over the Past 300 Years.* New York, NY: Cambridge University Press, 1990.

Turner, Monica G., William H. Romme, Robert H. Gardner, Robert V. O'Neill, and Timothy K. Kratz. "A Revised Concept of Landscape Equilibrium: Disturbance and Stability on Scaled Landscapes." *Landscape Ecology* 8, no. 3 (1993): 213-27.

Tusseau-Vuillemin, Marie-Hélène. "Do Food Processing Industries Contribute to the Eutrophication of Aquatic Systems?" *Ecotoxicology and Environmental Safety* 50, no. 2 (2001): 143-52.

UC Irvine Graduate School of Management Professor

Named to Taco Bell® Chair in Information Technology Management. UCI Communications Office, February 12, 1999 [cited August 19, 2002]. Available from http://www.today.uci.edu/releases/99releases/022aa99.html.

UCI Communications Office. *UC Irvine Graduate School of Management Professor Named to Taco Bell® Chair in Information Technology Management.* UC Regents, February 12, 1999 [cited August 7, 2002]. Available from http://www.today. uci.edu/releases/99releases/022aa99.html.

U.S. Census Bureau. *Statistical Abstract of the United States: 2000: The National Data Book.* Washington, D.C.: U.S. Census Bureau, 2000.

_____. *Statistical Abstract of the United States: 2001: The National Data Book.* Washington, D.C.: U.S. Census Bureau, 2001.

_____. *Statistical Abstract of the United States: 2002: The National Data Book.* Washington, D.C.: U.S. Census Bureau, 2002.

U.S. Coast Guard. *Pollution Incidents in and around U.S. Waters – Internet Version* [PDF]. August 2003 [cited March 19, 2004]. Available from http://www.uscg.mil/hq/g-m/nmc/response/stats/chpt 2001.pdf.

U.S. Department of Agriculture, Foreign Agricultural Service. "World Agricultural Production." Circular Series WAP 07-03 (2003).

U.S. Department of Energy. *Saving at the Office: Dollars and Energy.* U.S. DOE, 1996 [cited August 8, 2002]. Available from http://www.eren.doe.gov/cities_counties/saving.html.

U.S. Energy Information Agency. *Gasoline – a Petroleum Product.* U.S. Energy Information Agency, April 2005 [cited November 11, 2005]. Available from http://www.eia.doe.gov/kids/energyfacts/sources/non-renewable/gasoline.html.

_____. *Office Equipment.* 2004 [cited November 13, 2005]. Available from http://www.eere.energy.gov/buildings/info/components/appliances/office equipment.html.

U.S. Department of Energy, Office of Energy Efficiency and Renewable Energy, and U.S. Environmental Protection Agency. *Fuel Economy Guide.* 2005 [cited November 11, 2005]. Available from http://www.fueleconomy.gov/feg/FEG2006_Gasoline Vehicles.pdf.

U.S. Environmental Protection Agency. *Making the CFC Phaseout Profitable with the Energy Star Buildings Program.* Lawrence Berkeley Laboratory, April 1995 [cited August 6, 2002]. Available from http:/ /ateam.lbl.gov/coolsense/references/epacfc/epacfc. html.

_____. "EPA Press Statement." Washington, D.C.: US EPA, 2000.

_____. *Global Warming – Industry.* U.S. EPA, April 6, 2001 [cited August 6, 2002]. Available from http://www.epa.gov/globalwarming/actions/industry/index.html.

_____. *Global Warming – the Insurance Industry.* U.S. EPA, November 23, 2001 [cited August 6, 2002]. Available from http://www.epa.gov/globalwarming/actions/industry/insurance.html.

_____. *Clean Air Act* U.S. EPA, May 29th, 2002 [cited August 6 2002]. Available from http://www.epa.gov/region5/defs/html/caa.htm.

_____. *Clean Water Act.* U.S. EPA, March 26, 2002 [cited August 6, 2002]. Available from http://www.epa.gov/region5/water/cwa.htm.

_____. *Emergency Planning & Community Right to Know Act.* U.S. EPA, May 29, 2002 [cited August 6, 2002]. Available from http://www.epa.gov/region5/defs/html/epcra.htm.

_____. *Comprehensive Environmental Response, Compensation, and Liability Act (Superfund).* U.S. EPA, May 29, 2002 [cited August 6, 2002]. Available from http://www.epa.gov/region5/defs/html/cercla.htm.

_____. *Federal Insecticide, Fungicide, and Rodenticide Act.* U.S. EPA, May 29, 2002 [cited August 6, 2002]. Available from http://www.epa.gov/region5/defs/html/fifra.htm.

_____. *Resource Conservation and Recovery Act.* U.S. EPA, May 29, 2002 [cited August 6, 2002]. Available from http://www.epa.gov/region5/defs/html/rcra.htm.

_____. *Safe Drinking Water Act.* U.S. EPA, May 29, 2002 [cited August 6, 2002]. Available from http://www.epa.gov/region5/defs/html/sdwa.htm.

_____. *Toxic Substances Control Act.* U.S. EPA, May 29, 2002 [cited August 6, 2002]. Available from http://www.epa.gov/region5/defs/html/tsca.htm.

_____. *Liquid Assets 2000: The Business of Clean Water.* January 24, 2003 [cited November 13, 2005]. Available from http://www.epa.gov/water/liquidassets/business.html.

_____. *What Is the Toxics Release Inventory (Tri) Program.* U.S. EPA, June 13, 2002 [cited August 6, 2002]. Available from http://www.epa.gov/tri/whatis.htm.

_____. *Exxon Valdez.* August 25, 2003 [cited October 23, 2003]. Available from http://www.epa.gov/

oilspill/exxon.htm.

U.S. Environmental Protection Agency, Region 6. *Indoor Environments*. August 18, 2003 [cited October 30, 2003]. Available from http://www.epa.gov/earth1r6/6pd/iaq/iaq.htm.

U.S. Environmental Protection Agency. *Environmental Management Systems: Incorporating DFE into Your Gap Analysis – Draft*. 1999 [cited April 8, 2004]. Available from www.epa.gov/dfe/.

U.S. General Services Administration. *Ideas*. n.d. [cited August 8, 2002]. Available from http://policyworks.gov/org/main/mp/gsa/ics1.html.

U.S. Green Building Council. *Leed Rating System Version 2.1*. USGBC, July 25, 2002 [cited August 6, 2002]. Available from www.usgbc.org.

Ulanowicz, Robert E. "Contributory Values of Ecosystem Resources." In *Ecological Economics: The Science and Management of Sustainability*, edited by Robert Costanza, 253-68. New York, NY: Columbia University Press, 1991.

Ulhoi, John P., Henry Madsen, and S. Hildebrandt. "Green New World: A Corporate Environmental Business Perspective." *Scandinavian Journal of Management* 12, no. 3 (1996): 243-54.

UNEP – Production and Consumption Unit. *Background Information*. UNEP, Production and Consumption Unit, April 18, 2002 [cited August 6, 2002]. Available from http://www.uneptie.org/pc/sustain/lca/background.htm.

_____. *The Life Cycle Initiative*. UNEP, Production and Consumption Unit, July 17, 2002 [cited August 6, 2002]. Available from http://www.uneptie.org/pc/sustain/lca/lca.htm.

UNEP and WCMC. "82 State of the Environment and Policy Retrospective: 1972-2002," 62-89: UNEP and WCMC, 2002.

UNESCO-WWAP. *Water for People – Water for Life: The United Nations World Water Development Report*. New York, NY: UNESCO Publishing and Berghahn Books, 2003.

University of Cambridge, Department of Engineering, Institute for Manufacturing. *Gap Analysis*. n.d. [cited April 9, 2004]. Available from http://www-mmd.eng.cam.ac.uk/people/ahr/dstools/choosing/gapana.htm.

University of Hawaii. University of Hawaii, 2002 [cited August 6, 2002]. Available from http://www.hawaii. edu/gk-12/evolution/k-12%20project.htm.

University of Maryland, Department of Mechanical Engineering. *University of Maryland Green Manufacturing Initiative* [Web site]. 2002 [cited November 10, 2005]. Available from http://www.enme.umd.edu/greenmfg/areas.html.

University of Wisconsin – River Falls. *2001-2003 Course Catalogue*. University of Wisconsin – River Falls, n.d. [cited August 6, 2002]. Available from http://www.uwrf.edu/catalog/catalog_03/course/esm.htm.

Upton, Arthur C. and Eden Graber, eds. *Staying Healthy in a Risky Environment*. New York, NY: Simon & Schuster, 1993.

Valters, John. *Songbird Trade Threatens Rare Species*. BBC News, February 8, 2001 [cited August 6, 2002]. Available from http://news.bbc.co.uk/hi/english/uk/newsid_1159000/1159889.stm.

Van der Ryn, Sim and Stuart Cowan. *Ecological Design*. Washington, D.C.: Island Press, 1996.

van Gelder, Sarah. "The Next Reformation: An Interview with Paul Hawken." *In Context* 41 (1995): 17-22.

Van Patten, Peg. "The Mad Hatter Mercury Mystery." *Wrack Lines*, Fall-Winter 2002, online source – http://www.sp.uconn.edu/~wwwsgo/HATTER.HTML.

Volk, Tyler. *Gaia's Body: Toward a Physiology of the Earth*. New York, NY: Copernicus, 1998.

Wackernagel, Mathis and William Rees. *Ecological Footprint*. Philadelphia, PA: New Society Publishers, 1996.

Wasowski, Andy with Sally Wasowski. *Building Inside Nature's Envelope: How New Construction and Land Preservation Can Work Together*. New York, NY: Oxford University Press, Inc., 2000.

Waste Watch. *Waste Watch Environmental Report 2001*. Waste Watch, 2001 [cited August 6, 2002]. Available from http://www.wastewatch.org.uk/publicat/enviroreport.pdf.

Watts, Johnathon, Alan Senauke, and Santikaro Bhikkhu, eds. *Entering the Realm of Reality: Towards Dhammic Societies*. Bangkok, Thailand: International Network of Engaged Buddhists, 1997.

Webster. *Encyclopedic Unabridged Dictionary of the English Language*. Avenel, NJ: Gramercy Books, 1989.

Westerman, Martin. *The Business Environmental Handbook*. Grants Pass, OR: Oasis Press, 1993.

Westley, Frances, Steven R. Carpenter, William A. Brock, C.S. Holling, and Lance H. Gunderson. "Why Systems of People and Nature Are Not Just Social and Ecological Systems." In *Panarchy: Understanding Transformations in Human and Natural Systems*, edited by Lance H. Gunderson and C.S.

Holling, 103-19. Washington, D.C.: Island Press, 2002.

Wheatley, Margaret J. and Myron Kellner-Rogers. *A Simpler Way.* San Francisco, CA: Berrett-Koehler Publishers, 1999.

_____. *Leadership and the New Science: Discovering Order in a Chaotic World.* San Francisco, CA: Berrett-Koehler Publishers, 1999.

Wheeler, David and Maria Sillanpaa. *The Stakeholder Corporation: The Body Shop Blueprint for Maximizing Shareholder Value.* London, England: Pitman Publishing, 1997.

White, Allen L. "Sustainability and the Accountable Corporation: Society's Rising Expectations of Business." *Environment* 41, no. 8 (1999): 30-43.

White, Gillian. *Grounded Theory and Qualitative Data Analysis – Comment 1.* Health Research Methods Advisory Service, 26 August 1998 [cited August 7, 2002]. Available from http://www2.auckland.ac.nz/mch//hrmas/qual2d.htm.

Wilcox, Andrew and John Harte. *Ecosystem Services in a Modern Economy: Gunnison County, Colorado.* Edited by Gretchen C. Daily, *Nature's Services: Societal Dependence on Natural Ecosystems.* Washington, D.C.: Island Press, 1997.

William McDonough Architects. *The Hannover Principles.* New York, NY: William McDonough Architects, 1992.

Williamson, Oliver E. and Sidney G. Winter. *The Nature of the Firm: Origins, Evolution, and Development.* New York, NY: Oxford University Press, 1993.

Wilson, Cynthia. *Chemical Exposure and Human Health: A Reference to 314 Chemicals with a Guide to Symptoms and a Directory of Organizations.* Jefferson, NC: McFarland & Company, Inc., Publishers, 1993.

Wilson, Robert C. "What Does It Take to Be an Iso 14001 Ems Auditor?" *Pollution Engineering* 30, no. 6 (1998): 49-51.

_____. "An Ems Audit Should Begin at Your Desk." *Pollution Engineering* 31, no. 7 (1999): 35.

Winsemius, Pieter and Ulrich Guntram. *A Thousand Shades of Green: Sustainable Strategies for Competitive Advantage.* Sterling, VA: Earthscan Publications, Ltd., 2002.

Wirzba, Norman, ed. *The Essential Agrarian Reader: The Future of Culture, Commodity, and the Land.* Lexington, KY: The University Press of Kentucky, 2003.

Wolfson, Adam. "The Costs and Benefits of Cost-Benefit Analysis." *Public Interest*, no. 145 (2001): 93-99.

Wolters, Teun, Mark Bouman, and Marc Peeters. "Environmental Management and Employment: Pollution Prevention Requires Significant Employee Participation." *Greener Management International*, no. 11 (1995): 63-72.

World Business Council for Sustainable Development (WBCSD). *About the WBCSD.* WBCSD, 2003 [cited October 30, 2003]. Available from http://www.wbcsd.org/templates/TemplateWBCSD1/layout.asp?type=p&MenuId=NjA&doOpen=1&ClickMenu=LeftMenu.

World Resources Institute. *About Wri.* WRI, August 05, 2002 [cited August 6, 2002]. Available from http://www.wri.org/wri.html.

World Resources Institute and Aspen Institute for Social Innovation through Business. *Beyond Grey Pinstripes 2001.* New York & Washington, D.C.: Aspen ISIB & World Resources Institute, 2001.

Worldwatch Institute. *How Much Is Enough?* New York, NY: W.W. Norton & Company, Inc., 1992.

Wright, Robert. *Nonzero: The Logic of Human Destiny.* New York, NY: Pantheon Books, 2000.

Yorque, Ralf, Brian Walker, C.S. Holling, Lance H. Gunderson, Carl Folke, Stephen R. Carpenter, and William A. Brock. "Toward an Integrative Synthesis." In *Panarchy: Understanding Transformations in Human and Natural Systems*, edited by Lance H. Gunderson and C.S. Holling, 419-38. Washington, D.C.: Island Press, 2002.

Index